Managing the Microsoft Internet Information Server

Wave Technologies International, Inc.
MNT4-ELE2-8041A
Release 2

Managing the Microsoft Internet Information Server
MNT4-ELE2-8041A
Release 2
©1988-1998 Wave Technologies International, Inc.
All rights reserved.

Trademarks:

10 9 8 7 6 5 4 3 2 1

Contents

SELF STUDY

Introduction

COURSE PURPOSE

This course is designed to provide system administrators with the knowledge they need to install and administer Web services using Internet Information Server. It covers the criteria for the MCSE elective exam #70-87, Implementing and Supporting Microsoft Internet Information Server 4.0.

Before studying this manual, students should have a solid understanding of both Windows NT Server and TCP/IP.

COURSE GOALS

This course will provide you with the information required to complete the following objectives:

- Arrange Internet connectivity.
- Select connectivity options.
- Configure Windows NT Server to support Internet Information Server 4.0.
- Configure TCP/IP on your Windows NT Server.
- Install Windows NT Service Pack 3.
- Install Internet Explorer 4.01.
- Install Windows NT 4.0 Option Pack.
- Identify minimum installation requirements for Internet Information Server 4.0.
- Describe the Microsoft Management Console.
- Configure the WWW Service.
- Configure the FTP Service.
- Implement security on your Web sites.
- Implement security on your FTP sites.

- Describe the Secure Sockets Layer protocol.
- Install and use Certificate Server.
- Describe HTTP Headers.
- Create virtual directories.
- Create virtual servers.
- Configure your server to use Active Server Pages.
- Discuss available options for accessing data from your Web pages.
- Describe the role of Microsoft Transaction Server.
- Install and configure Index Server.
- Install and configure SMTP.
- Install and configure NNTP.
- Describe how you can manage your Internet Information Server through a Web browser.
- Describe how you can run a script using the Windows Scripting Host.
- Install Microsoft Site Server Express.
- Analyze a Web site's content using Site Server Express.
- Analyze a Web site's usage using Site Server Express.
- Optimize the performance of your Web server.
- Use Performance Monitor to gather performance data.

HARDWARE AND SOFTWARE REQUIREMENTS

The exercises in this course have been written so that they can be performed on a single computer. However, it must meet the minimum hardware requirements as follows:

- CPU: Pentium 66 (minimum), Pentium 90+ (recommended)
- Hard disk: 1 GB (minimum), SCSI Controller with 2+ GB hard drive (recommended)
- Memory: 32 MB RAM (minimum), 64+ MB (recommended)
- CD-ROM drive
- VGA, Super VGA, or video graphics adapter compatible with Windows NT Server 4.0
- Microsoft mouse or other pointing device

In addition, you must have Windows NT Server 4.0 and the Windows NT 4.0 Option Pack CD-ROM.

Remember, there is always help available online. Please refer to the Support pages in Getting Started for further information regarding online support.

Overview

OBJECTIVES

At the completion of this chapter, you will be able to:

- Describe the World Wide Web (WWW).
- Describe the Microsoft Internet Information Server (IIS).
- Define the relationship between the IIS 4.0 and Microsoft Windows NT Server 4.0.
- Describe the different features available with IIS 4.0.
- List and describe the two browser products that are currently most popular.
- Describe the relationship between client and server systems.

PRE-TEST QUESTIONS

The answers to these questions are in appendix A at the end of this manual.

1. What does the Microsoft Internet Information Server do?

   ....

   ....

2. What are the two most popular browsers?

   ....

   ....

3. What is the current version of Microsoft Internet Explorer?

   ....

   ....

4. Which version of Windows NT Server is required by IIS 4.0?

   ....

   ....

INTRODUCTION

This chapter is designed to start laying the groundwork required for you to install, configure, manage, and use Microsoft products designed for the Internet environment. Keep in mind that this chapter is only providing an overview and introduction. More detailed information on the subjects introduced here is provided throughout the course.

During this chapter, you will be introduced to some basic concepts and to some of the tools you will be using. Some of this information may already be familiar to you. The chapter opens with a quick introduction to the World Wide Web (WWW) and Microsoft's Internet Information Server (IIS). It also describes a little about the client/server environment in which these operate.

Essential Terms

The following are brief definitions of Internet terms. Most of these are described in greater detail in the following paragraphs and chapters.

Dial-up Client

A computer with a temporary Internet connection that cannot act as a server and has a temporary IP address.

Domain Name

The textual name identifier for a specific Internet host, i.e., www.microsoft.com.

Domain Name Server

An Internet host dedicated to the function of translating fully qualified domain names into IP addresses.

File Transfer Protocol (FTP)

The protocol used to transfer files between TCP/IP hosts.

Home Page

The default HTML document returned by an HTTP server when a URL containing no specific document is requested.

Host

A node on a TCP/IP network. This term can be used to refer to a client, a server, or a computer that acts as both a client and a server. It can also be used to refer to other network devices that have at least one IP address, such as routers.

HyperText Transfer Protocol (HTTP)

A client/server interprocess communication protocol used by "Web sites" (server) and "Web browsers" (client).

HyperText Markup Language (HTML)

The language used to construct documents for distribution by HTTP servers.

Internet

The global interconnection of networks based on the TCP/IP protocol suite.

Internet Protocol (IP)

An Internet (Network) layer protocol used to perform route discovery, packet routing, fragmentation, and re-assembly of packets on TCP/IP internetworks.

Intranet

A privately owned network based on the TCP/IP protocol suite.

Java

A cross-platform programming language developed by Sun Microsystems used to create applications that can run in a Web browser or as stand-alone programs.

Java Virtual Machine (JVM)

Software that allows a computer to execute applications written in the Java programming language.

Multipurpose Internet Mail Extensions (MIME)

Extensions to standard electronic mail protocols that support rich content such as animation, audio, and video.

Request for Comments (RFC)

A document describing each existing/proposed Internet protocol. The Internet
Engineering Task Force (IETF) establishes subcommittees to evaluate Internet protocols.
RFC documents are circulated throughout the Internet community to elicit user
feedback. Each RFC document is assigned a unique number.

Search Engine

A Web site dedicated to responding to requests for specific information, searching
massive locally stored indexes of HTML documents. Popular search engines include
Yahoo!, Excite, AltaVista, and InfoSeek, among others.

Simple Mail Transfer Protocol (SMTP)

The protocol used to exchange electronic mail messages between TCP/IP e-mail servers.

Spider

A program that searches the Internet for Web servers, retrieves HTML documents found
on each server, indexes the documents, and stores the indices in a database used by search
engines.

Transport Control Protocol (TCP)

A connection-oriented transport layer packet transport protocol that utilizes virtual
circuits, packet sequencing, and acknowledgment to provide reliable packet delivery on
TCP/IP networks.

Uniform Resource Locator (URL)

A location and document specifier that uniquely identifies a resource on a server. URLs
contain the domain name of the Internet host serving the resource, the path to the
resource, and the resource name. URLs are defined in RFC 1738.

User Datagram Protocol (UDP)

A connectionless transport layer packet transport protocol designed to provide high-
performance, low-overhead packet delivery.

Web Browser

An application that requests documents from an HTTP server and formats HTML documents for display on user workstations. The most popular Web browsers are Netscape Navigator and Microsoft Internet Explorer.

Web Page

An HTML document on an HTTP server.

Web Site

A collection of HTML documents located on an HTTP server. Pages typically contain HyperText links that allow users to easily navigate through available pages.

World Wide Web

A collection of rich content documents maintained by millions of HTTP servers located throughout the world.

CONNECTING TO THE INTERNET

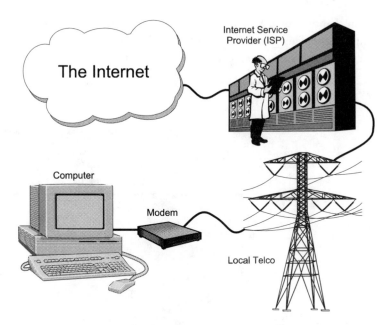

What do you need if you want to connect to the Internet? The answer depends on what you want to accomplish. While the vast majority of Internet users participate as clients who view available information, the number of servers on the Internet has exploded in recent years. Basic system requirements for Internet connectivity include:

- Computer
- Modem, Integrated Services Digital Network (ISDN), Asymmetric Digital Subscriber Line (ADSL), or cable adapter
- TCP/IP-capable operating system, such as UNIX, Windows 95, Windows NT, or Macintosh operating system
- TCP/IP Communications Protocol

- Archie, FTP, Gopher, SMTP mail, Telnet, or an HTML browser application
- Internet Service Provider (ISP)

This chapter provides an introduction to these tools and technologies, with more detailed information later in the course. Our emphasis in this course is server implementation, but any server discussion requires that you understand available clients as well.

WHAT IS THE WWW?

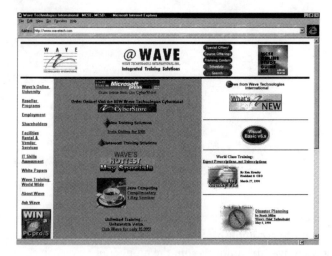

The Internet is the largest computer network in the world. It links computers of every model and operating system together to facilitate the sharing of information.

Every Web site (such as http://www.wavetech.com) on the Internet is assigned a unique address similar to the way that all of the buildings located on a particular street have an address. Computers that connect to the Internet use Internet Protocol (IP) addresses, which are understood by the TCP/IP protocol suite.

Each IP host is also assigned a Domain Name System (DNS) name. This is the name referred to by users who wish to access a particular host. Web servers typically have names in the following format:

```
www.domain_name
```

To access a particular Web server, users launch a Web browser application and specify the Uniform Resource Locator (URL) with which they wish to connect. URLs that refer to Web servers always begin with "http://". This is the URL designator for a HyperText Transfer Language (HTTP, a.k.a. "Web") server. The remainder of the URL refers to the host (typically "www") and domain information, such as "wavetech.com."

The client browser running on a user's computer generates HTTP requests for documents based on user selections.

Prior to the introduction of the HyperText Transfer Protocol and the World Wide Web (WWW), some universities and other agencies tried to organize information in a format that allowed you to find , view, and access information in a non-graphical format with protocols like Archie, Veronica, and Gopher. With the development of the WWW, HTML, HTTP, search engines, and graphical Web browsers, the Internet has become increasingly user-friendly. This has led to the explosive growth of Internet traffic in recent years.

The WWW provides access to text, pictures, sounds, and multimedia content from anywhere in the world. By using hypermedia and hypertext, users are able to retrieve information by a simple mouse click. Currently, there are over 34 million users accessing the Internet. Clearly, the WWW is the fuel feeding the incredible growth of the Internet.

Web Clients

The browser is the client component required to view documents stored on an HTTP Web server. When designing a Web site, your content should be formatted to support both of the popular browsers (Netscape Navigator and Microsoft Internet Explorer). Documents must provide consistent functionality across both application platforms.

Both Internet Explorer 4 and Netscape Navigator 4 provide support for Java applets and JavaScript. This allows you to create dynamic, moving Web pages. Java is becoming the language of choice for program development (like C++) and also for applet development. The primary reason for this is that, provided it does not depend on operating system Application Programming Interfaces (APIs), a Java program or applet can run on any platform that has a Java Virtual Machine. In other words, it is a platform-independent program requiring only a Java-enabled browser. JavaScript is the embedding of simple Java statements in your HTML code.

Microsoft Internet Explorer

In addition to support for the Java language, Internet Explorer 4 supports programs, or components, written to the ActiveX specification. This allows ActiveX components to be automatically downloaded to the browser and executed on a client. ActiveX components can be written in any Windows programming language, one of the most popular being Visual Basic 5.0, or its predecessor, Visual Basic–Control Creation Edition.

VBScript is similar to JavaScript in that it is the embedding of simple VB statements in your HTML code. Internet Explorer 4 supports VBScript.

Adding Support for Rich Content

One final way to enhance the client is called *Netscape Plugins*. These are programs that add functionality to the browser. They are downloaded from a server and installed on the client computer. Subsequently, Web browsers can use these programs to access documents containing an infinite variety of content types. Examples of popular plugins are Macromedia's Shockwave and Apple Computer's QuickTime.

Web Servers

A basic Internet server provides Web documents over HTTP and files over FTP. In addition, certain programs can run on the Web server to enhance the information sent to the browser. These are:

- Common Gateway Interface (CGI)
- Internet Server Application Programming Interface (ISAPI)
- Active Server Pages (ASP)

The primary difference between CGI and ISAPI is that with CGI programs, a new copy of the program is loaded into memory on the server every time a client browser requests the page containing the program. With an ISAPI program, one copy is loaded into memory and shared by all applications.

While CGI and ISAPI are usually written in either Perl or C (for CGI) or C++ (for ISAPI), an Active Server Page is a script that is interpreted by a dynamic link library that is loaded in the Internet Information Server's memory. This means that an Active Server Page can be written in any Active scripting language, including VBScript and JavaScript. An Active Server Page can also run ActiveX components, making it a very powerful tool for server-side Web solutions. Active Server Pages will be covered in more detail later in the course.

ASP, CGI, and ISAPI programs can provide many types of services to client browsers including:

- Database lookups
- Capturing information and updating a database
- Page hit counters
- Online shopping and order processing

What Happens When you Click on a HyperLink?

The following is a description of the events behind the operation of a typical HTTP server and client:

1. The client browser translates the URL embedded in the user-specified URL into a fully qualified domain name and path to the document.
2. The browser requests name resolution for the domain name and path from a DNS Server. The DNS server returns an IP address, which is the IP address of the server containing the requested document.
3. A TCP/IP connection is established to the server's IP address.
4. The browser uses HTTP to request the document from the server.
5. The server transmits the HTML document at the path indicated in the URL to the browser.

6. The TCP/IP connection to the Web server is broken. Each page request makes a unique, temporary TCP/IP connection.

7. The HTML document is formatted by the browser and presented to the user. Because HTML pages may contain many embedded objects such as graphics and frames, the request-response process is repeated until all objects have been retrieved.

   NOTE: *You can watch this process occur by watching the bottom left corner of your browser window. Connections are made and broken as the various elements of a document are retrieved.*

MICROSOFT INTERNET INFORMATION SERVER (IIS)

Microsoft provides support for Web applications through the Microsoft Internet Information Server. IIS transmits documents in HyperText Markup Language (HTML) pages using the HyperText Transfer Protocol (HTTP). It listens for requests from users and responds by providing the information that satisfies the request. With it you can provide a wide variety of services, including:

- Publish information about your business on the Internet.

- Publish a catalog and take orders.

- Create interactive programs that provide real time information to people visiting your site.

- Provide access to your databases for your employees and/or customers.

You can also use IIS in an intranet to provide internal access to company information, methods and procedures, and forms for your employees.

With IIS 3.0, Microsoft introduced server-side scripting. Many functions that formerly had to be done with a compiled application could now be done with text files that were interpreted by the Web server. Documentation and program example files are included with IIS 3.0 and IIS 4.0.

IIS 4.0 provides support for the Distributed Component Object Model (DCOM), JavaScript, Java applets, VBScript, and ActiveX programs that run on the server. (As opposed to being downloaded to the browser and running on the client.)

The latest version of IIS, version 4, offers so much flexibility in providing dynamic information, that previous versions should be used only until version 4 is installed.

Using Internet Information Server

Internet Information Server allows you to create powerful Web solutions, provided you understand the technologies available to you. For example, you could:

- Create client/server applications using the Microsoft Internet Server Application Programming Interface (ISAPI).

- Create and run Common Gateway Interface (CGI) applications.

- Create HTML scripts that interface with Microsoft SQL Server.

- Develop server-side scripts (ASP) to add dynamic information to your Web pages.

- Enhance your HTML pages with ActiveX, Java, VBScript, and JavaScript, on the server as well as the browser.

NOTE: Some of these terms and technologies may be unfamiliar to you. Don't let that concern you. At least initially, you only need a general understanding of many of these.

Microsoft Windows NT Server 4.0

The Microsoft Internet Information Server 4.0 runs on the Microsoft Windows NT Server 4.0 or higher operating system. Windows NT provides fast performance, good security, and the ability to integrate IIS with Microsoft's SQL Server.

IIS 4.0 requires that you first install Service Pack 3 and Internet Explorer 4.0. IIS 4.0 is available with the Windows NT 4.0 Option Pack, which can be downloaded from the Microsoft Web site at www.microsoft.com/windows/downloads/contents/products/nt4optpk/ or installed from the Microsoft TechNet or MSDN Universal CD-ROMs. These components are also included in Microsoft BackOffice Suite 4.0.

Microsoft Windows NT 4.0 Internet Client Tools

Windows NT 4.0 includes a complete set of Internet client application tools including:

- Internet Explorer

  This is a full-featured Web browser.

- Internet Mail/Exchange

  This is an e-mail utility that can be configured to send and receive e-mail over the Internet via the SMTP and POP protocols.

- FTP

  This is a standard File Transfer Protocol client utility.

- Telnet

  This is a utility that provides a command-line interface to connect to a remote host and access character-based applications as if connected via a local, serial terminal.

- Finger

  This is a utility used to look up information about users on a remote system.

- Ping

  This is a utility that is used to test connectivity to other systems. Ping is actually an acronym for Packet Internet Groper.

- Nslookup

  This is a utility used to resolve host names to Internet Protocol addresses.

- Rsh

  This is a utility that is used to access a remote shell program, allowing you to execute commands on remote UNIX hosts that support running the rsh service.

- Tftp

  The Trivial FTP utility allows you to upload and download files between two computers on a network.

- Tracert

  This is a utility that allows you to trace the route and track the number of router "hops" between your computer and any TCP/IP host computer.

SUMMARY

During this chapter, you were provided with an overview of Web-based solutions. This included:

- Web browsers
- Web servers
- HyperText Transfer Protocol
- Technologies for dynamic Web page development
- Internet Information Server 4.0 features

In the next chapter, you will look at some of the issues involved with connecting to the Internet.

POST-TEST QUESTIONS

The answers to these questions are in Appendix A at the end of this manual.

1. On what operating systems can the Microsoft Internet Information Server be run?

   ....

   ....

2. Anyone browsing a Web page from a server running IIS 4.0 must use the Microsoft Internet Explorer browser.

   A. True

   B. False

3. What must be unique for every server connected to the Internet?

    ....

    ....

4. If you are running IIS 4.0 and you have ActiveX components running on your server, which browsers will display your content properly?

    ....

    ....

5. What is the primary advantage of the Java programming language?

    ....

    ....

Arranging Internet Connectivity

OBJECTIVES

At the completion of this chapter, you will be able to:

*   List guidelines for locating an Internet Service Provider (ISP).

*   List interview guidelines for selecting an ISP.

*   List and describe the services you are most likely to need an ISP to provide.

*   List services that should be provided by an ISP.

*   Describe concerns when changing to a different ISP.

PRE-TEST QUESTIONS

The answers to these questions are in Appendix A at the end of this manual.

1. What is an Internet Service Provider?

    ....

    ....

2. Can you change ISPs?

    ....

    ....

3. What connectivity options are recommended when establishing a presence on the Internet?

    ....

    ....

4. What connectivity option provides the most bandwidth?

    ....

    ....

INTRODUCTION

Arranging the proper connections and finding the right Internet Service Provider (ISP) can take some time. This is one of the first steps in connecting to the Internet. The more you plan to do, the more involved the selection process may become. Make the initial calls as soon as you decide that you're going to connect to the Internet, even if you don't have all of the details of how quite yet. This will allow time to install the necessary phone lines (if new lines are required) and any special hardware, and prepare and process any necessary paperwork.

This chapter is designed to provide you with some guidelines, not only for locating an Internet Service Provider (ISP), but for selecting an appropriate ISP for your needs. There has been a surge in the number of ISPs competing for your business. Many are good, full-featured vendors. Some are less qualified and may have less sophisticated equipment. This chapter will help you ask the right questions and hopefully find a vendor that meets your needs the first time out.

ABOUT AN ISP

Your ISP selection can have a significant influence on your long-term reliability and capabilities on the Web. Issues include:

- Finding an ISP
- Connectivity Options
- Connections
- Terminal Adapter Versus Router
- Domain Name Server support
- How to change ISPs

Even if you already have an ISP, you need to review the services being provided before implementing a Web server.

Finding an ISP

There first step is to create a list of ISPs that serve your area.

There are three ways to find ISPs:

1. Whenever you attend an Internet conference or training, ask people who they're using.

2. Use the search engines on the Internet. Search for "ISP," "Internet Service Provider," and your city name.

3. Read your local newspaper. ISPs tend to advertise in the sports, business, and entertainment sections. You might have to search the paper for a week or two, but ISPs do advertise.

There are national ISPs, but usually they contract with a local ISP for their presence. Skip the nationals unless it is a big phone company and is a true provider instead of a middleman.

Connectivity Options

You should become familiar with connectivity terminology: The first thing that you want to be able to assess is your bit transfer rate requirements. You will need to weigh the cost of high transfer rates against the benefits. Next you'll want to look at options for sending and receiving those bits: ISDN, Frame Relay, and ATM.

The industry standard bit transfer rates for various transmission media are as follows:

T-Class Carriers

T-carriers are a type of high-speed leased telephone lines used for voice and data transmission. There are four service levels:

T1	1.544 Mbps	1 Channel
T2	6.312 Mbps	4 Channels
T3	44.736 Mbps	28 Channels
T4	274.176 Mbps	168 Channels

FT1

This is a subdivision of T1, which is less expensive and is based on 64 Kbps channels. This service is the most commonly used where you need an inexpensive, continuously open channel. This is called Fractional T1.

ISDN

This is a switched digital service that is usually sold on a time and distance rate schedule just like phone calls. Most ISDN is provided by phone companies that have converted some of their analog lines to integrated voice and digital. ISDN lines are available with bandwidth increments of 56/64 Kbps, 1.544 Mbps, and 2.048 Mbps.

The most common service options are Basic Rate and Primary Rate. Basic Rate divides its available bandwidth into three data channels: Two B channels and one D channel. The B channels transmit data at 64 Kbps each and the D channel transmits signaling and link management data at 16 Kbps. Since the third channel is used for signaling overhead instead of actual data transmission, the available bandwidth is 128 Kbps. In the United States, Primary Rate ISDN is 23 B channels at 64 Kbps and a D channel that operates at 64 Kbps. This yields a total of 1.544 Mbps T1 bandwidth. In Europe, Primary Rate ISDN includes 30 B channels and one D channel. This yields an available bandwidth of 2.048 Mbps.

> *NOTE: If your ISDN rate is a measured rate and ISDN is used continuously, it is generally more expensive than dedicated leased lines FT1 (Fractional T1) and T1.*

Frame Relay

This is a packet-switching network service that provides high-speed data transmission rates. Frame relay uses permanent virtual circuits (PVCs) to establish stable end-to-end circuits.

ATM (Asynchronous Transfer Mode)

This is a packet-switching network service that can transmit data in excess of 600 Mbps. Its high-speed advantage is due to the fact that it transmits uniform data packets that are subdivided into data frames. Each frame is enclosed within an addressable 53-byte cell and routed by hardware switching.

ATM is the backbone of major telecommunications companies. It is becoming more and more popular in private industry because prices are falling and hardware is more easily accessible.

> *NOTE: The above information is important to understand, but the bandwidths listed are those you will get under the best possible conditions. What you need from your ISP once you have chosen your data transfer rate and method of transfer is a guaranteed CIR (Certified Information Rate). A CIR guarantees that no matter how much traffic the lines support you are guaranteed that your data will always have a specific bandwidth.*

Check Them Out

Now that you have a list of ISPs contact each one and ask a few initial questions. Use a separate piece of paper for each and record who you are calling and when. A list of questions that you can use is included in this chapter. Keep in mind that picking the wrong ISP can ruin your Web site.

The people you will be talking to are often bright and know their business. They can be a great source of information. However, you need to realize that they sometimes are not the most tolerant people and get frustrated when they deal with the same (or similar) recurring questions.

ISPs usually do not mind sharing information with technical staff, but you have to ask the right questions. Your ISP can tell you what equipment you will need to connect to them and why. They can recommend additional software to make your site better and safer. After you have talked to one or two, you will feel comfortable when talking to others or when calling them back.

When you talk with an ISP you will start by telling them that you are setting up your own Web site for your company and are considering them as an ISP. Find out what kind of connections they recommend and what hardware they require.

Connection Concerns

Your biggest long-term cost will be what you pay your ISP each month for the connection and what you pay the phone company for the line. The type of phone line you choose is dependent on geography and politics. Some phone companies price services like ISDN cheaply; others charge much more. Your ISP should already have an intimate knowledge of the local phone company's structure and pricing policies and should guide you.

If your company is new to the Internet, you may be able to get by with a 56-Kbps connection to your ISP. You might choose a frame relay connection or an ISDN connection. A 56-Kbps connection will be the least expensive and will give you the opportunity to learn more about IIS and your ISP. Your ISP and your customers will alert you when more bandwidth is required.

Another area of concern is your ISP's connection to the Internet and how many people are using it. If your ISP only has a 56-Kbps line and is the ISP for a few companies, your throughput may not be very good. Access their Web site and check out the response.

How far is your ISP from the Internet backbone? The Internet backbone is the 12 (or so) Network Access Points (NAPs) in the United States that are connected to each other at 45 Mbps. Everyone else connects to these NAPs. For example, the best situation would be a provider who connects to one of these 12 backbone connections, such as StarNet (Washington University in St. Louis, Missouri). How many hops does your ISP have to go through to get to the backbone?

The three major long-distance companies all have their own version of the Internet backbone. Selecting one of these as your ISP can yield improved performance.

You will need to make sure your new ISP provides any add-on services, like mail, news, or DNS.

Terminal Adapter vs. Router

While talking with ISPs, they may mention using either a terminal adapter or a router for your connection. Each device connects to your network interface card and the telephone line. A router is more expensive but allows all of the computers on your network to connect directly to your ISP's router, then out to the Internet. A terminal adapter would connect one of your computers to one of your ISP's servers, then out to the Internet. With a terminal adapter, if the particular ISP server to which you are connected was to go down, your connection would also be down.

With ISDN, some routers can *spoof* the line. This means they actually connect to your ISP as needed while your server thinks the line is up all of the time. If your phone company is charging you for connection time, this can save money.

If you believe that your Web site has the potential to be very popular, consider buying a multiple ISDN connection router. Then as you grow, you can just add another ISDN line instead of having to purchase another router.

Domain Name System Server

The Domain Name System is described later in this course. Microsoft included a DNS server as part of the TCP/IP support shipping with Windows NT Server 4.0. In brief, a DNS server is a database of Internet domain names and their associated IP addresses.

You would normally run your own DNS to resolve any inquiries for your domain name, and any other names similar to it. For example, you can surf to www.wavetech.com, or you can surf to dhill.wavetech.com. If you surf to the latter, the DNS system will eventually contact the Wave DNS server to find out where dhill.wavetech.com is located.

Your ISP should provide your secondary DNS address which will point to your ISP's DNS server.

ISP Questions

Here are a few questions to keep in mind when interviewing potential ISPs:

1. How many rings before they answer the phone?
2. Are they too busy or rude?
3. What type of connection do they have to the Internet? How fast?
4. Do they have more than one local or long-distance carrier to get you to the Internet?
5. What connection do they recommend for connecting your IIS to them (the ISP)?
6. What is their fee structure?
7. What kind of equipment will you need? Where should you get it?
8. Who should you contact at your local phone company? What should you ask?
9. Is the equipment they are recommending expandable, in case your Web site gets popular?
10. Can they provide a DNS server for you?

11. Can they provide a mail server for your users?

12. Can they provide a news server for your users?

13. What are the terms of any agreements that will be signed?

14. What clauses are in the agreements that allow you to sever your relationship with this ISP?

Changing ISPs

If you become dissatisfied with your ISP, you can go through the process of finding another provider. It is important to register your own domain name. Smaller organizations are sometimes tempted to rely on an ISP's domain name as the path to their Web site. This leaves you locked into one vendor, or forces you to reroute anyone looking for your site.

In the long term, it is much easier if you have your own registered domain name. Once you find a new ISP, you can fill out an electronic form and submit it to have your domain name registered to the new ISP's network address. To do this, you must contact the InterNIC in Herndon, Virginia or submit your request electronically via the InterNIC Web site at http://www.internic.net.

SUMMARY

This chapter dealt with some of the decisions you will have to make before connecting to the Internet. These included:

•   Choosing an ISP

•   Choosing a connection method

The next chapter will focus on how to install a Windows NT Server that will run Internet Information Server 4.0.

POST-TEST QUESTIONS

The answers to these questions are in Appendix A at the end of this manual.

1. What are some of the problems caused by choosing the wrong ISP?

   ....

   ....

2. What is most important when designing your Internet connectivity?

   ....

   ....

3. How do you change ISPs after your site has been up for a while?

   ....

   ....

4. What are the bandwidth options offered by the T-class circuits?

   ....

   ....

5. Why is it important to register your own domain name?

   ....

   ....

6. How many 64-Kbps channels are provided with basic ISDN service?

   ....

   ....

7. Why is it more desirable to utilize an ISP that possesses a T3 connection to the Internet as opposed to a T1 circuit?

   ....

   ....

Microsoft Windows NT Server 4.0 Basic Configuration

▶ MAJOR TOPICS

OBJECTIVES

At the completion of this chapter, you will be able to:

- Set up Windows NT Server 4.0 to support Internet/Intranet connectivity.

- Describe guidelines for setting up FAT and NTFS disk partitions.

- Design a directory structure and set up directory sharing.

- Configure selected TCP/IP parameters.

- Describe the Windows NT 4.0 Service Pack 3.

- Install the Windows NT 4.0 Service Pack 3.

PRE-TEST QUESTIONS

The answers to these questions are in Appendix A at the end of this manual.

1. What are some of the advantages of an NTFS disk partition?

   ....

   ....

2. What protocol must be installed for IIS 4.0 to work properly?

   ....

   ....

3. Why might you have the DOS boot files on your NT server?

   ....

   ....

4. Why do you need to install Windows NT 4.0 Service Pack 3?

   ....

   ....

INTRODUCTION

This course assumes that you are familiar with both Windows NT Server and Microsoft's implementations of TCP/IP. This chapter does not attempt to provide a full discussion of all concerns when configuring your server or setting up TCP/IP support. Instead, it highlights a few key items required for Internet/intranet support.

The first area discussed in this chapter is disk support. Proper disk configuration is a key part of your security management. The chapter provides guidelines for setting up disk partitions, as well as some specifics relating to directory sharing.

The chapter also reviews TCP/IP configuration, focusing on those areas most significant to supporting IIS 4.0. You are also provided with instructions for downloading the most recent version of IIS 4.0 from Microsoft.

> *NOTE:*   *The procedures described in this course assume that you are logged on as a user having administrator rights and permissions. This is a requirement for running many of the Windows NT configuration utilities.*

WINDOWS NT SERVER INSTALLATION

The first step in preparing to install a Microsoft Internet Information Server is knowing how to install and configure Windows NT Server. You will also need to install Service Pack 3 and Internet Explorer 4.01.

Before installing Windows NT Server you need to determine if you will need a 10- to 20-MB FAT partition for DOS-based device drivers and utilities. With older motherboards that could not perform automatic detection or assign interrupts (IRQs) and I/O addresses to devices, it was necessary to create a FAT partition that could be used to run MS-DOS configuration and diagnostic utilities. These devices might include network adapters, modems, sound cards, CD-ROM drives, and SCSI controllers. With advances in motherboard and BIOS technology there is little or no need for a FAT boot partition.

Installing NT for an Internet Information Server

Windows NT currently ships with three setup diskettes, a Windows NT CD-ROM, and a Service Pack 3 CD-ROM. You can use the three setup diskettes to begin an NT installation. If you have a newer motherboard in which the BIOS supports a bootable IDE CD-ROM, you can install directly from the CD. If the latter is true you can configure the BIOS to boot to the CD-ROM drive first. The process for installing Windows NT Server by booting from the CD-ROM is the same, but faster than if you boot from diskette.

To install Internet Information Server 4.0 correctly, you must follow the appropriate installation order. That order is:

- Install Windows NT Server 4.0.

- Configure TCP/IP.

- Install Service Pack 3 (or a more recent version).

- Install Internet Explorer 4.01.

- Install Windows NT 4.0 Option Pack.

Exercise 3-1:
Installing NT Server 4.0

This exercise assumes that you will install Windows NT Server on a new unformatted hard drive, connected to a SCSI controller. If necessary, you may have a small MS-DOS boot partition. This exercise involves booting from the installation diskettes and installing from a supported CD-ROM.

It is strongly suggested that your server be attached to a training network to avoid any chance of interrupting normal operations. If it is necessary to attach to a production network, you should review this exercise and all of the other exercises in the course carefully with your Network Administrator before proceeding.

You will need a blank, formatted diskette.

1. Insert the Windows NT Server 4.0 CD-ROM in your computer's CD-ROM drive.

2. Insert the Windows NT Server Setup diskette (#1) in drive A.

3. Boot your system from the diskette.

4. When prompted, remove the diskette, place diskette #2 in the drive, and press *ENTER.*

5. When the "Welcome to Setup" screen displays, press *ENTER.*

6. When prompted to detect mass storage devices, press *ENTER.*

7. When prompted, remove diskette #2, insert diskette #3, and press *ENTER.*

8. Review the list of mass storage devices. Verify that the list is correct and press *ENTER.* If it is not correct or needs an additional device driver press *ESC,* insert the diskette with the driver in the A: drive and press *ENTER.* The supported devices are displayed. Leave the disk in the drive as it will be required by the Setup utility later on in the installation process.

   NOTE: *If you receive a warning that one of your hard disks has more than 1,024 cylinders, press ENTER to continue. You will also receive this warning on a new hard drive. Press C to continue. On a NEW SCSI hard drive, a 1-GB partition will be created. This will be discussed later in this section.*

9. When the Licensing Agreement displays, press *DOWN ARROW* until you reach the bottom of the agreement, then press *F8.*

   NOTE: *If there is an existing copy of Windows NT on your hard drive, you will be asked if you wish to upgrade.*

10. You are asked to verify the hardware configuration list and press *ENTER.* If you need to change a selection, scroll up to the item that requires modification and select the item. You will need to have the appropriate configuration diskette available.

    NOTE: *This will almost always occur with a DEC Alpha-based server. If you do not have the correct configuration diskette the installation may appear to proceed correctly but upon restarting the system will lock up.*

11. On a new installation you will be asked on what partition you want to install NT. If this is a new SCSI hard drive, it will only allow a 1-GB partition. If the drive was previously formatted or initialized by an Array Controller, the largest partition possible is 4,095 MB. If you try to create a larger partition you will be forced to return to this screen to delete and then re-create the partition.

    If you have a new SCSI hard drive and are forced to install in a 1-GB partition, proceed with the installation and formatting process. Once the file-copying process has completed, you will be prompted to reboot the computer. At this point you will need to start the installation process all over. When you are asked to select the partition on which you want to install NT, you will need to delete the existing 1-GB partition and create a new partition. This will allow you to create a partition greater than 1 GB but not greater than 4,095 MB.

12. After you create the partition you will be prompted to select a file system. When you install Windows NT you should choose NTFS as your file system. There is a higher probability of data loss and corruption of files with FAT. NTFS, on the other hand, is much more stable because of the transaction logs it maintains for the file system. Another important benefit for computers that host Web sites is that an NTFS partition allows you to set local user-level directory and file-access permissions.

13. Accept the default destination directory \WINNT, and press *ENTER*.

14. When prompted to perform an exhaustive examination of your hard disks, press *ENTER*.

    There will be a very small delay while setup makes an exhaustive check of your hard disk. Upon completion, the Setup utility will automatically begin to copy files to your hard disk.

15. After all files have been copied, remove the diskette and CD-ROM, then press *ENTER* to restart.

    On reboot NT will convert the file system to NTFS and the system will reboot once again.

16. Insert the Windows NT Server 4.0 CD-ROM when prompted. This will launch the graphical portion of the installation process.

17. When the Setup Wizard displays, click on **Next** or press *ENTER* to continue.

18. Enter the name of your corporate offices or other appropriate description and company information, then click on **Next**.

19. Enter the CD Key string located on the back of your Windows NT Server 4.0 CD case.

20. Enter the following as your computer name or other appropriate name, then click on **Next**:

        WEBSERVER

> *NOTE:* *If connecting to an existing network, ask your Network Administrator for a*
> *unique machine name.*

21. Select **Stand-alone server** as the **Server Type,** then click on **Next.**

22. Enter the password for the Administrator and confirm it, then click on **Next.**

23. When prompted to create an Emergency Repair Diskette, verify that the **Yes**
    option is selected, then click on **Next.**

> *NOTE:* *You are likely to repeat this procedure many times as a new diskette must be*
> *created whenever system configuration changes are made. This can also be*
> *performed via the Control Panel.*

24. When prompted to select the components to install, click on **Accessories,** then
    click on **Details.**

25. Select **Mouse Pointers,** then click on **OK.**

26. Click on **Next.**

27. When prompted to install Windows NT Networking, click on **Next.**

28. When prompted for your network connection, verify that **Wired to the network**
    is selected, then click on **Next.**

29. Deselect the **Install Microsoft Internet Information Server** option, then click on
    Next. (Do not install IIS at this time.)

> *NOTE:* *You will be installing Internet Information Server later in the course.*

30. When prompted to search for network adapters, click on **Start Search.** If the
    search does not produce a result, it means that the driver must be loaded from a
    manufacturer-supplied diskette *or* the card is not seated correctly in the PCI slot *or*
    there is an IRQ or other hardware-related device conflict.

> *NOTE:* *Be careful when using the Auto Search Driver load option. Some newer Intel*
> *cards require their own floppy-based drivers but Auto Search will load older*
> *NT drivers that do not function correctly but appear to bind properly.*

31. Verify that the correct network adapter is listed, then click on **Next.**

32. Select **TCP/IP Protocol,** deselect **NWLink,** then click on **Next.**

33. Click on **Select from list**. Scroll down to select **Simple TCP/IP Services**, then click on **OK**. Click on **Next**.

34. When prompted that the Setup utility is ready to install the selected components, click on **Next**.

35. Verify that the network adapter configuration information is correct, then click on **OK**.

36. When prompted to set your system up as a DHCP client, click on **No**.

37. When prompted to enter IP address information, obtain the values from your ISP, system administrator or use the following information:

IP Address	192.168.111.111
Subnet Mask	255.255.255.0
Default Gateway	192.168.111.253

38. Click on the **DNS** tab and enter the following information:

Domain	mydomain.com
Primary DNS Server	192.168.111.111
Secondary DNS Server	192.168.111.252

    NOTE: If connecting to an existing network, ask your Network Administrator for the DNS server's IP address.

39. Click on **Apply**, then click on **OK**.

40. To accept the default bindings, click on **Next**.

41. When you are prompted that the Setup utility is ready to start your network, click on **Next**.

42. Enter the following in the Workgroup field, then click on **Next**:

    WEB

43. Click on **Finish**.

44. Click on the time zone drop-down list. Locate and select your time zone, then click on **Close**.

45. When prompted that the display (video adapter) type has been detected, click on **OK**.

46. Click on **Test**, then click on **OK**.

47. After the sample color screen displays, click on **Yes**, then click on **OK** twice. Additional files are copied to the server.

48. Place a blank, formatted diskette in drive A, then click on **OK** to create the Emergency Repair Disk.

49. When informed that the installation was successful, remove the CD-ROM and the diskette, then press *ENTER* to restart your system.

50. Allow Windows NT Server 4.0 to load using the default settings. When prompted, press *CONTROL+ALT+DELETE*.

51. Verify that the User name field contains Administrator and the Workgroup field contains WEB.

52. Press *ENTER* to log in to the server.

OTHER PREPARATIONS

Installing Windows NT Server 4.0 is the first step in preparing to configure a Web server using IIS. Other preparation areas include:

- Directory Structures and Sharing
- Shared directories
- TCP/IP Installation and Configuration
- Name Resolution

A thorough understanding of the above concepts will help you to configure and maintain a secure, high-performance Web server.

Directory Structures and Sharing

An in-depth discussion of security issues will be provided later in the course. Click on the
Start button and select **Settings/Control Panel/Server/Shares**.

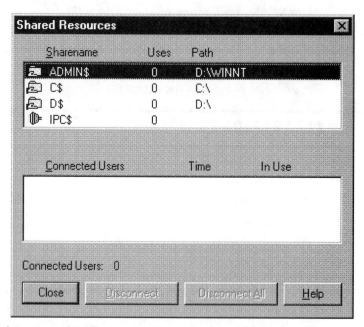

The Shared Resources list allows you to view the shared file systems on your
Windows NT Server computer. The drives and directories whose names end with a $ are
called administrative shares. There will always be some shares of this type present.

The significance of administrative shares is that they do not appear in browse lists. These
are used by the system and network for their own purposes. This does not mean,
however, that they are completely unavailable. In fact, you can set up your own *hidden*
shares by creating them as administrative shares. For users to access these shares, they will
have to know and manually enter the share name.

Initially, you will want to prevent all remote logins, except anonymous (more on this
later), so these administrative shares do not pose a security risk at this point.

User Management

Next, you should view information about the users and groups that have been defined on your server. Click on the **Start** button and select **Programs/Administrative Tools/User Manager for Domains**.

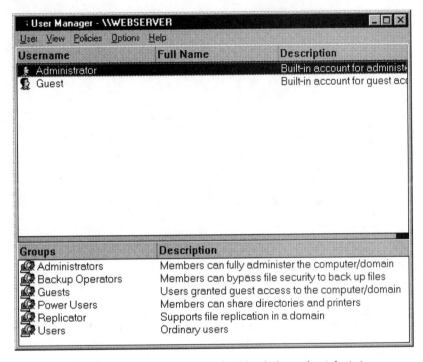

When User Manager for Domains launches, double-click on the Administrator user to display the User Properties page.

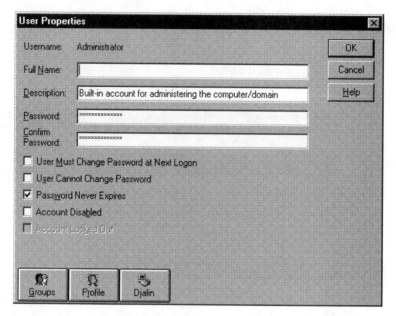

This is where you can change the password for the Administrator user. It is strongly recommended that you change your administrator password to something very difficult to guess.

For added security, you can change the Administrator account to a different name through User Manager for Domains.

In addition, review all user names on the system and make sure you don't have other administrators. The easiest way to do this is to view the member list of the Administrators (on a stand-alone server) or Domain Admins (on a domain controller) group.

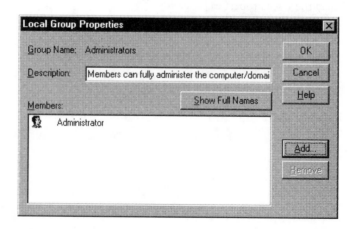

TCP/IP Installation and Configuration

You should have installed the TCP/IP protocol when you installed the Windows NT Server 4.0 operating system. If not, you can add TCP/IP support at any time, as long as you have access to the Windows NT Server installation files.

TCP/IP is the protocol you use when connecting your Windows NT Server computer to the Internet. Setup is straightforward once you have the necessary information from your Internet Service Provider (ISP).

TCP/IP installation and configuration tasks are performed using the Network utility.

You may also be using additional protocols such as NetBEUI or IPX to provide or gain access to resources on a LAN. It is recommended that you disable these other protocols before connecting your server to the Internet. Once you feel comfortable with the Windows NT Server security system, you can enable additional protocols as required.

Network Utility

To install or configure TCP/IP, click on the **Start** button and select **Settings/Control Panel/Network**. Or right-click on Network Neighborhood, then select **Properties**.

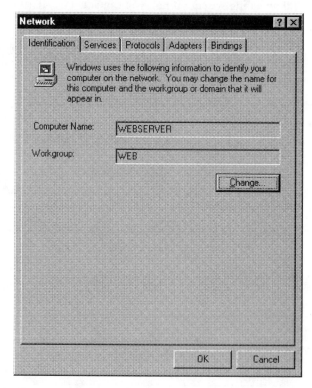

You can view the Computer Name and Workgroup values that were assigned during the server installation process. To edit these values, click on **Change** and enter the new information.

Network Adapters

Click on the **Adapters** tab. You should notice one or more entries in the Network Adapters field. If it is blank, you will need to click on **Add** and install the appropriate drivers. The drivers are located on the Windows NT Server 4.0 CD-ROM.

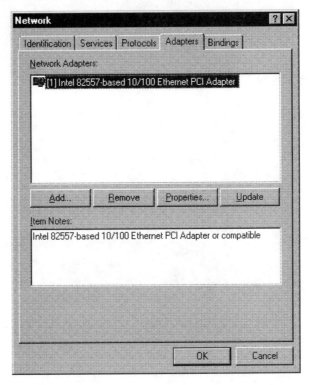

If you are using an unsupported network interface card you will need access to the Windows NT Server 4.0 driver diskette supplied by the card's manufacturer.

Communications Protocols

Click on the **Protocols** tab. Scroll through the list to locate the TCP/IP Protocol entry. If it is not listed, click on **Add** and install the appropriate files. The files are located on the Windows NT Server 4.0 CD-ROM.

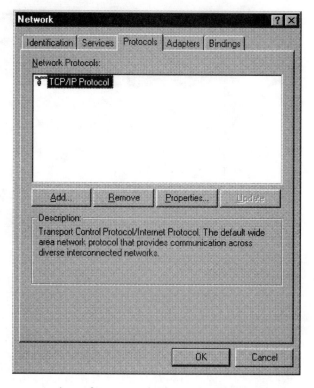

Depending on your server's configuration there may be additional communications protocols listed. The only protocol required to use Internet Information Server is TCP/IP.

TCP/IP Properties

To check your TCP/IP configuration, select TCP/IP Protocol, then click on **Properties**.

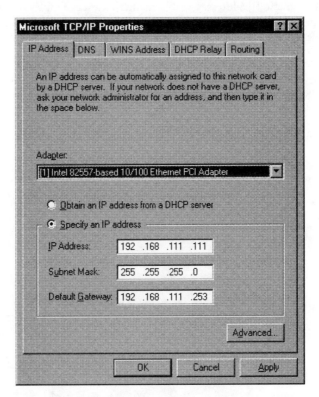

The listed Adapter should be the network interface card that you will be using to connect to your ISP. Do not enable **Automatic DHCP Configuration**. Your ISP should have provided you with values for the IP Address, Subnet Mask, and Default Gateway fields.

> *NOTE: Do not connect your server to the Internet until these values are properly configured!*

Domain Name System Configuration

The Domain Name System is a client/server protocol that translates TCP/IP host names into numeric IP addresses. DNS maintains a set of tables that map host names to IP addresses. If a certain DNS server does not find a host name in its tables, it passes the DNS query to another DNS server for resolution.

A DNS server can be installed on your Windows NT Server 4.0 computer, on one of your ISP's servers, or elsewhere on the Internet. A typical configuration maintains a local DNS for your LAN, in addition to a DNS provided by your ISP, for resolving Internet host names.

To view Domain Name System information, click on the **DNS** tab.

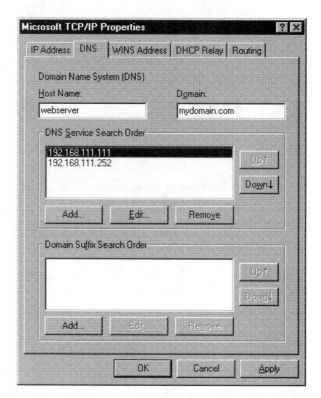

Your ISP should have provided you with the addresses of one or more DNS servers. You will need to enter the information in the DNS Service Search Order list. Also enter a host and domain name. If you have registered a domain name with InterNIC, enter it here.

Click on **OK** when done. Return to the Network Settings window, then click on **OK**. If any parameters were modified you will be prompted to restart the server.

NAME RESOLUTION AND WINS

A critical issue in networking is the resolution of host names, especially in a Microsoft networking environment. Microsoft's implementation of TCP/IP supports the following:

- HOSTS file

    This method uses a text file to associate a host name with an IP address. This method does not support NetBIOS-based applications.

- DNS

    The Domain Name System supports fully qualified host names including an IP domain, subdomain, and host name.

- NetBIOS broadcasts

    This method resolves NetBIOS names and IP addresses through broadcasts. However, broadcasts are not propagated past the local subnetwork, severely limiting the usefulness of this method.

- LMHOSTS file

    Similar to the HOSTS file method, this method specifically supports NetBIOS names. Name resolution is maintained via a text file located on the local machine or accessed through network shares.

- WINS

    This is an automated NetBIOS name resolution method. WINS clients automatically register themselves with the WINS server, which can then be queried for name resolution. NetBIOS names can also be manually entered into the database.

Each of these methods will have its place in a mixed network environment.

Additonal Utilities

Microsoft includes three tools with Windows NT Server 4.0 that are vital for testing your TCP/IP installation and Internet connectivity. These are:

- PING.EXE

    The Packet Internet Groper utility is used to test TCP/IP connectivity by transmitting ICMP packets to a TCP/IP host. The host should then echo the packets back to the originating IP address.

- IPCONFIG.EXE

    The Internet Protocol Configuration utility is used to view TCP/IP configuration information from a command prompt.

- TRACERT.EXE

    This utility is used to check the availability of routes to a given destination network. It also provides timing information that can be used to identify bottlenecks in an internetwork or on the Internet.

Each of these utilities is located in the \WINNT\SYSTEM32 subdirectory.

Exercise 3-2:
Viewing TCP/IP Configuration

In this exercise you will verify proper configuration and operation of the TCP/IP communications protocol on your Windows NT Server 4.0 computer.

1. Click on **Start**, then run **Settings/Control Panel/Network**. Or right-mouse click on Network Neighborhood, then select **Properties**.

2. Click on the **Adapters** tab.

3. Check to see that your network interface card is shown in the Network Adapters list. If it is blank, click on **Add** and install the appropriate drivers.

4. Click on the **Protocols** tab. Check to see if TCP/IP is already installed. If it is not listed, you will need to click on **Add** and install the appropriate files.

5. Click on TCP/IP Protocol, then click on **Properties**. The network interface card in the Adapter list should match the network interface card that you will be using to connect to your ISP.

6. If your ISP supplied you with an IP address, subnet mask, and gateway, enter that information now. If you do not have this information enter the following:

   IP Address: 192.168.111.111

   Subnet Mask: 255.255.255.0

   Gateway: 192.168.111.253

7. Click on **Apply**.

8. Click on the **DNS** tab.

9. Enter a Host Name of WEBSERVER. If your ISP has registered a domain name for you, enter it in the Domain field. If you do not have a registered domain name, enter mydomain.com.

10. Click on Add in the DNS Search Order list.

11. Your ISP should have provided you with primary and secondary DNS server addresses. Enter them now. If you do not have a valid DNS address, you can enter 192.168.111.111 for the primary DNS server and 192.168.111.252 for the secondary DNS server. Bear in mind that without access to a DNS server, anytime that you enter a URL, such as www.wavetech.com, your browser or FTP client will fail to find the server. If you receive an error at this point, click on **OK**.

12. After you enter the DNS address, click on **Add**.

13. Click on **OK** to close the TCP/IP properties window.

14. Click on **OK** to close the Network properties window.

15. If prompted to reboot your computer, select **Yes**. If you are returned to your desktop without being asked to reboot, click on **Start/Shutdown/ Restart the computer.**

You can also view TCP/IP configuration information using the IPCONFIG command-line utility. This utility reports on your current TCP/IP configuration and can also be used to change settings.

16. Click on **Start/Programs/Command Prompt**.

17. Enter the following command and press *ENTER*:

    ```
    ipconfig
    ```

18. Does the information displayed coincide with the information you viewed in the Control Panels?

19. Enter the following command to close the window:

    ```
    exit
    ```

Exercise 3-3:
Verifying TCP/IP Operation with PING and TRACERT

In this exercise you will use the PING utility to verify proper TCP/IP operation.

1. Click on **Start/Programs/Command Prompt**.

2. Enter the following commands:

    ```
    ping  192.168.111.111   (substitute your IP address)
    ping  localhost          (the local network interface)
    ping 192.168.111.253    (the default gateway/router)
    ping 192.168.111.111    (the primary DNS server)
    ping 192.168.111.252    (the secondary DNS server)
    ping www.microsoft.com (the Microsoft Web site)
    ```

NOTE: *If you are successful on all of these, your TCP/IP stack is working properly. If you are not connected to the Internet or do not have access to a gateway or DNS server, some of these commands will fail. You should always be able to ping your local interface and IP address, however.*

Next, you will use the TRACERT utility to view the route used between your server and another IP address. This exercise won't work if you are not properly connected to the Internet and using an operational DNS server for host name resolution.

3. If you are connected to the Internet, enter the following command:

```
tracert www.microsoft.com
```

4. Enter the following command to close the window:

```
exit
```

WINDOWS NT 4.0 SERVICE PACK 3

The Windows NT 4.0 Service Pack 3 is required by Internet Information Server 4.0. This is a self-installing Service Pack that *must* be reapplied anytime changes are made to operating system services or hardware configuration.

Service Pack 3 contains the following components:

- Updated Dynamic Link Libraries (.DLL)
- Windows NT Kernel Updates
- Windows NT Driver Updates
- Windows NT Service Updates

Because several parts of Internet Information Server must run as a service, if IIS 2.0 is already installed, Service Pack 3 will automatically update the service to IIS 3.0. Service Pack 3 is available on Microsoft's Web site or on the Windows NT 4.0 Option Pack CD-ROM.

Exercise 3-4:
Installing the Windows NT 4.0 Service Pack 3

In this exercise you will install the Windows NT Server 4.0 Service Pack 3.

1. Insert the Windows NT 4.0 Option Pack CD into your CD-ROM drive.

2. Allow the AutoPlay to execute. If it doesn't, open Explorer and right-click on your CD-ROM drive. Choose **AutoPlay**.

3. Maximize your browser window.

4. Click on **Install**.

5. Click on the Windows NT Service Pack 3 hyperlink for your appropriate platform.

6. Select **Run this program from its current location** and click on **OK**.

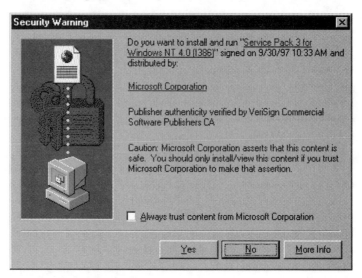

7. Click on **Yes** to begin installation.

8. At the Welcome screen, click on **Next** to continue.

9. Click on **Yes** to accept the license agreement.

10. Ensure that **Install a Service Pack** is selected and click on **Next**.

11. Ensure that **Yes, I want to create an Uninstall directory** is selected and click on **Next**.

12. Click on **Finish**.

13. Click on **OK** to restart the computer.

The Microsoft Internet Explorer (IE)

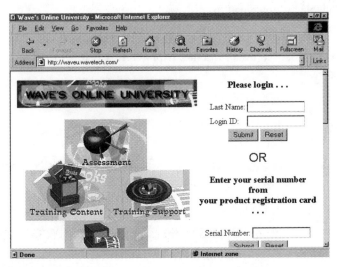

Included on the Windows NT Server 4.0 CD-ROM is an earlier version of the Microsoft Internet Explorer Web browser. This is a tool for navigating and accessing information on the Web. Web surfers can use any Web browser for accessing your site and this is a major consideration when designing your Web pages. Internet Explorer is also available for the Macintosh.

Microsoft Internet Explorer 4.0 and higher supports HTML 1 through HTML 4.0. Netscape Navigator currently supports HTML 1 through HTML 3.2. Each browser may display pages slightly differently. Both also have special enhancements that enable *cooler* looking pages and better functionality, but are proprietary to that particular browser.

If you use HTML commands that are browser specific, you may restrict many potential customers from gaining access to you. Later in the course, publishing information is discussed in more detail.

The latest version of IE can be downloaded from the Microsoft Web site (http://www.microsoft.com/ie). According to Microsoft, IE Service Packs will be made available for download from the same site.

Internet Explorer 4.01 is also available on the Windows NT 4.0 Option Pack CD-ROM. It is necessary to install Internet Explorer 4.01 before installing Internet Information Server.

Exercise 3-5:
Install IE 4.01

In this exercise you install the browser on your Windows NT server. You will need the Option Pack CD-ROM in your CD-ROM drive.

1. Launch Explorer.

2. Expand your CD-ROM drive, then open IE401\X86.

    NOTE: If you are installing on an Alpha computer, open the Alpha directory instead.

3. Double-click on IE4Setup.

4. Confirm the product ID and click on **Next**.

5. Click on **I accept the agreement** and click on **Next**.

6. Make sure Standard Installation is selected and click on **Next**.

7. Click on **No** to disable the desktop update.

8. Click on **Next**.

9. Select the region most appropriate to your location and language. Click on **Next**.

10. Accept the default destination. Click on **Next**.

11. After the files have been copied, click on **OK**.

12. Click on **OK** to restart your computer.

SUMMARY

In this chapter you prepared your computer for installing Internet Information Server 4.0. This included:

- Installing Windows NT Server 4.0
- Configuring and testing TCP/IP
- Testing your TCP/IP settings using PING, TRACERT, and IPCONFIG
- Installing Service Pack 3

In the next chapter you will learn about the features of Internet Information Server and install Internet Information Server 4.0.

POST-TEST QUESTIONS

The answers to these questions are in Appendix A at the end of this manual.

1. How big should the FAT boot partition be on an NT Server?

   ....
   ....

2. Why should you have a DOS floppy with network and CD-ROM drivers on it?

   ....
   ....

3. What is the correct setup and installation order for NT and IIS in order to use IIS 4.0?

   ....
   ....

4. What are some TCP/IP properties to check before connecting your IIS to the Internet?

    ....

    ....

5. Name three utilities included with Windows NT Server 4.0 that can be used to verify TCP/IP configuration and network connectivity.

    ....

    ....

CHAPTER 4

Installing the Microsoft Internet Information Server

OBJECTIVES

At the completion of this chapter, you will be able to:

- List the minimum requirements for installing IIS 4.0.

- Download and install the Windows NT 4 Option Pack, which contains IIS 4.0.

- Set up initial configuration.

- Install Internet Information Server.

PRE-TEST QUESTIONS

The answers to these questions are in Appendix A at the end of this manual.

1. What is the minimum available hard disk space required to install the Windows NT 4.0 Option Pack?

    ....

    ....

2. What type of file system is recommended as the location for your wwwroot directory?

    ....

    ....

3. After installing Internet Information Server, you launch a browser and navigate to the URL http://localhost. What document is displayed?

    ....

    ....

INTRODUCTION

IIS 4.0 is tightly integrated with the Windows NT operating system. For access control, IIS 4.0 shares user security information with Windows NT, rather than forcing NT-server and Web-server administrators to maintain separate user databases. When configuring IIS 4.0, you typically limit file system access for Web and FTP users to directories related to those respective services. For more granular security requirements, you can use Windows NT file security permissions to restrict access for individual users and groups.

NOTE: *If you elect to store HTML documents on a FAT partition, you lose most of the ability to restrict access to those directories. It is strongly suggested that when installing IIS 4.0, you select an NTFS partition for the HTML content directories.*

WINDOWS NT 4.0 OPTION PACK AND IIS 4.0 SYSTEM REQUIREMENTS

Most Internet Information Servers will probably be up and running 24 hours a day, 7 days a week. It is important to select a high-quality hardware platform. The following is a list of the minimum hardware and software requirements for running IIS 4.0. You may also have additional requirements depending on the applications you are running or services you want to support.

Minimum IIS 4.0 Requirements

The following is a list of minimum and recommended requirements for an Internet Information Server:

- CPU: Pentium 66 (minimum), Pentium 90+ (recommended)
- Hard Disk: 200 MB of disk space (minimum), SCSI Controller with 2+ GB hard drive (recommended)
- Memory: 32 MB RAM (minimum), 64+ MB (recommended)
- CD-ROM drive

- VGA, Super VGA, or video graphics adapter compatible with Windows NT Server 4.0

- Microsoft mouse or other pointing device

- Windows NT Server 4.0

- Windows NT Service Pack 3

- Internet Explorer 4.01 (or greater)

- Windows NT 4 Option Pack

- Network Interface Card

- An Internet connection and an Internet Protocol (IP) address from your Internet Service Provider (ISP), unless you're setting up an intranet

- Router or terminal adapter for connecting to your ISP

- A registered Internet Domain Name

Obtaining Windows NT 4.0 Option Pack

IIS 4.0 ships with the following Microsoft BackOffice products:

- Microsoft BackOffice Server 4.0

- Microsoft BackOffice Enterprise Server 4.0

IIS 4.0 is also a component of the Windows NT 4.0 Option Pack, which can be obtained from:

- http://www.microsoft.com/msdownload/ntoptionpack/askwiz.asp

- Requesting it on CD-ROM from Microsoft

It is generally considered more convenient to have a CD-ROM on hand when something isn't working right and you need to find a driver or file. Besides, Windows NT Option Pack is 27 MB, which will be a lengthy download if you are using a modem.

Exercise 4-1:
Install Windows NT 4.0 Option Pack/IIS 4.0

In this exercise, you will install the IIS 4.0 from the Windows NT 4.0 Option Pack CD-ROM. The exercises in Chapter 3 are a prerequisite.

1.   Open Explorer.

2.   Right-click on the CD-ROM and run **AutoPlay**.

3.   Click on **Install**.

4.   Click on **Install Windows NT 4.0 Option Pack**.

5.   Select **Run this program from its current location** and click on **OK**.

6.   If you receive the following security warning, click on **Yes**.

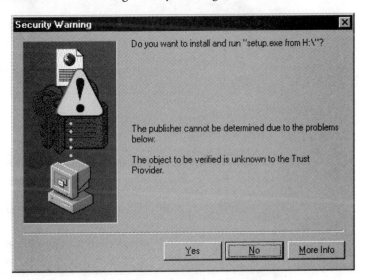

7.   Click on **Next**.

8.   Click on **Accept**.

9. Click on **Custom**.

10. Scroll down the list and notice the components that are available. Keep the default selections. You will add some additional components later in the course. Click on **Next**.

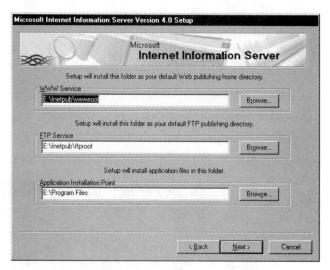

11. Keep the default publishing directories. Click on **Next**.

    NOTE: The default path for the directories that Setup creates will be the Inetpub directory on the drive where Windows NT is installed.

12. Keep the default path for Microsoft Transaction Server. Click on **Next**.

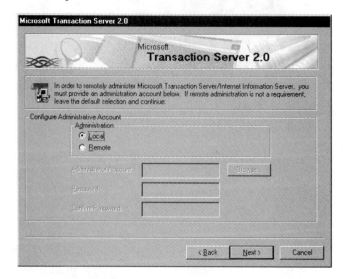

13. Keep administration local. Click on **Next**.

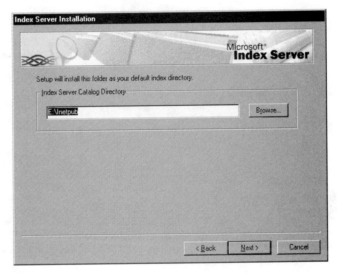

14.   Keep the default Index Server directory. Click on **Next**.

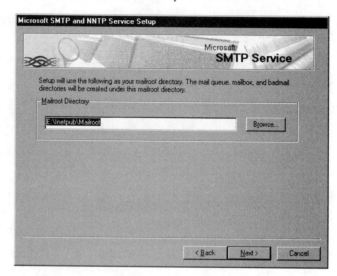

15.   Keep the default mailroot directory. Click on **Next**.

16.   Click on **Finish**.

17.   Click on **Yes** to restart your computer.

IIS Directory Structure

By default, the Windows NT 4.0 Option Pack/IIS 4.0 installation process creates the following directory structure on the drive where Windows NT was installed:

\InetPub\wwwroot

\InetPub\ftproot

\InetPub\scripts

\InetPub\Mailroot

\InetPub\nntpfile

\InetPub\Catalog.wci

\InetPub\iissamples

\InetPub\Mail

\InetPub\News

NOTE: *You are provided with the option of installing to a different drive but most installations use the default IIS parent directory of \InetPub.*

Making Sure It's Running

To verify that your installation was successful, launch Internet Explorer and type the following URL:

```
http://localhost
```

If your Web service is running, the default document on the local machine will be displayed.

You can also tell if the Web service is running by opening the Services utility in Control Panel.

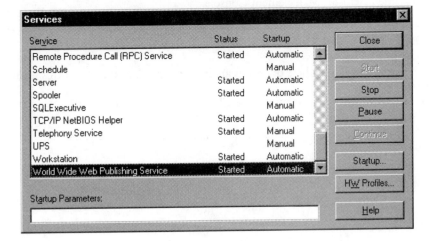

SUMMARY

During this chapter you learned how to install the Windows NT 4.0 Option Pack. This included:

- Installation requirements
- Custom installation
- Directories created during installation
- Testing your installation

In the next chapter, you will learn how to manage Internet Information Server through the Microsoft Management Console.

POST-TEST QUESTIONS

The answers to these questions are in Appendix A at the end of this manual.

1. What are the minimum CPU requirements for IIS 4.0?

    ....

    ....

2. What is the minimum memory requirement for IIS 4.0?

    ....

    ....

3. What is the default root directory for the WWW service?

    ....

    ....

4. What service must be running in order for you to display a Web page by typing the command:

    ```
    http://localhost
    ```

    ....

    ....

CHAPTER 5

Managing Your Microsoft Internet Information Server

OBJECTIVES

At the completion of this chapter, you will be able to:

- Use the Internet Service Manager and Microsoft Management Console to configure installed Services.
- Set WWW directory properties.
- Describe the information logged when logging is enabled.
- Configure FTP Service properties.

PRE-TEST QUESTIONS

The answers to these questions are in Appendix A at the end of this manual.

1. What is the function of the Microsoft Management Console?

    ....

    ....

2. What NT username is referred to as the anonymous user account?

    ....

    ....

3. What happens when someone browses to a directory that does not have a default document?

    ....

    ....

4. Where can you change the default settings for all of the new sites you create on your server?

    ....

    ....

INTRODUCTION

The previous chapters have led you through the installation processes for the Windows NT 4.0 Server operating system and the Internet Information Server.

This chapter describes IIS 4.0 configuration parameters, the Internet Service Manager, and Microsoft Management Console utilities. You will use these tools to configure and manage the operational parameters of the IIS 4.0 Web and FTP Servers.

MICROSOFT MANAGEMENT CONSOLE

Windows NT 4.0 Option Pack installs a new management interface called the Microsoft Management Console (MMC), as well as snap-ins to handle various services. This section will show you how to use and customize the MMC. This includes:

- Benefits of the MMC

- MMC Feature Tour

- Saving Consoles

- Getting Help

Let's look first at what the MMC is and how it can make administering your network easier.

Benefits of the MMC

In Windows NT 4.0, every management tool you use has a different interface. This requires you to think about how to use the tool's interface. By consolidating all management functions into a uniform interface, you can more easily concentrate on the job that needs to be done instead of worrying about which menu or button you need to select to get you where you want to go.

The Microsoft Management Console solves that problem. The MMC is a shell that provides the user interface to management tools called *snap-ins*. Windows NT 4 Option Pack installs the snap-ins that are used to manage the services you select to install. For example, the Internet Service Manager snap-in allows you to administer the Internet Information Server. The Microsoft Transaction Server snap-in allows you to administer the Microsoft Transaction Server.

MMC Feature Tour

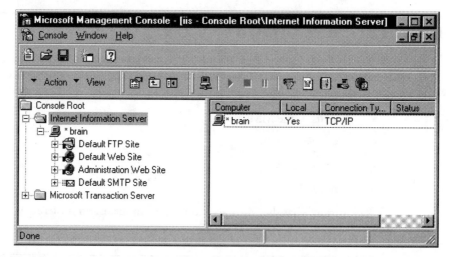

To launch the Microsoft Management Console utility, run **Start/Programs/Windows NT 4.0 Option Pack/Microsoft Internet Server/Internet Service Manager**.

The MMC has an Explorer-like interface with a hierarchical TreeView control on the left-hand side and a ListView control on the right-hand side. The left-hand side is known as the *scope* pane. The right-hand side is the *contents* pane. As with Explorer, the information in the contents pane can be displayed in either Large Icon, Small Icon, List, or Detail views.

The snap-ins that have been added to the console are listed under the Console Root folder in the scope pane. They can be expanded to reveal the objects they contain. To change which snap-ins are displayed, run **Add/Remove Snap-In** from the **Console** menu.

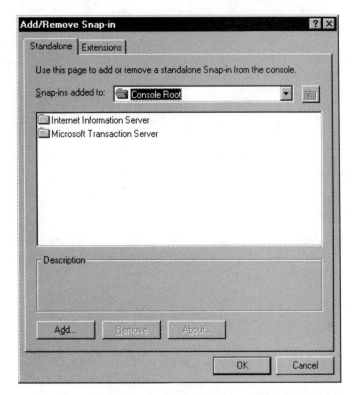

You can add either a stand-alone snap-in, such as the Microsoft Index Server snap-in, or an extension, like the SMTP extension for Internet Information Server. If you choose to add a stand-alone snap-in, you will be prompted to select whether the snap-in will be used to manage a local service or a service on another computer.

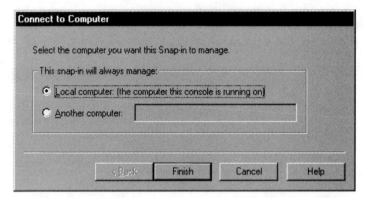

Once you click on **Finish**, the snap-in will be added to the scope pane of the current console.

Saving Consoles

When MMC is first loaded, the default console is displayed. However, you can customize consoles for yourself and for other administrators and users. Benefits of doing this include:

- Using your customized console on various machines.

- Limiting which snap-ins a particular user can load.

To save a console you have created, run **Save As** from the **Console** menu. Give the console a name. The file will be saved with the .msc extension. It can then be copied to a disk or to the network and shared with the appropriate permissions. One example of this would be if you have developers who need to manage the Microsoft Transaction Server and you want to restrict them from accessing other servers. In this case, you could create a console with only the Microsoft Transaction Server snap-in and save it to a shared directory. Then give the Developers group read-only access to that directory.

Getting Help

The **Help** menu of the Microsoft Management Console allows you to access help files for the console itself, as well as for the currently selected snap-in.

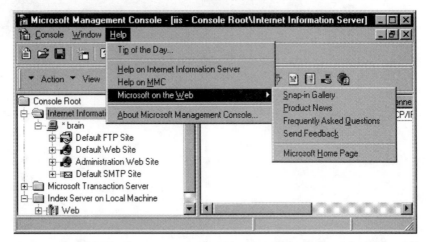

If you are connected to the Internet, you can also select **Microsoft on the Web** to directly access URLs that provide you with access to a gallery of snap-ins, product news, frequently asked questions, and the ability to send feedback on the product. You can also access Microsoft's Home Page.

INTERNET SERVICE MANAGER

The Internet Service Manager is the snap-in that allows you to administer the Internet Information Server on the local machine or on a remote machine. This section will overview what you can do with this snap-in. The discussion will include:

- Management Tasks
- Objects and Icons
- Inheritance
- Computer Properties

Management Tasks

Examples of common management tasks you might need to perform through the Internet Service Manger include:

- Controlling anonymous login
- Configuring authentication methods
- Configuring directory restrictions
- IP Filtering

NOTE: *When using NT Explorer to alter directory permissions, User Manager to add or change user names and groups, or the Internet Service Manager to configure IIS 4.0, it may be necessary to stop and restart the WWW and FTP services for changes to take effect.*

Objects and Icons

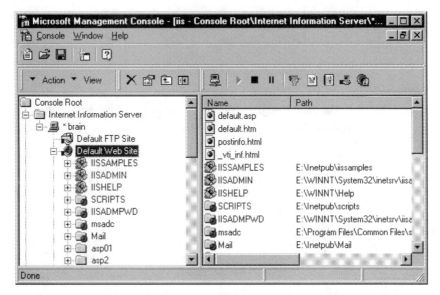

Before you can use the Internet Service Manager to administer your Web server, you need to understand some of the objects that are created beneath the Internet Information Server. These are:

*   Computer

    This object's icon resembles a computer. It is used to set properties that apply to all of the sites running on a particular computer. Some of these properties can be overridden by properties set on child objects.

- Sites

    Beneath the Computer object are all of the sites running on that server. One of the powerful features of Internet Information Server 4.0 is that you can run multiple sites on the same computer and manage them easily through the MMC. When Internet Information Server is installed, the following sites are created automatically:

    Default FTP Site

    Default Web Site

    Administration Web Site

    If you installed extension services, such as SMTP, a site for that service will appear as well. In addition, you can add multiple sites to your server. You will see how that is done later.

- Applications

    Applications can be added to each Web site. In Web usage, an application defines the directories in which a file being executed runs. All files within an application can share context information and variables. For example, you may have an order entry application that includes several forms. By including those forms in an application, each form can have access to variables set on the other forms. An application is defined by its starting point. Directories added beneath that starting point belong to the application. However, if an application starting point is added inside of one of those directories, a new application tree is started.

- Virtual Directories

    A virtual directory is a directory that can be located on the local computer running Internet Information Server or on a different machine. They will be discussed in detail later in the course.

- Directory

    A directory is a path on the local computer or one that can be accessed by a URL.

Inheritance

Each object has a set of properties associated with it. By default, all child objects inherit properties from the parent object. For example, when Internet Information Server is first installed, the Connection Timeout value for the FTP connections on the Computer object is set to 900. Therefore, all FTP sites beneath the server have a Connection Timeout set to 900 as well. You can change this default value on the Computer object. If you do, it will affect any FTP site objects that have not had their Connection Timeout value set explicitly.

However, if you set a property on a child object explicitly, that value will override any value set on an object above it in the hierarchy. In the previous example, suppose you were supporting an FTP site for users that you knew would be dialing over poor lines with slow modems. You could increase the timeout value for that site only to 1500. Even if the Computer object's Connection Timeout value was later changed to 300, the site with the explicitly set value would remain unchanged.

It is important to note that for properties that contain lists of values, such as users who have permission to an object, the lists are replaced, not merged.

Server Properties

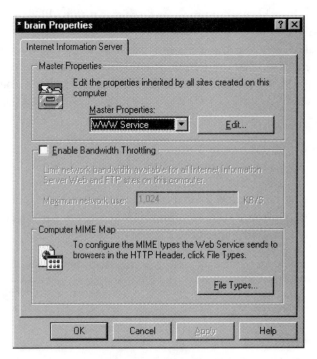

You can display the Computer object's properties by right-clicking on the Computer object and running **Properties** or by selecting the Computer object and clicking on the **Properties** button. To set default properties for either WWW sites or FTP sites, select the appropriate service from the drop-down list and click on **Edit**. The appropriate property pages will be displayed.

You can also set bandwidth throttling properties and mime types globally from this property page. Keep in mind that these are global to all sites running on the server except those for which properties have been explicitly set.

WWW SERVICE PROPERTIES

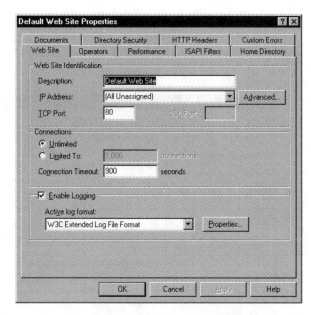

This section will overview the property pages for the WWW Service. These are:

- Web Site
- Operators
- Performance
- ISAPI Filters
- Home Directory
- Documents
- Directory Security

- HTTP Headers
- Custom Errors

Let's look at each of them. Right-click on the Default Web Site and select **Properties**.

Web Site

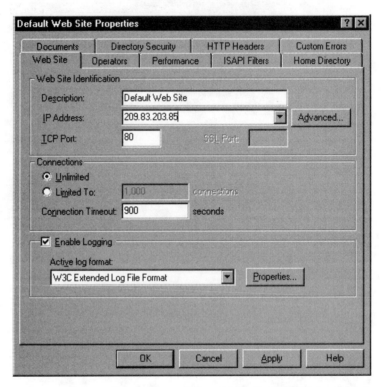

The Web Site property page allows you to define the Web site name, specify the IP address of the Web server, control the number of connections, enable/disable logging, and configure the TCP Port number used for the Web site and any SSL you may have selected.

The IP address can be selected from those configured in the Network utility. A special value of All Unassigned is the default. This means that the site will respond to any IP address that is configured in the Network utility, but that is not being used by another WWW site on the server. This is useful for computers with multiple network adapter cards.

The Port is another important field. The default port for the WWW service is port 80. If you change the port number for a particular Web site, users will have to append the port number to the URL in order to reach the site.

Operators

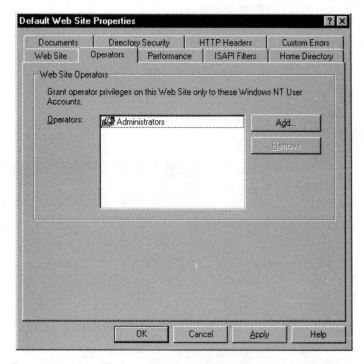

This page allows you to specify the users who possess rights to control certain aspects of the Web site. By default, the Administrators group is given this right.

Operators cannot do everything. They are not allowed to:

- Modify a Web site's host header, IP Address, or port.

- Make changes to the IUSR_*ComputerName* account.

- Change bandwidth throttling settings.

- Create virtual directories.

- Relocate virtual directories.

In order to be assigned as an operator, a user account must be created in either User Manager (for a stand-alone system) or User Manager for Domains (for a domain member).

Performance

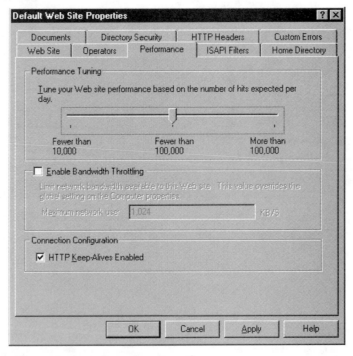

This property page allows you to configure the performance of the Service based on the expected number of users per day. If you are a corporation that has an Internet link you can configure the bandwidth that you are willing to allow for the Web server so that e-mail and other network traffic is not adversely affected by Web traffic. Performance properties will be discussed in more detail later in the course.

ISAPI Filters

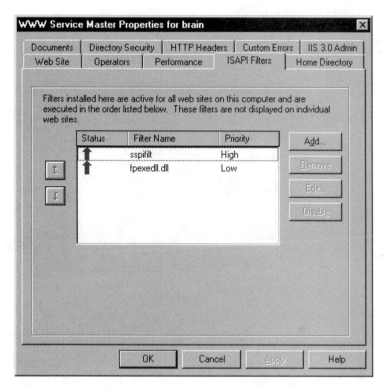

An ISAPI filter is a dynamic link library that executes in response to a particular event. ISAPI filters can be specified on a Server level or on a Site level. When they are specified at both levels, the lists are merged. When you configure an ISAPI filter, you must specify the path to the DLL, the event with which the filter is associated, and the filter's priority. If an event is associated with multiple filters, the filter with the highest priority executes first. If two filters have the same priority, the filter that was loaded first is the one executed first.

A filter loads into memory when the server or site that uses it starts. They are loaded in the order in which they appear in the list. To promote or demote a filter, use the arrow buttons to the left of the list.

Home Directory

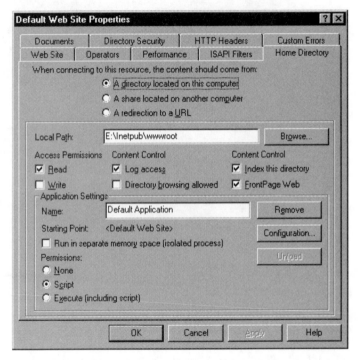

This property page allows you configure the home directory for your Web site. The default directory for IIS 4.0 is *systemdrive:*\Inetpub\wwwroot. This directory could exist as a share on a separate Windows NT Server computer by enabling redirection. You can also control user rights and permissions to the contents of this directory along with application settings.

The Home Directory property sheet is used to configure the default directory for your home page and other Web content. When a user enters the URL for your Web site such as http://www.wavetech.com, a default document is returned to them. If the URL specifies a subdirectory on your server without specifying a particular document, a default document from that subdirectory is returned to them, if available.

Documents

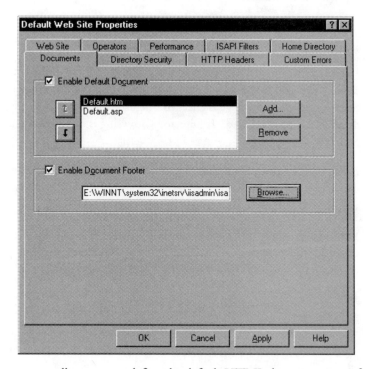

This property page allows you to define the default HTML document name for your Web site. When users connect to your Web site, if they haven't asked for a specific document, your server will send them the default document from your \Inetpub\Wwwroot directory.

Two sample HTML pages are created in \InetPub\wwwroot directory during the NT 4.0 Option Pack installation process. They are:

- default.htm
- default.asp

If more than one document is specified, IIS 4.0 goes down the list until it locates one of them. If you don't specify a default document and the Directory Browsing property on the Web site property page is checked, the user will receive a directory listing when a document is not specified. If Directory Browsing is disabled, the user will receive an error.

In the UNIX world, the default document name is index.html. In the world of IIS 4.0, the default document name is generally default.htm. You can change this name to anything you desire (usually index.html).

You can also specify a file containing a footer on this property page. This is useful in a situation where you want to have an identical footer on every Web page that is displayed. For example, you might use a footer to display a copyright notice on all content.

Directory Security

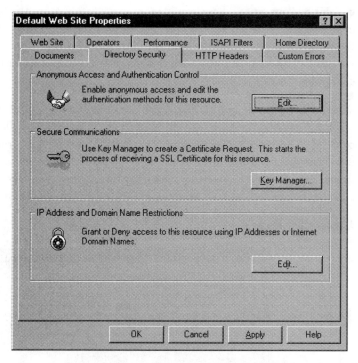

This allows you to configure the type of security that is established on the Web site. You can also choose to make global directory security changes to other IIS 4.0 Services. You can configure anonymous logon, Windows NT logon with directory security, IP restrictions, or combinations of all three. Security will be discussed in detail later in the course. However, let's take a brief look at it now.

Anonymous Access

The anonymous user account is the account that the WWW Service uses when accessing content on your server. The default anonymous user account IUSR_*Computername* is appropriate for most situations. During creation, this user is added to the member lists of the local Guests group and the Domain Users global group. Later in this chapter, you will see how to verify that the Windows NT permissions for this account are properly configured.

When a user clicks on a URL that points to your server, the IUSR_*Computername* account is used by IIS 4.0 to determine access to directories and files containing Web content. Access is controlled by the Windows NT and IIS 4.0 permissions granted to this account. If you wish to limit site access to certain users, you can require users to supply a valid account name and password. If you enable this option, all users that connect to your Web server will require NT user accounts and passwords.

Authentication Methods

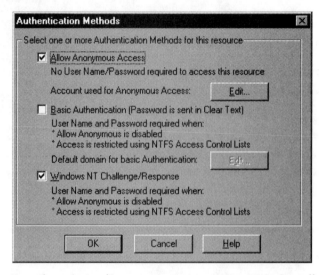

Authentication is used to restrict directory access to certain users. Overall user access is determined by the combination of IIS security, Windows NT directory permissions, and user rights.

For example, if you wish to enable access to your Web site for Internet users you would configure the directory permissions to the wwwroot directory for the IUSR_*Computername* account to Read. If you then wanted to prevent anonymous users from accessing certain subdirectories below wwwroot, you would not grant any NTFS permissions to the IUSR_*Computername* account for those subdirectories. If you have a user that requires access to a restricted subdirectory, you will need to create a Windows NT user account, assign a password, and grant the user Read permission in the subdirectory.

IIS 4.0 provides two user-level authentication options:

Basic Authentication

Basic Authentication can be used by all browsers. This authentication method transmits usernames and passwords through a network as simple unencrypted ASCII text. This might be considered a security problem since anyone with a network analyzer could capture packets containing usernames and passwords. However, if you do not select this option, you will disallow access to secured directories for users with a browser other than Internet Explorer. When you enable this option, you are warned that this is a possible security issue. Ignore the warning and enable Basic Authentication.

Windows NT Challenge/Response

This authentication method is for users who use the Internet Explorer browser. This method encrypts usernames and passwords during transmission and is considered secure.

HTTP Headers

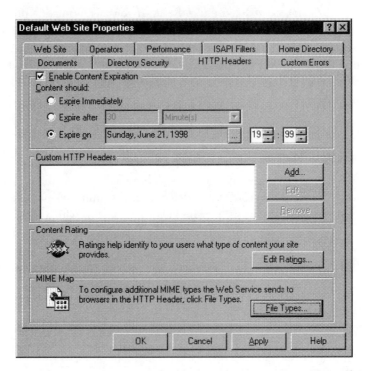

Allows you to configure custom HTTP headers, Multipurpose Internet Mail Extensions (MIME types), content expiration, and content ratings. These will be discussed later in the course.

Custom Errors

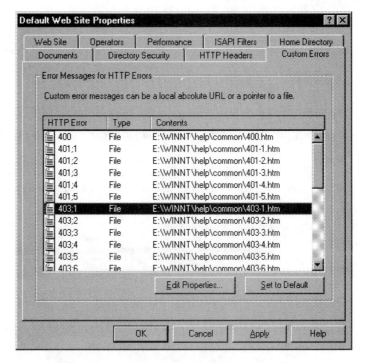

This property page allows you to create custom error messages for your Web site.

Exercise 5-1:
Configuring Authentication and the Default Document

In this exercise you will enable Basic Authentication, change the default document parameters, and verify directory permissions. Exercise 4-1 is a prerequisite.

1. Click on **Start/Programs/Windows NT 4.0 Option Pack/Microsoft Internet Server/Internet Service Manager** to launch the Internet Service Manager.

2. Open the Internet Information Server folder, then open the Web server computer icon.

3. Right-click on Default Web Site and select **Properties** or single-click Default Web Site and click the **Properties** button on the button bar.

4. Click on the **Directory Security** tab. Click on the **Edit** button for Anonymous Access and Authentication Control.

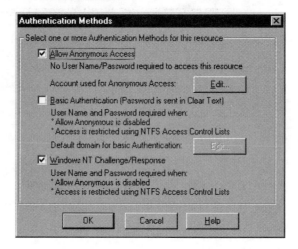

5. Select **Basic Authentication**. Read the following message, then click **Yes**.

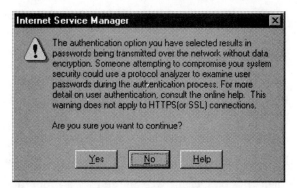

6. Click on **OK** to close the Anonymous Access and Authentication Control window.

7. Click on **Apply**. Read the message in the Inheritance Overrides dialog box.

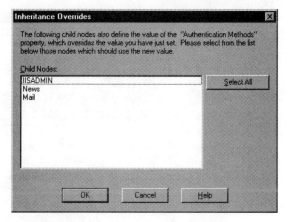

8. Click on **Select All**, then click **OK**.

9. Click on the **Document** tab.

10. Select default.htm and click on **Remove**. Click on **Add** and enter the following file name:

    ```
    index.html
    ```

11.   Click on **Apply**, then click on **OK**.

12.   Minimize the Microsoft Management Console window.

13.   Click **Start/Programs/NT Explorer** and browse to locate the following directory and file:

```
\InetPub\wwwroot\default.htm
```

14.   Right-click the default.htm file and select **Rename**. Enter the following name, then click on **OK**:

```
index.html
```

15.   Exit NT Explorer and maximize the Microsoft Management Console utility.

16.   Right-click on Default Web Site and select **Properties** or single-click on Default Web Site and click on the **Properties** button on the button bar.

17.   Click on the **Home Directory** tab.

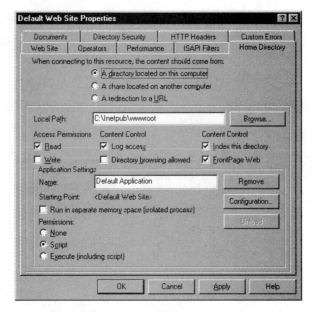

18.   Verify that the wwwroot directory only allows Read access. This permits anyone accessing your site to view documents but prevents them from making changes. Click on **OK**.

19. Double-click on Default Web Site. Select the SCRIPTS folder in the Name/Path list, then click on the **Properties** button on the tool bar.

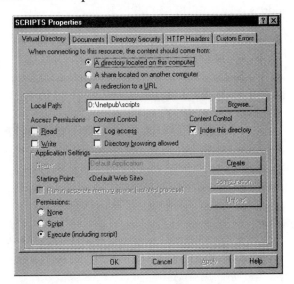

20. Verify that the scripts directory only allows Execute access. The scripts directory is where your CGI, ISAPI, Active Server scripts, and so on, reside. These files are programs that execute on the server. Do not download someone else's CGI, ISAPI, or other program and run it on your server without first testing it thoroughly.

   NOTE: Execute permission is used so that these programs can run, but no one can remotely view or download the contents of the scripts directory.

21. Click on **OK** to return to the Microsoft Management Console. Minimize the application.

22.   Launch your Web browser and enter the IP address that you assigned to your server. If you followed the installation procedure in Chapter 3 your server's IP address is 192.168.111.111.

23.   Are you able to view your server's default home page?

24.   Exit from your Web browser.

FTP SERVICE PROPERTIES

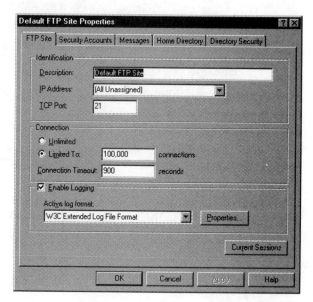

You configure the FTP Service through a collection of five properties pages. These are:

- FTP Site
- Security Accounts
- Messages
- Home Directory
- Directory Security

Let's look at each of them.

FTP Site

In the **FTP Site** properties page you can:

- Enter a description of the FTP Site and the IP address of the FTP server.
- Configure the TCP/IP Port on which the service is listening. This defaults to Port 21.
- Limit the maximum number of concurrent connections the site should allow.
- Enable or disable logging.
- Display a list of users who are currently connected to the site.

Security Accounts

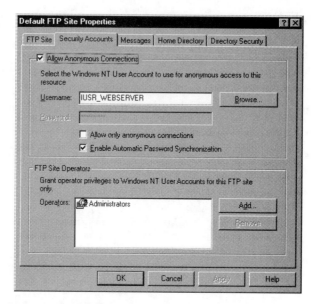

In the **Security Accounts** properties page you can:

- Allow anonymous connections using the Internet guest account IUSR_*Computername*.

- Enable or disable automatic password synchronization and allow only anonymous logons.

- Assign FTP site operators.

By enabling the **Allow Anonymous Connections** option you allow browsers and FTP clients to connect to your server without an explicit user account name and password. You must use NTFS permissions in conjunction with FTP server directory permissions to control access to the FTP server.

If you enable the **Allow only anonymous connections** option you prevent anyone from logging on to your server with a valid username and password. For example, with this option disabled, a user might successfully guess your Administrator password and would have access to directories with the same permissions as the Administrator user.

Messages

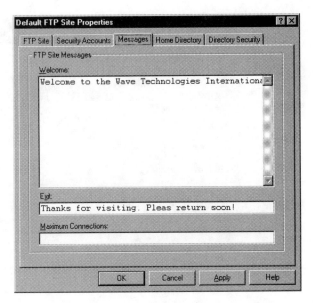

In the **Messages** properties page you can configure three types of messages to be displayed by your FTP server:

- A Welcome message that is displayed when a client connects to the FTP server.

- An Exit message that is displayed when a client disconnects from the FTP server.

- A Maximum Connections message that is displayed when the site has reached the maximum number of user connections allowed.

Home Directory

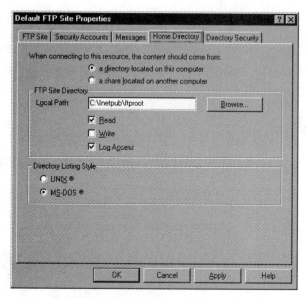

In the **Home Directory** properties page you can:

- Specify where FTP content is stored, either locally or on another server.

    If the FTP content is stored on another server it is accessed through a share.

- Configure the default parent directory for the FTP Service.

    This is the path to the directory that will store the files. It is recommended that it be on an NTFS partition.

- Configure the access permissions for the FTP root directory.

    The initial default configuration for this directory is read-only with logging enabled. There may be a time when you want to designate a subdirectory to allow clients to upload files. Then you would select both read and write for that subdirectory only.

    If the directory is on an NTFS partition and the permissions set here do not match the NTFS permissions granted to the user, the most restrictive settings will be applied. For example, if the IUSR_*ComputerName* account is granted read-only permission to the directory and the FTP Site is set up with write permission, an anonymous user will only be granted read permission to this site.

- Directory-style listing

   Select from either UNIX or MS-DOS directory-style listings. The default is MS-DOS.

When a user connects to your FTP server with a valid Windows NT user account and password, the FTP service will look for a subdirectory under \InetPub\ftproot or a virtual directory that matches the user's name. If one exists, the FTP service will set that directory as the default for this user.

Directory Security

The **Directory Security** properties page allows you to configure IP Filtering.

When most people connect to the Microsoft FTP site, they do so anonymously. The username is "anonymous" and the password is usually their e-mail address. By allowing anonymous connections, Microsoft can distribute updates and new software without having to maintain millions of user accounts. Many companies allow read permission to some directories for the anonymous user and limit writing to one directory called incoming.

The anonymous user account (IUSR_*Computername*) is created during the Windows NT 4.0 Option Pack installation process and is the default user account used by the FTP Service. The Internet standard username used by clients is "anonymous" and IIS 4.0 recognizes this.

Exercise 5-2:
Configure FTP Messages

In this exercise you will configure welcome and exit messages for your FTP server.

1. Click **Start/Programs/Windows NT 4.0 Option Pack/Microsoft Internet Server/ Internet Service Manager** to launch the Internet Service Manager.

2. Open the Internet Information Server folder, then open the webserver computer icon.

3. Right-click on Default FTP Site and select **Properties** or single-click on Default FTP Site and click on the **Properties** button on the button bar.

4. Click the **Messages** tab.

5. Enter the following text in the Welcome field:

   Welcome to My Company's FTP Site.

6. Enter the following text in the Exit field:

   Thank you for visting My Company.

7. Enter the following text in the Maximum Connections field:

```
Site is busy, please try later.
```

8. Click on **Apply**, then click on **OK**.

9. Double-click on the Internet Explorer icon on your desktop.

10. Enter the following text in the Address field:

    ```
    ftp://192.168.111.111
    ```

    (or substitute your server's IP address)

    Was the welcome message that you configured for your FTP server displayed?

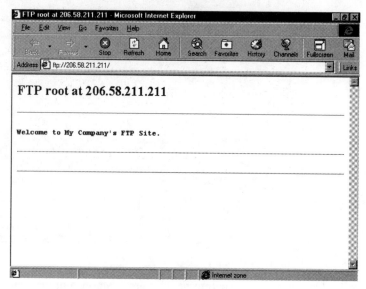

11. Exit from the Internet Explorer application.

12. Click on **Start/Programs/Command Prompt**.

13. Enter the following text at the command prompt:

    ```
    ftp 192.168.111.111
    ```

    (or substitute your server's IP address)

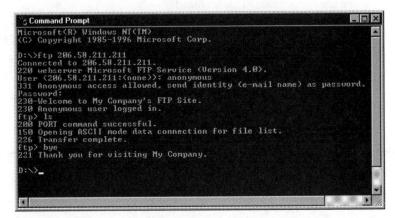

14. When prompted for a user name, enter the following:

    ```
    anonymous
    ```

15. When prompted for a password, enter your e-mail address, then press *ENTER*.

16. Was your welcome message displayed?

17. Enter the following command to view a directory listing:

    ```
    ls
    ```

18. Enter the following command to end your FTP session:

    ```
    bye
    ```

19. Was your exit message displayed?

20. Enter the following command to close the **Command Prompt** window:

    ```
    exit
    ```

SUMMARY

During this chapter, you were introduced to the Internet Service Manager and Microsoft Management Console. This included:

- Adding snap-ins
- Object hierarchy
- Configuring the WWW service
- Configuring the FTP service

In the next chapter, the discussion will focus on security issues.

POST-TEST QUESTIONS

The answers to these questions are in Appendix A at the end of this manual.

1. What is the default document that is loaded when a user requests just a directory?

   ....

   ....

2. Your marketing department is responsible for managing your company's presence on the Internet. You would like them to be able to manage the Internet Information Server, but nothing else. How can you do that?

   ....

   ....

3. The remote users in your company access the corporate intranet across the Internet. They all use Internet Explorer as their browser. What authentication method should you use to keep their passwords from being sniffed on the wire?

   ....

   ....

4. You would like to display a corporate disclaimer on the bottom of each Web page on your Beta Products Web site. How can you do this?

....

....

5. What password is usually used when a user logs on to your FTP site anonymously?

....

....

6. How can you determine who is currently connected to your FTP site?

....

....

7. Your company has recently changed its FTP site from a UNIX host to Internet Information Server. Many of the employees do not like the way directory listings are displayed because it is different than what they are used to seeing. What change should you make?

....

....

Security

OBJECTIVES

At the completion of this chapter, you will be able to:

- Set appropriate access permissions to Web server directories.
- Review user account settings for the anonymous user.
- Set account rights to help limit unauthorized access.
- Set Web and FTP permissions.
- Enable IP Filtering.
- Configure Secure Sockets Layer communication.
- Install and configure Certificate Server.

PRE-TEST QUESTIONS

The answers to these questions are in Appendix A at the end of this manual.

1. What are the default permissions assigned to a directory upon creation?

   ....

   ....

2. Which utility is used to manage Account and User Rights policies?

   ....

   ....

3. What feature would you use to grant access to a particular directory only to one particular subnet?

   ....

   ....

4. What do you need to install in order to act as a Certificate Authority?

   ....

   ....

INTRODUCTION

Security is an important issue when implementing an Internet or intranet site. This chapter looks at some of the key concerns. It begins with a brief look at physical security. Next, resource security is covered. This discussion includes a look at the criteria you can use to determine who is given access to a particular site or directory. The chapter continues with a look at the Secure Sockets Layer (SSL) protocol. Finally, you will be introduced to Microsoft Certificate Server.

PHYSICAL SECURITY

If your Internet Information Server is connected to the corporate network, you need to think about how it is connected and the possible security risks the connection presents. Let's look at two possible scenarios:

- Connecting Without a Firewall
- Connecting With a Firewall

Connecting Without a Firewall

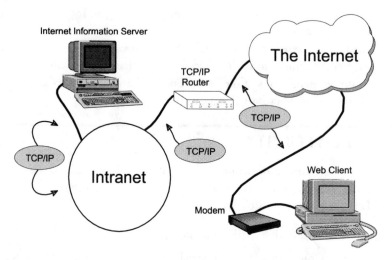

There are many options available for connecting your Web server to the Internet. In the example shown above, the Web server is connected to the corporate intranet. The intranet is connected to the Internet via a TCP/IP router. This configuration allows access to the server by both internal users and Internet users. Although flexible and easy to implement, this configuration may be difficult to secure from outside intruders.

Connecting With a Firewall

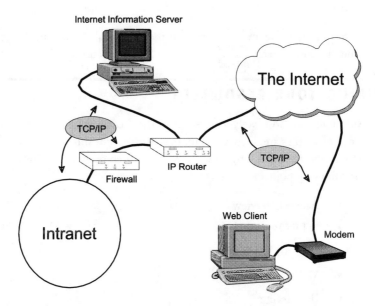

In the above example, the corporate intranet connects first to a firewall and then to a port on a TCP/IP router. The Web server connects to a different router port and is located on a separate subnet. This configuration also allows access to the Web server by internal corporate users as well as external Internet users. The primary difference between this configuration and the previous example is the introduction of a firewall to secure the corporate intranet.

A firewall is capable of providing a much more sophisticated level of security than is available in most routers or the Windows NT Server 4.0 operating system. IP Filtering is the primary method available to IIS 4.0 administrators for keeping out unwanted intruders. Most firewalls combine IP Filtering, circuit-level proxy, and application-level proxy functions to virtually eliminate network security breaches.

A circuit-level proxy operates at the OSI Session layer by substituting the firewall's IP address in place of the client computer's. All packets leaving the firewall appear to the Internet as coming from a single IP address.

An application-level proxy operates at the OSI Application and Presentation layers and is generally considered to offer the highest level of security.

SECURING YOUR RESOURCES

Although you most likely want some of the files on your Web site to be available to all users, other files are likely to be more sensitive. For this reason, it is important that you understand the criteria by which access to a Web resource is granted. Let's take a look at the following points:

- Access Overview
- NTFS Permissions
- User Authentication
- Web Permissions
- IP Filtering

Understanding these points will give you the foundation you need to begin to design a security infrastructure for your Web server.

Access Overview

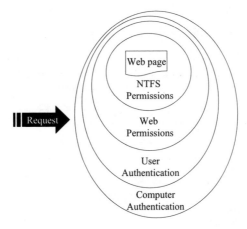

Depending on your needs, you can enable up to four layers of security to protect a document on a Web server. If all four layers are implemented, an access request must be approved at each of them. If any of the security criteria are not met, the request for access will be denied. The four criteria you can use to configure access are:

- Computer authentication

    You can select to grant or deny access based on the identity of the computer making the request.

- User authentication

    You can select to grant or deny access to the Web site based on whether the user can correctly enter the user name and password of a known Windows NT domain user. Another way to provide user authentication is through verifying that the user holds a valid certificate that grants him or her access. Certificates will be discussed later in the chapter.

- Web permissions

  You can specify that a Web site, directory, virtual directory, or file has a particular set of permissions, regardless of who is trying to access it.

- NTFS permissions

  You can take advantage of Windows NT's security model by assigning NTFS permissions to resources. This provides you with the ability to control access based on a user's identity.

Let's look at each of these, beginning with NTFS permissions.

NTFS Permissions

NTFS permissions consist of two components:

- Directory Access Permissions

  Directory Access permissions determine a user's rights to a directory or subdirectory.

- File Access Permissions

  File Access permissions determine a user's rights to a particular file.

Directory Access Permissions

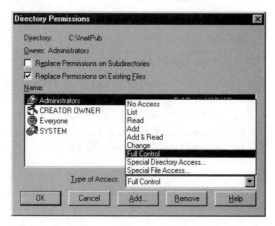

Windows NTFS security includes several pre-configured directory permissions sets. These make it easy to assign directory rights without needing to select individual permissions.

You can set the following directory permissions:

- No Access (None) (None)

  Prevents access to the directory. If a user or group to which a user belongs is assigned No Access, the user will not be able to access the directory, regardless of the permissions specified by other group memberships.

- List (RX) (Not Specified)

  Allows viewing file names, subdirectory names, and changing to the directory's subdirectories. Does not provide access to files.

- Read (RX) (RX)

  Allows viewing file names, subdirectory names, and changing to the directory's subdirectories. Allows viewing of file contents and program execution.

- Add (WX) (Not Specified)

  Allows adding files and subdirectories to the directory. Does not provide access to files.

- Add & Read (RWX) (RX)

  Allows viewing file names, subdirectory names, and changing to the directory's subdirectories. Allows adding files and subdirectories to the directory. Allows viewing of file contents and program execution.

- Change (RWXD) (RWXD)

  Allows viewing file names, subdirectory names, and changing to the directory's subdirectories. Allows adding files and subdirectories to the directory. Allows viewing and changing of file contents and program execution. Allows deletion of the directory and its files.

- Full Control (All) (All)

  Allows viewing file names, subdirectory names, and changing to the directory's subdirectories. Allows adding files and subdirectories to the directory. Allows viewing and changing of file contents and program execution. Allows deletion of the directory and its files. Allows deletion of the directory and its files. Allows changing ownership and taking ownership of the directory and its files.

NOTE: *When you set a directory permission, a set of abbreviations for individual permissions is displayed next to it. For example, when you set Add & Read permissions on a file, you see (RWX) (RX), signifying Read, Write, and Execute permissions.*

Special Directory Access

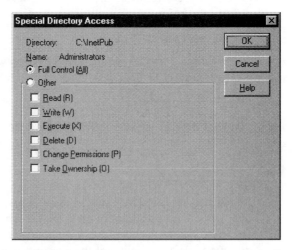

You can also configure Special Directory Access permissions, which allow you to select from a list of permissions rather than use one of the pre-configured Type of Access sets. Special Directory Access permissions are:

- Full Control (All)

  Includes Read, Write, Execute, Delete, Change Permissions, and Take Ownership permissions.

- Read (R)

  Allows viewing of file names and subdirectories.

- Write (W)

  Allows adding files and subdirectories to the directory. Does not provide access to files.

- Execute (X)

  Allows changing to subdirectories in the directory.

- Delete (D)

  Allows deletion of the directory.

- Change Permissions (P)

  Allows changing the directory permissions.

- Take Ownership (O)

  Allows taking ownership of the directory.

File Access Permissions

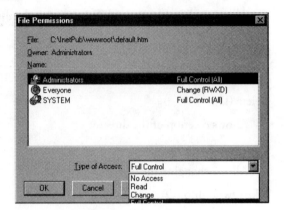

Windows NTFS security also includes several pre-configured file permissions sets. These simplify the assignment of file rights. You can set the following file permissions:

- No Access (None)

   Prevents access to the directory.

- Read (RX)

   Allows viewing of file contents and execution.

- Change (RWXD)

   Allows viewing of file contents and execution. Allows writing to the file and file deletion.

- Full Control (All)

   Allows viewing of file contents and execution. Allows writing to the file and file deletion. Allows changing ownership and taking ownership of the file.

- Special Access

   Allows user-selectable permissions.

Special File Access

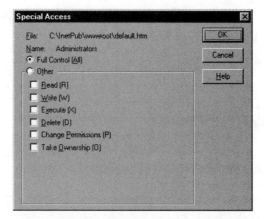

You can also configure Special File Access permissions, which allow you to select from a list of permissions rather than use one of the pre-configured Type of Access sets. Special Directory Access permissions are:

- Full Control (All)

    Includes Read, Write, Execute, Delete, Change Permissions, and Take Ownership permissions.

- Read (R)

    Allows viewing of the file's contents.

- Write (W)

    Allows changing the file's contents.

- Execute (X)

    If the file is a program, allows execution of the file.

- Delete (D)

    Allows deletion of the file.

- Change Permissions (P)

  Allows changing the file's permissions.

- Take Ownership (O)

  Allows taking ownership of the file.

Exercise 6-1:
Working with NTFS Permissions

In this exercise you will create a directory structure and configure NTFS permissions for the structure.

1. Double-click on My Computer.
2. Double-click on the icon for drive C:.
3. Run **File/New/Folder**.
4. Name the folder Parts.
5. Double-click on the Parts folder.
6. Click on **File/New/Folder**.
7. Name the folder Chevrolet.
8. Click on **File/New/Folder**.
9. Name the folder Chrysler.
10. Click on **File/New/Folder**.
11. Name the folder Ford.
12. Close the Parts folder.
13. Right-click on the Parts folder and select **Properties**.
14. Click on the **Security** tab, then click **Permissions**.
15. Select the group Everyone from the Name list.
16. Change the Type of Access to Special Directory Access.
17. Select the **Read** option, then click on **OK**.
18. Click on **Add**. Give the Administrator's group Full Control.

   NOTE: *You can prevent files from inheriting the permissions you set for their parent directories. To do this, select the **Special File Access** option and click on **Access Not Specified** in the Special File Access dialog box.*

Default Directory Access Permissions

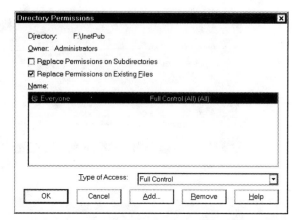

The above graphic shows the default permissions that the Windows NT 4.0 Server operating system assigns to an NTFS directory upon creation. These permissions are inappropriate for a Web server. From a security standpoint, Web server access is treated as local access. Anyone who visits your Web site could add, change, and delete files. Obviously, you are going to want to change these permissions.

Securing Your File System

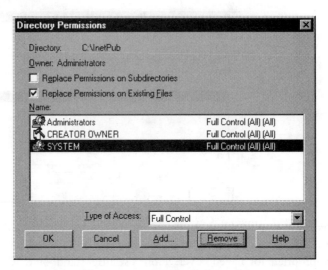

By definition, the anonymous user account is a member of the group Everyone. In this example, the group Everyone has been removed from the Directory Permissions list.

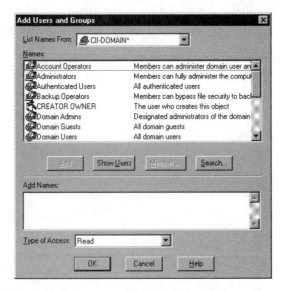

Click on **Add** and select a user or group. To view users, click on **Show Users**. Select the user or group and click on **Add**, select the Type Of Access, then click on **OK**.

The above example shows the addition of a group named WebUsers to the Access Control List for the C:\InetPub directory. This group's members are users who will be administrators of the Web site. Click on **OK** to save the new settings.

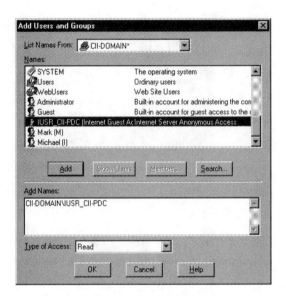

Next, give Directory Access permissions to the IUSR_*Computername* user account. This is because we removed the permissions for the group Everyone. This is the account Windows NT will use to allow anonymous access to Web resources.

Assign Read (RX) (RX) permissions to the IUSR_*Computername* user account.

The revised permissions list for the C:\InetPub directory is shown below.

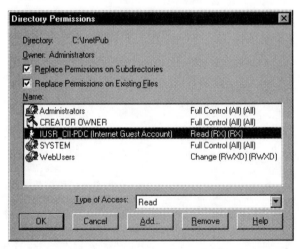

Depending on your requirements you may need to assign permissions for additional users and groups.

Exercise 6-2:
Managing Directory Permissions

In this exercise you will use the Windows NT User Manager for Domains utility to create a new group. You will then assign permissions to the group allowing its members to access your Web site.

1. Click on **Start/Programs/Administrative Tools/User Manager for Domains**.

2. Select **New Local Group** from the **User** menu. Enter the name WebUsers and the description WWW Users. Click on **Add**, then click on **OK** twice.

3. Close the User Manager for Domains utility.

4. Launch the Windows NT Explorer and browse to the root directory of drive C:.

5. Right-click on the C:\InetPub directory and select **Properties**.

6. Click on the **Security** tab.

7. Click on the **Permissions** button.

8. Click on **Add**. Select the Administrators group in the Names list.

9. Click on **Add**. Set the Type of Access to Full Control, then click on **OK**.

10. Click on **Add**. Select the WebUsers group in the Names list.

11. Click on **Add**. Set the Type of Access to Read, then click on **OK**.

12. Click on **OK** to close the Add Users and Groups window.

13. Click on **Add**. Click the **Show Users** button.

14. Scroll down and highlight the IUSR_*Computername* user account.

15. Click on **Add**. Set the Type of Access to **Read**, then click on **OK**.

16. Click on **OK**.

17. Select the group Everyone in the Name list, then click on **Remove**.

18. Verify that the **Replace Permissions on Subdirectories** and **Replace Permissions on Existing Files** options are selected, then click on **OK** twice.

User Authentication

You have already been introduced to the anonymous user and to two of the options available for user authentication. However, let's take a closer look at some key points.

IUSR_Computername

By default, the Internet Guest account is named IUSR_*Computername*, where *Computername* is the machine name of your Internet Information Server. When you install Internet Information Server, this account is created automatically. You can modify the account in User Manager for Domains, but if you change the username or password, you will have to change it in Internet Information Server as well. Select the server or site for which you want to change the guest user. Display **Properties**. Click on Directory Security. Click on the **Edit** button for Anonymous Access.

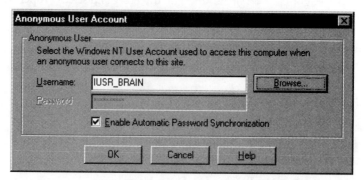

Browse to select the new account. Notice that you can synchronize the passwords so that if the anonymous user's password is changed in User Manager for Domains, the change will automatically be changed in Internet Information Server.

Basic Authentication

If you need to support browsers other than Internet Explorer, you will only be able to validate users with Basic Authentication. This method involves sending a username and password as clear text and is not as secure as using Windows NT Challenge/Response. However, this security hole can be eliminated by requiring that password information be sent over Secure Sockets Layer (SSL). SSL will be discussed later in the chapter.

Windows NT Challenge/Response

When a user is validated through Windows NT Challenge/Response, the username and password are not actually sent across the wire. Instead, the browser and the server communicate using a cryptographic technique. This is more secure than Basic Authentication, but requires that users have Internet Explorer 2.0 or higher. If a browser supports both Windows NT Challenge/Response and Basic Authentication, Windows NT Challenge/Response is used as the preferred authentication method.

Client Certificates

You can associate a client certificate with a particular Windows NT user account. Public key encryption and certificates are discussed in detail later in the chapter.

When is Authentication Used?

Users are prompted for logon when the site they request does not allow anonymous access. This is configured through the Web Site property page. Users will also be prompted for logon if they attempt to access a resource for which NTFS permissions have been configured, but the anonymous user has not been granted the necessary permission.

Windows NT User and Group Security

In this section we will review Windows NT user and group security considerations. Areas of specific interest include:

- Internet User Configuration
- Passwords
- Miscellaneous security notes

Internet User Configuration

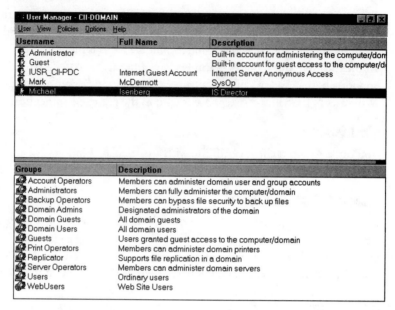

Windows NT user management is performed using the User Manager for Domains utility. To launch this utility, run **Start/Programs/Administrative Tools/User Manager for Domains**.

Now check the properties of the anonymous user account, IUSR_*Computername*.

Double-click on the IUSR_*Computername* user account.

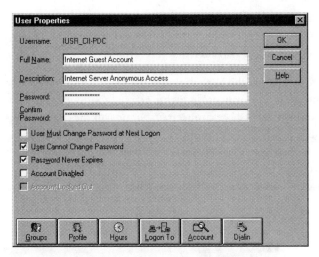

Click on the **Groups** button.

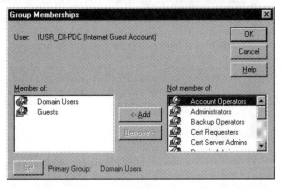

Verify that the anonymous username is a member of only the Guests group. If the Web server has an account in a Windows NT Domain, the Domain Users group will also be listed.

> *NOTE:* *Even though not explicitly listed, membership in the group Everyone is assumed for all users.*

When you are setting file and directory access permissions, you can set them for Everyone, Guests, or just for the anonymous username. From a security standpoint, it would typically be considered best to avoid assigning any permissions to Guests.

Next, we'll check the User Rights policy for the anonymous user account. The User Rights policy determines the rights granted to groups and user accounts. A right authorizes a user to perform certain actions on the system. A user who logs on to an account to which the appropriate rights have been granted can carry out the corresponding actions. When a user does not have appropriate rights, attempts to carry out those actions are blocked by the system. User rights apply to the system as a whole and are different than permissions, which apply to specific objects.

Select **User Rights** from the **Policies** menu.

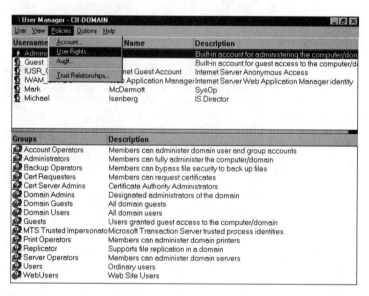

Set the Right option to Log on locally. Verify that the IUSR_*Computername* user account is listed. This is the only special rights assignment that should be given to the anonymous user. If you continue to view the different policy rights you will notice that the IUSR_*Computername* user account is listed only under Log on locally.

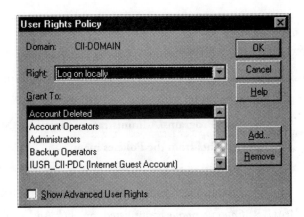

The rights granted to a group are also provided to the members of that group. In most situations, the easiest way to provide rights to a user is to add that user's account to a group that already possesses the needed rights.

NOTE: *If an appropriate group does not exist, create one. It is more efficient to manage the server on a group basis than managing individual user rights.*

If you choose to create a new group, assign the group the following rights:

• Log on locally

• Access this computer from a network

Exercise 6-3:
User Rights Policy Management

In this exercise you will use the User Manager for Domains utility to view and change User Rights assignments.

1. Click on **Start/Programs/Administrative Tools/User Manager for Domains**.

2. Select **User Rights** from the **Policies** menu.

3. Set the Right option to Log on locally.

4. Verify that the IUSR_*Computername* user account is listed.

5. If IUSR_*Computername* is not listed, on click **Add**. Click on the **Show Users** button and select the IUSR_*Computername* user account. Click on the **Add** button, then click on **OK**.

6. View all of the other Right options to verify that the ISR_*Computername* user account is not listed elsewhere, except for Access this computer from a network.

7. When finished, click on **OK**.

8. Close User Manager for Domains.

User Account Passwords

Even though the Web server is primarily accessed via the anonymous user account, it is important to review all of your Windows NT domain and server security policies when setting up for Internet access. Make it as difficult as possible for someone to guess another user name and password on your server.

It is common knowledge that the default superuser account on a Windows NT Server computer is Administrator. It is critical that this account is always password protected. You could also rename this account for additional protection.

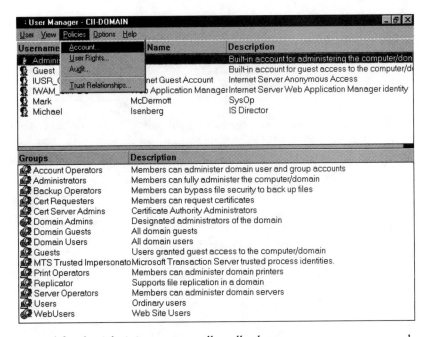

The password for the Administrator, as well as all other users on your server, needs to be difficult to guess. If this is a new Windows NT Server computer that is used only for Internet connectivity, you should have only a handful of user accounts to review.

You can configure the Account Policy for your server with the User Manager for Domains utility. Select **Account** from the **Policy** menu.

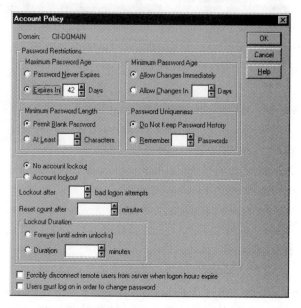

The above figure shows recommended settings for username and password policies. Though a detailed discussion of policy issues is beyond the scope of this course, some areas of concern should be mentioned:

- Always force periodic password changes.

- Minimum password ages should be used.

- Force a minimum length long enough to help make passwords difficult to guess.

- Keep a password history to limit reuse of passwords.

- Use account lockout to detect attempts to break into your system.

While these will not make your system impenetrable, they will help. Remember that part of your protection plan is teaching users to create good passwords.

Miscellaneous Security Issues

Limit the members of the Administrators group–the fewer the better. Also limit membership of other default groups to only those users needing special rights or access permissions.

By default, when an NTFS directory is created, the group Everyone has full control of all files in it. Change or remove the permissions for the group Everyone by using **Properties/Security/Permissions**.

Enable auditing if you suspect that a user is attempting to hack into your system. You can enable auditing by using **Properties/Security/Auditing**. You should audit any NTFS directories where you are concerned about user access. You can have auditing track successful attempts, failed attempts, or both.

Exercise 6-4:
Account Policy Management

In this exercise you will use the User Manager for Domains utility

1. Click on **Start/Programs/Administrative Tools/User Manager for Domains**.

2. Select **Accounts** from the **Policies** menu.

3. Enable Maximum Password Age and set the value to 45 days.

4. Set Minimum Password Age to allow changes in 7 days.

5. Require a Minimum Password Length of 7 characters.

6. Set Password Uniqueness to remember 4 passwords.

7. Enable Account Lockout and accept the default values.

8. Click on **OK** to save your changes.

9. Close the User Manager for Domains utility.

Web Permissions

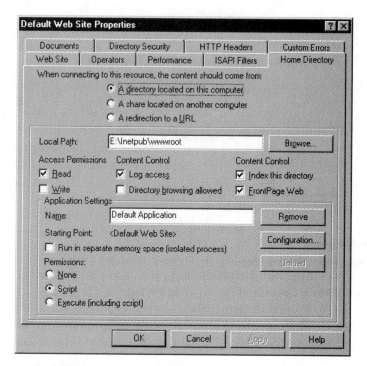

Permissions that are not sensitive to user identification can be granted on the Home Directory property page. Most of these settings will be discussed later in the course. For now, let's look at those that specifically apply to whether a user is granted access.

Access Permissions

You can specify whether the contents of a directory are available for Read (download) access or Write (upload) access. Most HTML documents should only be available for Read access. FTP sites and directories can also be assigned Read and/or Write access.

Application Permissions

You can configure whether or not the applications or server-side scripts that exist in the directory can be run. Available settings are:

- None

    This prevents files located in the directory from being executed. This does not prevent HTML from being downloaded and executed by the browser. This is the default value.

- Script

    This allows scripts, such as CGI scripts, Internet Data Connector (IDC), and ASP scripts, to be executed by the server.

- Execute

    This allows both applications, dynamic link libraries, and scripts to be executed in this directory. This setting should never be combined with the Write permission because it would effectively allow a hacker to upload an application and execute it on your Web server.

These settings are only available for Web sites and directories. They do not apply to FTP sites.

Directory Permission Guidelines for IIS 4.0

The following guidelines will help you determine which permissions to assign for various Web server content directories. The following options are configured using the Web site's Home Directory properties page.

- HTML Content

    These are directories containing HTML content.

    Set the Access Permissions value to **Read** and the Applications Settings Permissions to **None**.

- Executable Programs

    These are programs that users can run.

    Set the Access Permissions value to **Read** and the Applications Settings Permissions to **Execute**.

- Scripts

    These are CGI or other types of scripts that users can run.

    Set the Access Permissions value to **Read** and the Applications Settings Permissions to **Script**.

- Database Files

    These are SQL or other types of database files.

    Set the Access Permissions value to **Read** and **Write** and the Applications Settings Permissions to **None**.

IP Filtering

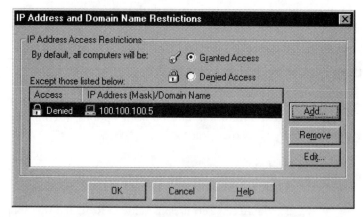

You may have a situation that warrants either granting or restricting access based on the IP address or domain name of the machine sending the request. You can choose to either grant access to all computers except those explicitly listed or deny access to all computers except those explicitly granted. This option is available on the Directory Security property page.

To add an entry to the list, click on the **Add** button.

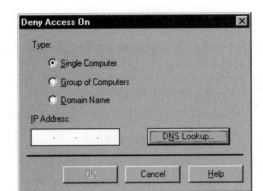

You can choose to add:

- A single computer

    Specify the IP address of the computer you wish to add. If you don't know the IP address, you can click on **DNS Lookup** to specify it by host name.

- A group of computers

    You will need to specify the Network ID and the subnet mask of the group of computers you wish to add. This option is useful if you are building a Web site that should be accessed only by members of a particular department and that department is in its own subnet.

- A domain name

    You can specify that computers with a particular domain name be granted or denied access. However, this will adversely affect performance, since the DNS server will have to be consulted for a reverse lookup with each access request.

Exercise 6-5:
IP Filtering

In this exercise you will configure IP Filtering on your Windows NT Server computer.

1. Click on **Start/Programs/Windows NT 4.0 Option Pack/Microsoft Internet Server/Internet Service Manager** to launch the Internet Service Manager

2. Right-click on Default Web Site and select **Properties**.

3. Click on the **Directory Security** tab.

4. Click the **Edit** button for IP Address and Domain Name Restrictions.

5. To prevent a specific computer from connecting to your Web server, click on **Add**.

6. Select **Single Computer** and enter the following IP address:

    `192.168.222.222`

7. Click on **OK**.

8. Click on **OK**.

9. Right-click on Default FTP Site and select **Properties**.

10. Click on the **Directory Security** tab.

11. Click on **Add**.

12. Select **Single Computer** and enter the following IP address:

    `192.168.222.222`

13. Click on **OK**.

14. Click on **OK**. IP Filtering has now been enabled.

15. Finally, stop and restart the Web and FTP Services for the changes to take effect.

THE SECURE SOCKETS LAYER (SSL) PROTOCOL

The Secure Sockets Layer (SSL) protocol is a low-level authentication and encryption method used to secure transactions in higher-level protocols such as HTTP and FTP. It is supported by IIS 4.0 and both Netscape Communicator/Navigator and the Microsoft Internet Explorer browsers.

To properly configure and manage the IIS 4.0 Secure Sockets Layer (SSL) implementation you must understand the following concepts:

- Securing transmissions
- Keys
- Generating a key pair
- Certificates

SSL is an available option for supporting encrypted communications across the Internet.

Securing Transmissions with Secure Sockets Layer

The SSL protocol uses an initial client/server handshake process to decide on the type of security to be used during a conversation. Once the security level has been determined, all subsequent communications between the server and client are encrypted.

SSL includes provisions for server authentication (verifying the server's identity to the client), encryption of data in transit, and optional client authentication (verifying the client's identity to the server).

By employing SSL-enabled servers and clients, it is possible to send encrypted messages across the Internet without fear of interception. In order to implement SSL you must first apply for and obtain a verification certificate from a certificate authority (CA), such as Verisign (www.verisign.com) or Cardservice (www.cardservice.com). You can also use Microsoft Certificate Server to act as your own certificate authority. This will be discussed later in the chapter.

SSL should be enabled only for virtual directories containing highly sensitive information, as SSL encrypted transmissions are slower due to the overhead of the encryption/decryption process.

The latest version of SSL, version 3, offers improved performance over earlier versions due to a streamlining of the client/server handshaking process. SSL3 is compatible with SSL version 2.

Clients requesting documents stored in SSL-enabled directories must use the https://
URL format instead of the standard http:// format.

Digital Envelopes

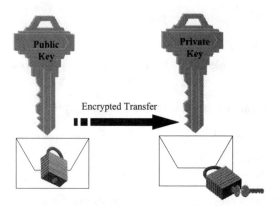

SSL works by utilizing the concept of digital envelopes. In order for a digital envelope to
work, a key pair is required. One of the keys is a public key and is used to lock the
envelope before it is sent. The other key is a private key and is used to unlock the
envelope after it is received. This guarantees that the only one who can open the
envelope is the recipient who has the private key. Let's look at a practical example.

Suppose you have a Web page that accepts credit card information from clients. In order
to secure that transaction, you send the client the public key of your key pair. The client
then uses that key to lock the envelope containing his credit card information. No one
except the owner of the private key (you) can unlock that envelope. When you receive
the envelope from the client, you use your private key to unlock it.

Implementing SSL

The tasks required to implement SSL are:

- Generate a key pair and a request file.
- Request a certificate from a certificate authority (CA).
- Install the certificate on your server.
- Enable the SSL security on a folder.

Generate a Key Pair and Request File

The first step in implementing SSL is to generate a key pair and request file. The key pair is created with the Key Manager. When generating the key pair, you provide the following information:

- Key name
- Password
- Encryption key length
- Organization
- Organizational unit
- Common name
- Country
- State
- City
- Administrator name, e-mail address, and phone number

You can elect to save this information in a file, which you must then send to the selected CA or allow the Key Manager utility to automatically send the request to an online CA. The CA will then send you a certificate to be installed on your server.

To generate a key pair and request file, run **Start/Programs/Windows NT 4.0 Option Pack/Microsoft Internet Server/Internet Service Manager**.

Right-click on Default Web Site and select **Properties**. Click on the **Directory Security** tab. Click on the **Key Manager** button.

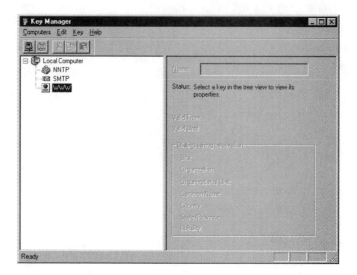

Single-click on WWW. From the **Key** menu, select **Create New Key**.

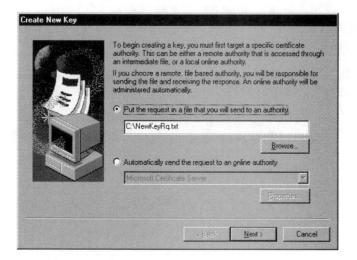

Select a request file option and click on **Next**.

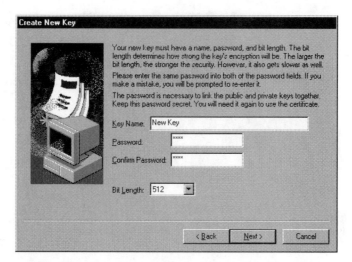

The Key Name field is used to assign a name to the new key. You might have multiple keys if you are hosting Web sites for other companies. The password is used to encrypt the key. If you downloaded the International version of IIS 4.0 from the Microsoft Web site, your only choice will be a key that is 512 bits. The key pair in the U.S. version can be up to 1,024 bits long. Enter the appropriate values, then click on **Next**.

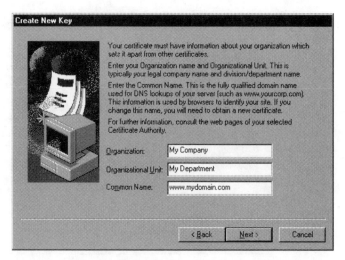

Enter your company name in the Organization field. Enter your department or division in the Organizational Unit field.   Enter the DNS name for your Web server, such as www.wavetech.com, in the Common Name field. Click on **Next**.

Enter the two-letter ISO country code in the Country field. Enter your state or province and city information in the appropriate fields. Click on **Next**.

Enter your site administrator's name, e-mail address, and phone number. Click on **Next**.

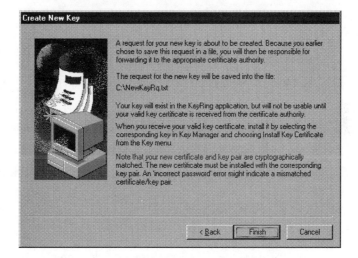

After all information has been entered, click on **Finish**. Depending on the request file option you selected, a request file will be created locally or one will be automatically sent to the CA you specified.

Key Request Tips

- Never use commas in any of the fields. Commas signal the end of a field and will cause an improper certificate request to be created.

- VeriSign will not accept any punctuation or abbreviations. For Example:

    You must spell out "Street" instead of "St."

    You must spell out "Incorporated" instead of "Inc."

    You must spell out "Saint Louis" instead of "St. Louis," and so on.

Exercise 6-6:
Generating a Key Pair and Request File

In this exercise you will generate a key pair and a request file.

1. Click on **Start/Programs/Windows NT 4.0 Option Pack/Microsoft Internet Server/Internet Service Manager**.

2. Right-click on Default Web Site and select **Properties**.

3. Click on the **Directory Security** tab.

4. Click on the **Key Manager** button.

5. Single-click on WWW. From the **Key** menu, select **Create New Key**.

6. Select the **Put the request in a file you will send to an authority option**, then click on **Next**.

7. In the Key Name field enter:

    FirstKey

8. In the Password and Confirm Password fields enter:

    password

9. Click on **Next**.

10. In the Organization field enter:

    My Company

11. In the Organizational Unit field enter:

    My Department

12. In the Common Name field enter:

    www.mydomain.com

13. Click on **Next**.

14. In the Country field enter:

    US

15. In the State/Province field enter:

    Oregon

16. In the City/Locality field enter:

    My City

17. Click on **Next**.

18. Enter your name, e-mail address, and phone number in the appropriate fields. Click on **Next**.

19. Read the text in the Create New Key Dialog box, then click on **Finish**.

20. You should see the key you just created listed below WWW in the Key Manager list window. The key is displayed with two red lines through it, as it has not yet been activated with a certificate from a CA.

Acquiring a Certificate

When you contact either VeriSign or Cardservice, you will need to enter information about your organization and your server. The current cost for a server ID certificate from Verisign is $349.00 (U.S.) for the first server and $249.00 for each additional server.

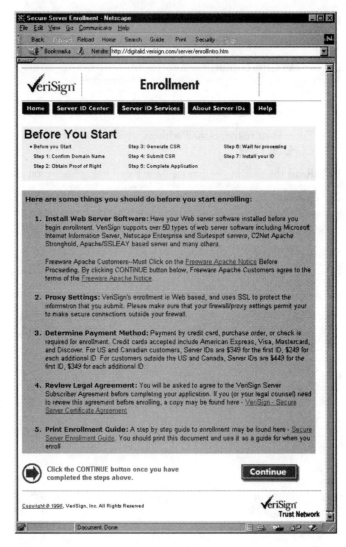

You can also apply for a certificate by filling out the appropriate online forms at Verisign or another CA.

The online application process at Verisign presents you with a seven-step process.

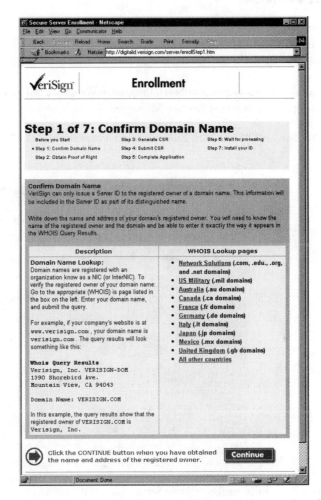

You will need to provide the CA with all of the information discussed in this section.

Installing a Certificate

Once your application has been processed by the CA, the certificate digital ID file will be e-mailed to you. After you receive your certificate file, you must run the Key Manager utility and select the key to which you will be adding the certificate.

To install the certificate, run **Start/Programs/Windows NT 4.0 Option Pack/Microsoft Internet Server/Internet Service Manager**.

Right-click on Default Web Site and select **Properties**. Click on the **Directory Security** tab.

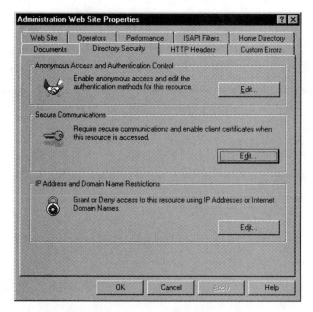

Click on the **Edit** button next to Secure Communications.

> *NOTE:*   *After you have created a key using Key Manager, this dialog box changes and the **Key Manager** button is replaced by the **Edit** button.*

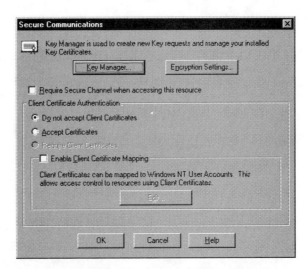

The default encryption strength is 40 bits. If you require 128-bit encryption, click on the **Encryption** button, select the **Require 128-bit encryption** option, then click on **OK**. At the time of this writing, 128-bit encryption was only available in the United States and Canada.

The Client Certificate Authentication option allows you to configure your Web server to accept, require, or reject client certificates as a method of establishing a connection to Web content directories that are SSL enabled.

If you select the **Enable Client Certificate Mapping** option, certificate-bearing clients who connect using a valid Windows NT user account name and password will be automatically mapped to that account and its corresponding access restrictions.

Click on the **Key Manager** button.

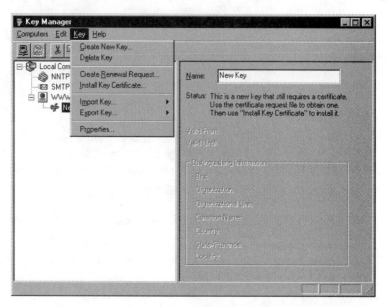

Click on the key you wish to authorize, then select **Install Key Certificate** from the **Key** drop-down menu.

Browse to locate the certificate file. When you select the file, you will be prompted to enter the same password that you specified when you created the key pair. Enter the IP address for your server or use the Any Unassigned option to apply the certificate to all of the unassigned IP addresses on your server. Click on **OK.**

> *NOTE:*   *If you use a proprietary e-mail system, the text file containing your digital ID could be corrupted when received. If you try to install your key and you get a message about an invalid password, the digital ID might have been corrupted by the mail system, or in transit. To resolve this problem, contact Verisign Technical Support and request that they send the digital ID to a standard SMTP/POP3 mail server.*

The double red line that was displayed through your key should now be gone indicating that the key has been certified.

Select **Commit Changes Now** from the **Computers** menu, then click on **OK.** Restart your server to continue.

Enabling SSL

After completing the process of obtaining a certificate and installing it on the server, enable SSL on a per directory basis.

To enable SSL, launch the Internet Service Manager utility and open the properties for your Web site. Right-click on any of the folders in your Web server's directory structure and select **Properties**. Click on the **Directory Security** tab, then click on the **Edit** button next to Secure Communications.

Select the **Require Secure Channel when accessing this resource** option. Finally, select the desired Client Certificate Authentication option and select **Enable Client Certificate Mapping**, if required.

> *NOTE:*   *From this point on, all client references to documents in this directory must specify a URL format of "https://" instead of "http://."*

Back Up Your Key File

You will want to back up your key file and keep it in a safe place. Key Manager allows you to export your key from the registry into a file.

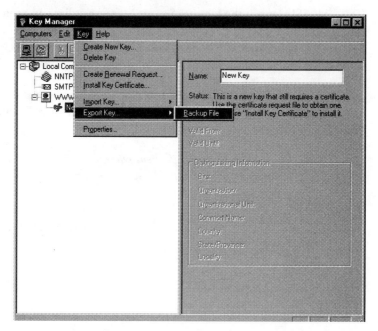

Select the key you wish to back up and click on the **Key** menu. Select **Export Key**, then **Backup File**. Specify a destination and click on **OK**.

Exercise 6-7:
Back up Your Key File

In this exercise you will back up the key pair request file you generated in Exercise 6-6.

1. Click on **Start/Programs/Windows NT 4.0 Option Pack/Microsoft Internet Server/Internet Service Manager**.

2. Right-click on Default Web Site and select **Properties**.

3. Click on the **Directory Security** tab.

4. Click on the **Edit** button next to Secure Communications.

5. Click on the **Key Manager** button.

6. Click on FirstKey in the Key list.

7. From the **Key** menu, select **Export Key**, then **Backup File**.

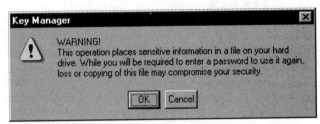

8. Read the warning, then click on **OK**.

9. Browse to select the destination path, then click on **OK**.

10. Close.

CERTIFICATE SERVER

One of the components of Windows NT 4 Option Pack is the Certificate Server. It allows you to create certificates to configure valid key pairs for Internet Information Servers, Internet Explorer, and Netscape Navigator clients. Let's look at how it is used. Our discussion will include:

- Suggestions for Using Certificate Server

- Installing Certificate Server

- Customizing Certificate Server

- Processing a Certificate Request

- Certificate Server Tools

- Configuring a Browser to Recognize a CA

Running your own certificate server is not the best solution for every need. Let's look at when it is appropriate.

Suggestions for Using Certificate Server

If your goal is to use SSL to enable you to accept credit cards from users over the Internet, running your own certificate server is probably not your best option. In order for a certificate to be accepted, the client needs to trust the authority. Internet Explorer is already configured to trust several well-known certificate authorities.

However, if you need to use SSL to provide a secure channel to your corporate intranet or if you have a well-known set of customers for whom you'd like to provide a secure site, you might want to consider creating your own certificates by using Certificate Server.

While the architecture of Certificate Server is beyond the scope of this course, it is important to point out that the policies for granting certificates are entirely at your discretion. You can write applications that interface with Certificate Server to perform any sort of business logic you require to validate a user. They can even be written so that they store the certificate request so that you can perform manual validation.

Installing Certificate Server

Before you install Certificate Server, you will need to create a shared directory in which you will store the configuration information.

Certificate Server is part of Windows NT 4.0 Option Pack. To install it, insert the Option Pack CD-ROM in your CD-ROM drive. It automatically displays Internet Explorer. Click on **Install**. Click on **Install Windows NT 4.0 Option Pack**. Select to open the file from its current location and click on **OK**. When the Option Pack welcome screen displays, click on **Next**. Click on **Add/Remove**.

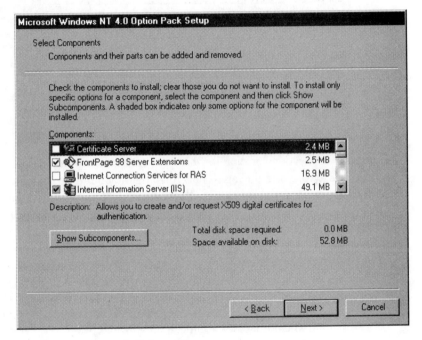

Select Certificate Server and click on **Next**.

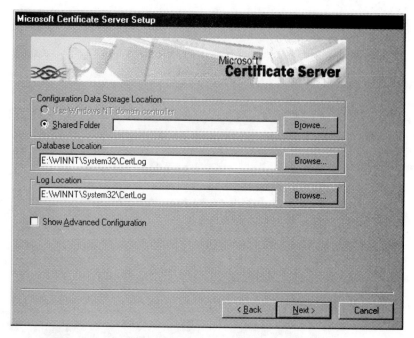

Here you can select the location in which to store the CA configuration information, the certificate database, and the log. The CA configuration information includes the CA certificate that users can download and install in their browsers. This information must be stored in a shared directory on the machine where Certificate Server is installed.

If you select **Show Advanced Configuration** and click on **Next**, you will be prompted to select the following options:

- Cryptographic Service Provider

    This allows you to select alternate CSPs. By default, the CSP installed will be Microsoft Base Cryptographic Provider.

- Hashing algorithm

    Hashing is a numeric computation that is used to encrypt the data. Different CSPs will support different hashing algorithms. You can even develop your own CSP to provide a custom hashing algorithm.

NOTE: The current release of Certificate Server only supports Microsoft Base Cryptographic Provider and the MD5 hashing algorithm

- Use existing keys

  This option is useful if you are upgrading an existing Certificate Server. If Certificate Server can find a matching certificate in the store, it will use that to generate the keys.

- Make this Certificate Server the default

  Select this option if you want this Certificate Server to be the default server when a certificate is requested.

- Choose Certificate Hierarchy

  In future releases, you will be able to select whether you are generating a root certificate authority or a non-root certificate authority. This option is not supported in this release.

If you did not choose to go through the advanced options or after you have finished setting them, you will be prompted to enter identification information. This information will be contained in the certificate authority certificate users will download and install in their browsers.

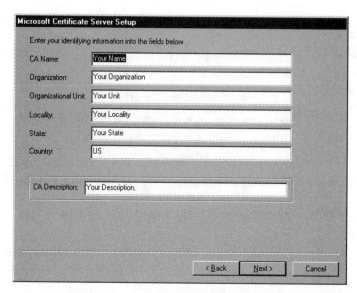

After you have entered the appropriate information, click on **Next**. Your computer will be configured for Certificate Server and the necessary files will be downloaded. After it finishes copying files, click on **Finish** to complete the installation. The Certificate Server will be loaded as a service. It will be configured to start automatically as soon as the computer starts.

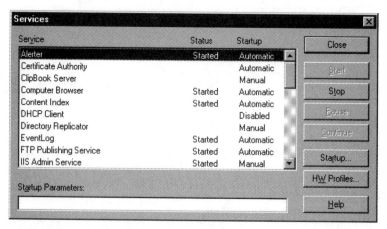

You will need to restart your computer or manually start the Certificate Authority service before you can issue certificates.

Exercise 6-8:
Installing Certificate Server

In this exercise, you will install Certificate Server.

1. Using Windows Explorer, create a directory on your NTFS partition and name it Certs. Share it using the same name.

2. Insert the Windows NT 4.0 Option Pack CD-ROM in your CD-ROM drive. If it is already in the drive, launch Explorer, right-click on your CD-ROM drive and run **AutoPlay**.

3. Click on **Install**.

4. Click on **Install Windows NT 4.0 Option Pack**.

5. Click on **Open this file from its current location** and click on **OK**.

6. Click on **Next**.

7. Click on **Add/Remove**.

8. Select Certificate Server and click on **Next**.

9. Browse to locate the Certs directory you created in step 1.

10. Accept defaults for the other locations and click on **Next**.

11. Enter your identifying information and click on **Next**.

12. Click on **Next**.

13. Click on **Finish**.

14. Restart your computer.

Customizing Certificate Server

By default, Certificate Server uses the policy file Certpdef.dll,. However, you can configure it to use a custom policy. To do so:

- Obtain or build a policy DLL.

  Certificate server exposes some COM interfaces that programmers can use to build policy modules in C++, Visual Basic, or Java. These interfaces are beyond the scope of this course.

- Unregister the current policy file.

  Like any COM server, the policy file is unregistered through the command:

  ```
  regsvr32 /u certpdef.dll
  ```

- Register the new policy file.

  Copy the custom policy module to the *systemroot*\System32 subdirectory and run the **regsvr32** command. For example, to register the policy named corpplcy.dll, you would type the following:

  ```
  regsvr32 corpplcy.dll
  ```

The same basic procedure can be used to customize the way in which the certificate is delivered to the recipient. The module that controls this is known as the *exit module*. The default exit module is certexit.dll. Exit modules are optional.

Processing a Certificate Request

Once you have a certificate request, like the one generated by using Key Manager, you can easily process it. To do so, run **Start/Programs/Windows NT 4.0 Option Pack/ Microsoft Certificate Server/Process Certificate Request File.** You will be prompted to locate the .req or .txt file containing the request. After you locate it, you will be prompted for a file name and directory containing the certificate. A valid certificate will be generated, containing the appropriate public key. You can now distribute it for installation or use the Key Manager to install it, as described earlier in the chapter.

Certificate Server Tools

Certificate Server is managed through a Web page named *certsrv*. To open it, launch Internet Explorer and type the following URL:

```
http://localhost/certsrv
```

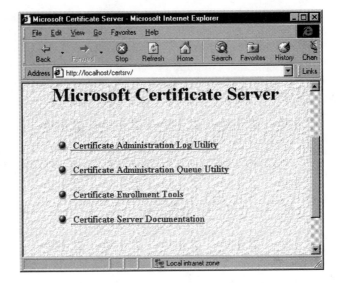

This page provides hyperlinks to the following tools:

- Certificate Administration Log Utility

    This utility allows you to view information about the certificates that have been processed and their status. You can view either a list of certificates or view certificates one at a time.

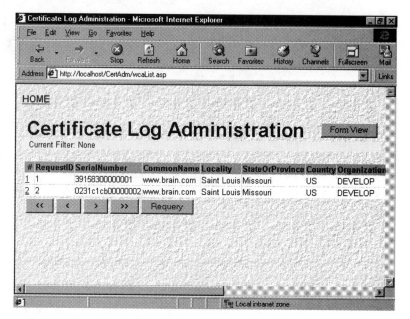

- Certificate Administration Queue Utility

    This utility allows you to get information on the status of issued and pending certificate requests.

- Certificate Enrollment Tools

    This utility allows you to install CA certificates, process certificate requests, and request a client authentication certificate.

- Certificate Server Documentation

    This hyperlink will display help on using Certificate Server.

Configuring a Browser to Recognize a CA

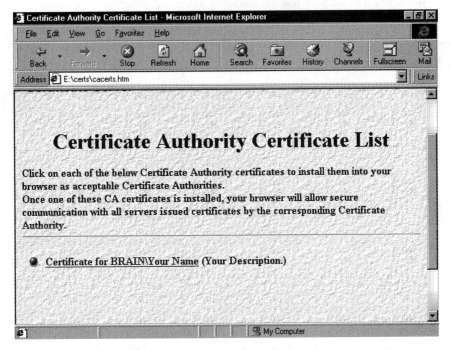

Before a browser will accept a certificate issued by a particular Certificate Authority, that browser must obtain a valid CA Certificate. When Certificate Server was installed, that certificate was created in the shared configuration directory. One of the files created is an HTML document named cacerts.htm. By navigating to that document, users can install the CA Certificate for your server simply by clicking on the hyperlink. Select to open the file. You will be prompted to select whether or not to enable authentication and for which types of services. You will need to close and restart your browser for changes to take effect.

Exercise 6-9:
Installing a Certificate and Establishing SSL

In this exercise, you will use Certificate Server to create a valid certificate, install it in Internet Information Server using Key Manager, and configure SSL communication on a directory.

1. Run **Start/Programs/Windows NT 4.0 Option Pack/Microsoft Certificate Server/Process Certificate Request File**.

2. Browse to select the request file named FirstKey that you created in Exercise 6-6. Click on **Open**.

3. Save the certificate as FirstCert in the same directory.

4. Launch Internet Service Manager.

5. Right-click on Default Web Site. Select **Properties**.

6. Select **Directory Security**. Click on the **Edit** button for Secure Communications.

7. Click on **Key Manager**.

8. Select FirstKey.

9. Run **Key/Install Key Certificate**.

10. Locate FirstCert and click on **Open**.

11. Type the password as follows and click on **OK**:

    password

12. Select Any Unassigned port and click on **OK**.

13. Close Key Manager.

14. Click on **Yes** to commit all changes now.

15. Click on **OK** to close the Default Site property page.

16. Expand Default Web Site.

17. Right-click on the CertSrv directory. Select **Properties**.

18. Click on **Directory Security**.

19. Click on the Secure Communications **Edit** button.

20. Click on **Require Secure Channel when accessing this resource.**

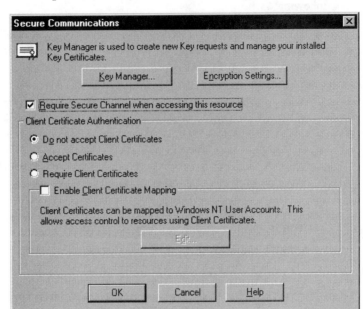

21. Click on **OK.**

22. Click on **OK.**

23. Open Internet Explorer and navigate to the URL http://localhost/certsrv.

   NOTE: *You should receive an error 403. You now can only access this virtual directory*
   using SSL.

24. Navigate to https://localhost/certsrv.

25.   Click on **OK** to view pages over a secured connection. You should receive the following warning:

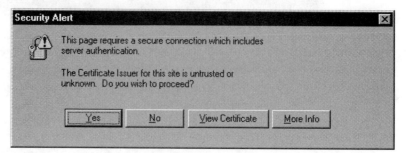

26.   If you are prompted with another warning, click on **Yes**.

27.   Click on **Certificate Enrollment Tools**.

28.   Click on **Install Certificate Authority Certificates**.

29.   Click on the hyperlink for your CA certificate.

30.   Select **Open this file from its current location**. Click on **OK**.

31.   Clear the check from **Secure e-mail** and **Software Publishing**.

32.   Click on **OK**.

33.   Click on **Yes** to add the certificate to the root store.

34.   Close Internet Explorer.

35.   Open Internet Explorer and navigate to the URL https://localhost/certsrv.

36.   Click on **Yes** to confirm that you'd like a secure connection.

37.   If you receive a warning that the site name and the certificate name do not match, click on **Yes**.

SUMMARY

In this chapter, you were introduced to basic security concepts necessary for the management of an Internet Information Server. This included:

- Physical security

- NTFS security

- User management

- Web and FTP security

- IP Filtering

- SSL

- Certificate Server

The next chapter will focus on implementing Web content.

POST-TEST QUESTIONS

The answers to these questions are in Appendix A at the end of this manual.

1. The password for the anonymous username entered into Internet Service Manager must:

    ....

    ....

2. Why is it probably not a good idea to filter access by domain name?

    ....

    ....

3. A directory named Acctg contains HTML documents. The Accountants group is granted NTFS Read and Write permission. The Employees group is granted Read permission. The Contractors group is granted No Access. The **Directory Permissions** tab for the directory specifies Read and Write Access permissions and None for Application permissions. Sally belongs to the Contractors group and the Accountants group. What happens when she attempts to access the site?

    ....

    ....

4. A directory named Acctg contains HTML documents. The Accountants group is granted NTFS Read and Write permission. The Employees group is granted Read permission. The Contractors group is granted No Access. The **Directory Permissions** tab for the directory specifies Read Access permissions and None for Application permissions. Dan belongs to the Employees group and the Accountants group. What happens when he attempts to access the site?

....

....

5. You have a certificate from Verisign on your Internet Server. You have configured the keys and enabled secure communication for the OrderEntry Web site. However, when customers click on the link to get there, they receive an error 403. What is the problem?

....

....

6. You have established secure communication on your corporate intranet using an in-house Certificate Server. When users in your branch office try to connect to the site, they receive an error that the server is untrusted. What should they do?

....

....

7. Your users all use Internet Explorer 4.0. You want access to be granted based on user identification. Which authentication method will be used by default?

....

....

CHAPTER 7

Content-Related Configuration

OBJECTIVES

At the completion of this chapter, you will be able to:

- Describe the use of HTTP headers.

- Describe the purpose and use of virtual directories.

- Identify situations where it would be appropriate to use virtual directories.

- Set up and configure virtual directories.

- Redirect a URL to a virtual directory.

- Describe the purpose and use of virtual servers.

- Set up and configure a virtual server.

- Identify ways in which you can access data from a Web site.

- Configure your Web server to use ISAPI filters.

- Configure your Web server to run ASP scripts.

- Configure your Web server to access a SQL database.

- Describe how Microsoft Transaction Server simplifies server-side solutions.

PRE-TEST QUESTIONS

The answers to these questions are in Appendix A at the end of this manual.

1. What is the main reason for setting up a virtual server?

    ....

    ....

2. Where can a virtual directory be located?

    ....

    ....

3. Which type of HTTP header would contain information about content expiration?

....

....

4. Which data access technology allows you to create disconnected result sets?

....

....

5. Which Windows NT 4.0 Option Pack server provides a thread pool?

....

....

INTRODUCTION

Internet Information Server gives you a great deal of flexibility in how you organize and distribute content on the Web or on your corporate intranet. This chapter will examine several powerful features that make IIS 4.0 a powerful and scalable solution that can be customized for a wide variety of situations.

The chapter begins with a look at HTTP 1.1, the protocol that carries HTML from the server to the browser. This discussion will focus on the types of information that can be transmitted in the HTTP header.

Following that, you'll be introduced to virtual directories. You will see how you can use virtual directories to run Web sites with pages distributed across multiple drives and even across multiple servers.

From there, the discussion will examine the use of virtual servers. You will see the three ways in which you can host multiple Web sites on a single computer.

Finally, the chapter will cover server-side content. This will include a brief discussion of database connectivity, ISAPI filters, Active Server Pages, and Microsoft Transaction Server.

HTTP 1.1

Internet Information Server uses HTTP 1.1 as its Web protocol. This section will look at the HTTP protocol, including:

- The HTTP Protocol
- HTTP Headers
- Content Expiration
- Content Ratings
- MIME Types
- Custom Errors

Let's start with an overview of how an HTTP header works.

The HTTP Protocol

HTTP Conversation

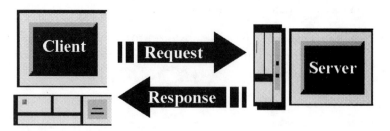

A Web server and Web client communicate by using the HTTP protocol. The client (browser) initiates the communication by sending a Request. The server parses the request and sends a Response. Traditionally, the connection between them would be terminated as soon as the response was sent.

However, since more and more requests result in a number of Response packages, later versions of HTTP made it possible (and in HTTP 1.1, recommended) to keep the connection open until some action indicates that the conversation is over. One of the important features of the HTTP 1.1 specification is that it made persistent connections the default. This is known as HTTP Keep-Alives. In Internet Information Server 4.0, this is turned on by default. It is recommended that you keep it in almost all situations. However, if your scenario warrants turning it off, you can do so on the Performance property page of the appropriate Web objects. However, keep in mind that establishing and closing connections is costly, not only for the client and server machines, but for the network itself.

HTTP Headers

Every HTTP Request or Response has both a header and a body. They can be sent together or the header can be sent independently.

The Request header contains important information the server needs to locate the requested resource and fulfill the response. For example, it contains the Uniform Resource Identifier (URI) for the resource being requested. It can also contain information about preferred languages, conditions on which the content should be downloaded, and information that identifies the type of browser sending the request. The type of browser is passed in the field called the User Agent. One of the most important Request header fields introduced with HTTP 1.1 is the Host field. You'll see more how that is used later in the chapter.

The Response header contains information the client needs to determine whether to accept the response and to properly display the content. For example, it might include information about when the content on a particular Web page expires or which application should be used to display it. Response headers can be set on the HTTP Headers property page of any Web site or directory object.

A number of important fields are defined by the HTTP 1.1 specification. It is available on the Internet at http://www.w3.org/Protocols/rfc2068/rfc2068. Although it is possible to configure additional fields, keep in mind that both the client and the server will need to understand their significance.

Content Expiration

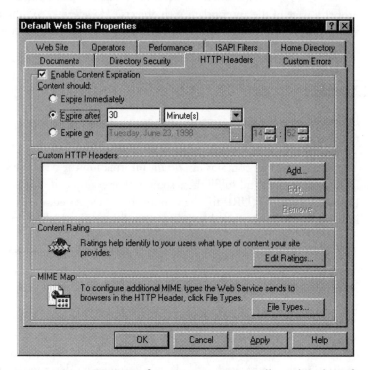

When a browser receives a Response from a server, it normally caches the information so that the next time the page is accessed, the browser simply displays the cached page instead of sending another request. However, depending on how dynamic the information on your Web page is, you may want the cached information to expire after a particular period of time. For example, if you have a special offer that is going to last until July 4th, 1998, you will want the cached page to expire on July 5th, 1998 at 12:01 a.m. If, however, your Web site is updated hourly to show the latest company news bulletin, you will want the cached page to expire after 1 hour.

When a user requests a URL, the browser checks to see if that URL is in the cache. If it is, the browser will check to see if the content has expired. If it has, the browser will request an update from the server. If it has not, the cached content will simply be displayed.

Content Ratings

Depending on the type of data you display on your site, you might want to provide content ratings. If a user is using a browser that supports content ratings, appropriately identifying your content can allow users to filter it out.

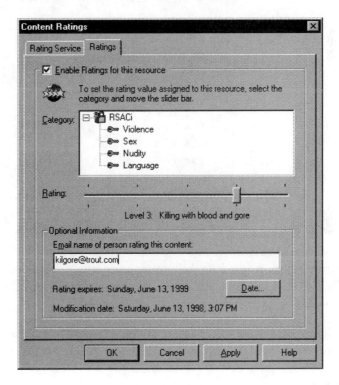

You can rate your site based on the level of violence, sex, nudity, or language it uses. This voluntary rating system was developed by the Recreational Software Advisory Council as a way to help parents screen the content their children can access on the Internet. More information is available at www.rsac.org.

MIME Types

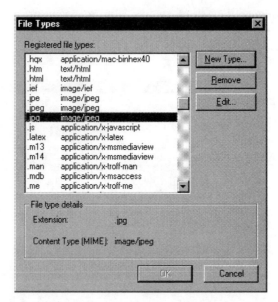

A Multipurpose Internet Mail Extension (MIME) type associates a file extension with a particular data type to help the browser know how it should be handled. For example, a file with the extension .jpg is associated with the image/jpeg MIME type by default. You can add new types, remove types, or edit existing types.

A list of MIME types is configured at the computer level. If you add a MIME type to a dependent object, the addition *replaces* the list defined at the computer level. Remember, with the exception of ISAPI filters, properties that are actually lists are replaced, not merged.

Custom Errors

When a Request cannot be fulfilled or if there is additional information, the server will send back a Response containing an error. The error will have an error number that browsers can use to determine the course of action they should take and a user-readable message to let the user know why the request was denied. However, the standard user-readable messages are not very user-friendly or explanatory. Therefore, you can use the Custom Errors property page to reference files or URLs to be used in place of the standard error messages.

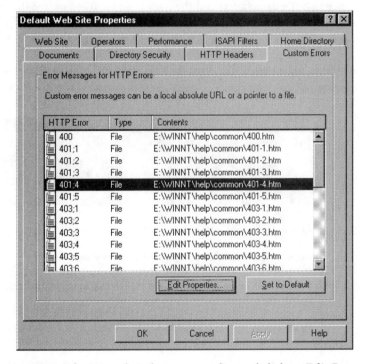

To change a message reference, select the error number and click on **Edit Properties**. You will receive the following dialog:

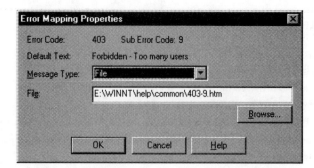

Notice that the default text and the error code are listed on the dialog. You can choose whether to use the default text or to reference a file by path or a URL. The URL must point to a resource on the local server.

Microsoft has supplied user-friendly error messages for many errors. These are installed at *systemroot*\help\common\. The Microsoft message for Error 403.9 is shown below:

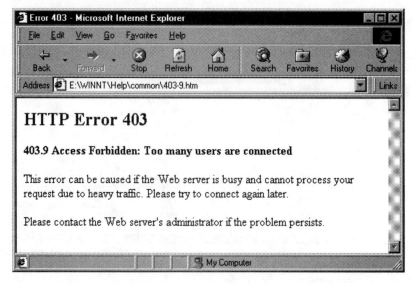

However, you still may find it beneficial to provide your own messages for some errors. For example, if your site is geared toward children, you may want to have an error message with simpler language. Another situation where you might want a custom message would be to provide error messages in the same language as the text on the site.

VIRTUAL DIRECTORIES

Virtual directories provide you with maximum flexibility for storing your Web and FTP resources. This section will examine the following:

- Uses for Virtual Directories
- Creating Virtual Directories
- Directory Browsing
- Redirection

Let's start by looking at what virtual directories are and some practical uses.

Uses for Virtual Directories

When a client connects to your Web site, IIS 4.0 uses HTTP to send your home page (usually default.asp, default.htm, or index.html) to a browser application. This file is stored in the wwwroot directory. Directories that hold content for the Web server are called *publishing directories*. However, suppose you want to store content in a directory that is not beneath the wwwroot directory. For example, you may want to store content on a second hard drive or even on different servers on your network. These directories are known as *virtual directories*.

Some reasons to use virtual directories are:

- Load Distribution

  When browsers send requests to your IIS 4.0, the server has to retrieve data from its hard drive (or cache RAM). If the requested data must be read from disk, it is then temporarily cached in server memory. This process consumes server memory resources and imposes CPU and bus overhead. Increasing numbers of client requests leads to greater server utilization. By distributing the processing load across multiple servers you can manage the utilization of any given server.

- Content Distribution

    Content distribution is as important as load distribution. For example, if you were a distributor of auto parts you might configure a server that contains an inventory and vendor database. Another server might store information about employees and payroll. A third server could act as a query server, allowing intranet users to access realtime inventory and human resources data.

- Enhanced Security

    You can enhance your system's security by storing content and data on physically separate servers. Users never directly access virtual directories.

Virtual Directory Scenario

Let's examine a scenario that describes virtual directories:

A user points his Web browser to http://www.autoparts.com. Because no specific directory or document name was supplied by the client, IIS 4.0 responds by sending the contents of the default home page, which is located in the C:\InetPub\wwwroot directory.

The auto parts distribution company that owns the Web site maintains inventory information on a separate server named Auto1. The path to the directory containing the inventory information on Auto1 is C:\Parts\Chevrolet. It is shared to the network as ChevyParts. The IIS 4.0 administrator creates a virtual directory below wwwroot on the *AutoWeb* server that references the \\Auto1\ChevyParts share. The administrator also supplies an alias of *Chevy* for the virtual directory.

When Web clients select a hypertext link that points to documents stored on Auto1, the user is unaware that the documents are located on a different Web server. The URL to documents on Auto1 would be entered in the following format:

```
http://www.autoparts.com/Chevy/document_name
```

where *document_name* is the name of an HTML document stored in the C:\Parts\Chevrolet subdirectory on Auto1. If no document name is provided, the document specified as a default document will be used.

Universal Naming Convention

To successfully create and manage virtual directories you need to be familiar with the syntax specified by the Universal Naming Convention (UNC) system. The format for a UNC is:

```
\\servername\sharename
```

The *servername* refers to the NetBIOS name of the server containing the desired resource and *sharename* refers to the shared resource used.

For example, the UNC name for the ChevyParts share on the Auto1 server would be:

```
\\Auto1\ChevyParts\
```

Creating Virtual Directories

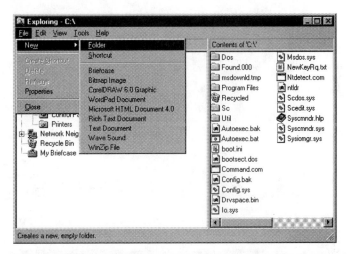

Let's see how to create a virtual directory on IIS 4.0. First, create a directory named Parts1. Set the appropriate NTFS permissions for the folder. If it is on a computer other than the one running Internet Information Server, share the directory to the network. Make sure the Sharing permissions are the same as the NTFS Security permissions. If they are different, the most restrictive access permissions will be used.

In Internet Service Manager, right-click on the Web site that should contain the virtual directory and select **New/Virtual Directory**.

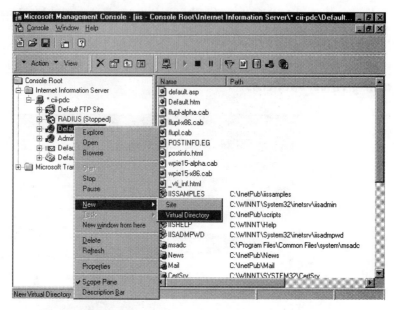

Enter an alias name for the virtual directory, then click on **Next**.

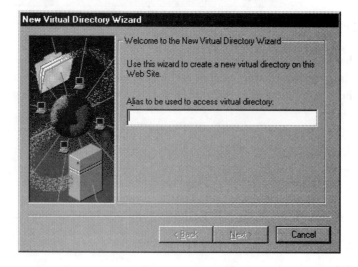

If the physical directory is on the local machine, enter a path. If it is on a different machine, enter the UNC name. Click on **Next**.

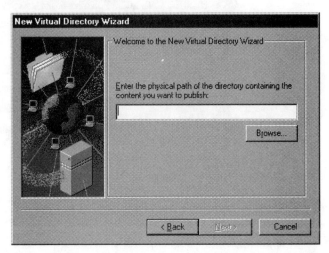

You can also click on **Browse** to locate the directory. Select the desired directory, then click on **OK**. Click on **Next**.

After selecting the physical directory, click on **Next** to continue.

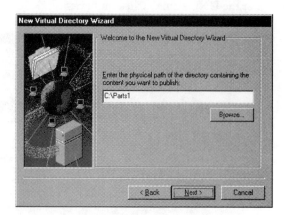

Select the access permissions you wish to assign to the new virtual directory. The default permissions are **Allow Read Access** and **Allow Script Access**. This is appropriate for server-side applications, but the Script access should be cleared for virtual directories that contain HTML files. Clear **Allow Script Access** and click on **Finish**.

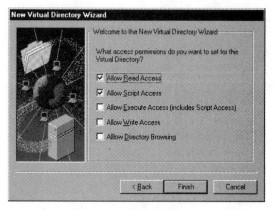

The virtual directory is now created and can be viewed with the Internet Service Manager utility.

This is how the virtual directory appears in Internet Service Manager:

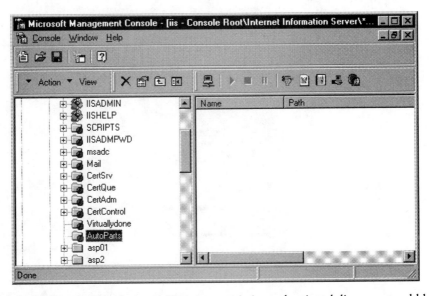

If you had selected either Script or Execute permissions, the virtual directory would have been configured as an application starting point. Applications will be discussed later in the course.

Right-click on the virtual directory and select **Properties** to view the Virtual Directory properties sheet.

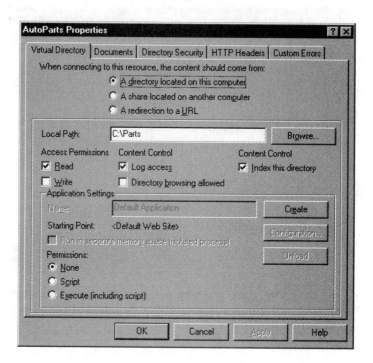

Exercise 7-1:
Creating Virtual Directories

In this exercise you will create virtual directories on the IIS 4.0.

Creating a Local Virtual Directory

You will create a virtual directory on the local computer.

1. Launch the Windows NT Explorer and browse to the root directory of drive C:.

2. Select **New Folder** from the **File** menu. Name the folder Parts2.

3. Run **Start/Programs/Windows NT 4.0 Option Pack/Microsoft Internet Server/ Internet Service Manager**.

4. Open the Internet Information Server folder, then open the Web server computer icon.

5. Right-click on Default Web Site and select **New/Virtual Directory**. Enter AutoParts in the alias field, then click on **Next**.

6. Click on **Browse** to locate the physical directory. Browse to select C:\Parts2, then click on **OK**. Click on **Next**.

7. Clear the check from **Allow Script Access** permissions, then click on **Finish**.

8. Right-click on the AutoParts virtual directory and select **Properties** to view the Virtual Directory properties sheet. Click on **OK**.

Enable Directory Browsing

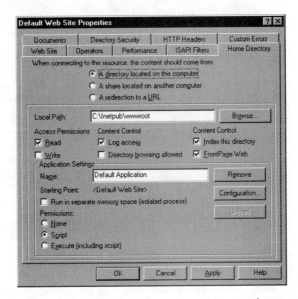

Virtual directories will not appear in your directory structure unless you enable the **Directory browsing allowed** option. This option is located on the Home Directory properties sheet.

Redirection

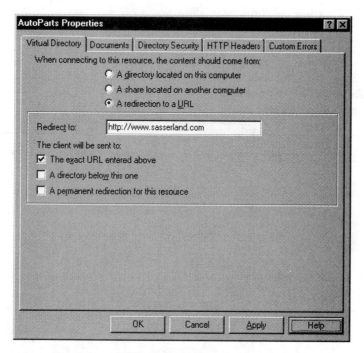

Often when you reorganize your Web site, you find that you have many links that need to be fixed. One way that you can provide your users with the continuing use of your Web site while you find those links is to use browser redirects. The Virtual Directory, Home Directory, and Directory property pages allow you to configure the virtual directory, site, server, or directory to redirect access attempts to a different URL.

VIRTUAL SERVERS

By creating virtual servers, a single computer can host multiple Web sites. This is particularly useful for ISPs. Another example of how it can be used is to provide a separate Web presence for corporate customers than for individuals. There are four ways to create a virtual server:

- Multiple Network Adapters
- Multihoming

- Specifying a Host Header
- Specifying a Unique Port

Let's look at each of these.

Multiple Network Adapters

This method requires that you install a separate network interface card (NIC) for every IP address/Web server that you are hosting.

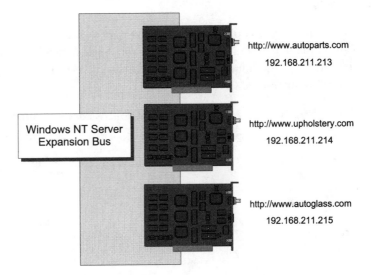

This method requires a separate hub port connection for each individual NIC. You also need a free expansion slot for each board.

The decision to install multiple network interface cards depends on several factors including:

- Available bandwidth on your Internet connection
- Router speed
- Overall network traffic
- Disk channel usage.

Multihoming

Another method of implementing virtual servers is called *multihoming*. This method requires you to bind multiple IP addresses to a single network interface card. Each assigned IP address/domain name is associated with a virtual server possessing a specific home directory on the server. For example:

- 192.168.211.213 = http://www.autoparts.com = c:\autoparts
- 192.168.211.214 = http://www.upholstery.com = c:\upholstery
- 192.168.211.215 = http://www.autoglass.com = c:\autoglass

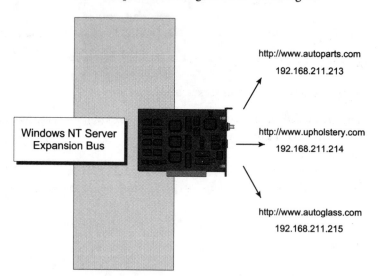

This method requires only one hub port connection and a single expansion slot in the host computer. However, because all network traffic funnels through a single NIC, the NIC is a likely source of data transmission bottlenecks.

Exercise 7-2:
Configure Multihoming

In this exercise you will bind multiple IP addresses to a single network interface card.

1. Right click on Network Neighborhood and select **Properties**.

2. Click on the **Protocols** tab, select **TCP/IP Protocol**, then click on **Properties**.

3. Click on the **Advanced** button.

4. Click on **Add** and enter 192.168.211.213 for the IP Address value and 255.255.255.0 for the Subnet Mask value. Click on **Add**.

5. Click on **Add** and enter 192.168.211.214 for the IP Address value and 255.255.255.0 for the Subnet Mask value. Click on **Add**.

6. Click on **Add** and enter 192.168.211.214 for the IP Address value and 255.255.255.0 for the Subnet Mask value. Click on **Add**.

7. Click on **OK**, then click on **Close**. This will bind the new IP addresses to your server's NIC. When prompted to reboot, click on **OK**.

8. Go to a remote computer and Ping each of the IP addresses you assigned to verify that they are bound to the NIC.

Exercise 7-3:
Create Web Sites for Virtual Servers and Home Directories

In this exercise you will create several virtual servers.

1. Launch Windows NT Explorer and browse to the root directory of drive C.

2. Select **New Folder** from the **File** menu. Name the folder AutoParts.

3. Select **New Folder** from the **File** menu. Name the folder AutoGlass.

4. Select **New Folder** from the **File** menu. Name the folder Upholstery.

5. These three folders will act as the root directories for three different Web sites.

    NOTE: If you were configuring these Web sites for actual use, you would configure NTFS permissions at this point.

6. Exit Windows NT Explorer.

7. Run **Start/Programs/Windows NT 4.0 Option Pack/Microsoft Internet Server/ Internet Service Manager**.

8. Open the Internet Information Server folder, then right-click on the Web server computer icon.

9. Select **New/Web Site**.

10. Enter AutoParts for the Web Site Description value, then click on **Next**. This will start the Web Site Wizard.

11. Select IP address 192.168.211.213. Accept the default TCP Port value, then click on **Next**.

12. Click on the **Browse** button and browse to select C:\AutoParts. Verify that the **Allow anonymous access to this web site** option is selected. Click on **OK**, then click on **Next**.

13. Accept the default Access Permissions by clicking on **Finish**. You should see the new AutoParts Web site listed in the MS Management Console.

14. Right-click on AutoParts and select **Start**.

15. Right-click on the Web server computer icon and select **New/Web Site**.

16. Enter Upholstery for the Web Site Description value, then click on **Next**. This will start the Web Site Wizard.

17. Select IP address 192.168.211.214. Accept the default TCP Port value, then click on **Next**.

18. Click on the **Browse** button and browse to select C:\Upholstery. Verify that the **Allow anonymous access to this web site** option is selected. Click on **OK**, then click on **Next**.

19. Accept the default Access Permissions by clicking on **Finish**. You should see the new AutoGlass Web site listed in the MS Management Console.

20. Right-click on Upholstery and select **Start**.

21. Right-click on the Web server computer icon and select **New/Web Site**.

22. Enter AutoGlass for the Web Site Description value, then click on **Next**. This will start the Web Site Wizard.

23. Select IP address **192.168.211.215**. Accept the default TCP Port value, then click on **Next**.

24. Click on the **Browse** button and browse to select C:\AutoGlass. Verify that the **Allow anonymous access to this web site** option is selected. Click on **OK**, then click on **Next**.

25. Accept the default Access Permissions by clicking on **Finish**. You should see the new Upholstery Web site listed in the MS Management Console.

26. Right-click on Upholstery and select **Start**.

   NOTE: *The Default Web Site needs to be redirected to make all of the virtual servers function properly.*

27. Right-click on Default Web Site and select **Properties**.

28. Click on the **Home Directory** tab. Click on the **Browse** button and browse to select C:\AutoGlass. Click on **OK**, then click on **Apply**.

29. Click on the **Web Site** tab. Enter AutoGlass for the Description value and 192.168.211.213 for the IP Address. Click on **Apply**, then click on **OK**.

Specifying a Host Header

One of the most powerful new features of HTTP 1.1 is the ability to run multiple Web
sites off a single IP address. This is done through the use of a new field in the HTTP
Request header, the Host field. To configure a virtual server using Host Headers:

Right-click on the Computer object. Run **New/Web Site**.

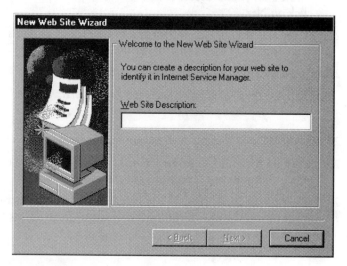

Enter a description for your site.

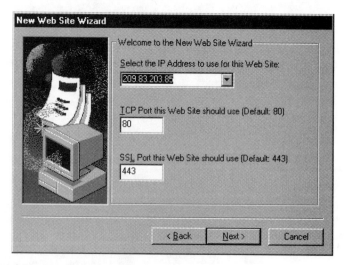

Select an IP Address (or keep it at Any Unassigned).

Configure the path for the site's home directory and select whether the site can be accessed anonymously.

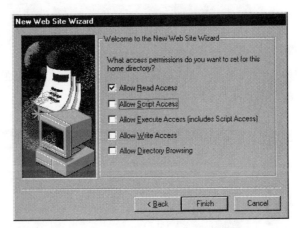

Configure access permissions. Once again, Read and Script access are the defaults. However, if you are going to be using strictly HTML, you can clear the Script access. Click on **Finish**. At this point, the new site will be created, but it will not be started.

Right-click on the new Site icon and run **Properties**.

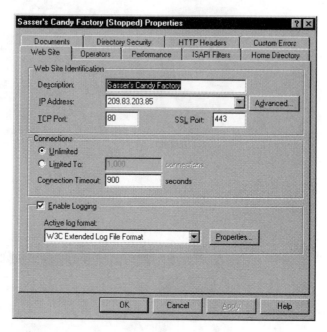

Click on **Advanced**.

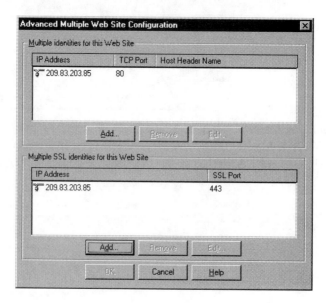

Now you can edit the identity for the site. Select the item in the Multiple identities for this Web site list. Click on **Edit**.

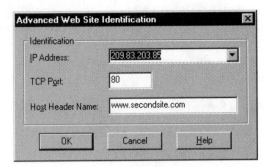

Enter a fully qualified domain name as the Host Header Name and click on **OK**. Close all of the dialogs and property pages. Click on the **Start** button to start the site.

> *NOTE: You cannot use host headers to provide multiple sites that use SSL. This is because the host name is associated with the SSL certificate.*

A Note on Name Resolution

As with any Web site, you will need to implement the appropriate host name resolution to enable users to access your Web site. If you are using HOSTS for name resolution, provide an alias to each additional Web site on the line with the IP address. If you are using DNS, you will need to create an additional A record for each host name your Web site supports.

Specifying a Unique Port

You can also create multiple Web sites by specifying unique ports for each site, instead of using the default port of 80. While this works from a technical point of view, it is not as friendly for users because the port must be specified as part of the URL.

However, using ports to identify unique sites is one way to support multiple SSL sites on the same IP address.

SERVER-SIDE APPLICATIONS

So far most of the discussion has focused around providing access to HTML files that will be executed on the client. However, more and more Web sites are taking advantage of server-side technologies to provide their customers and employees with powerful data-driven solutions. This section will focus on using Active Server Pages to provide a server-side solution. These include:

- Active Server Pages Benefits

- Intrinsic Active Server Pages Objects

- Creating an Active Server Page

- Scripting an Active Server Page

- Creating Object Instances

- URL Arguments

- Directory Permissions

Since this is a course in IIS 4.0 administration, the focus will be on when it is appropriate to use each of these and how to configure IIS 4.0 to take advantage of them. The details of implementing server-side solutions are beyond the scope of this course.

Active Server Pages Benefits

Active Server Pages were introduced earlier in the course. However, it is important to revisit their benefits before talking about their specifics. An Active Server Page is compiled by Internet Information Server. Regardless of the scripting language or components used in its code, its output to the client (browser) is vanilla HTML. For this reason, using Active Server Pages will provide you with the following benefits:

- Browser compatibility

    Provided your output is only standard HTML, your Web page can be viewed with any Web browser. In fact, Internet Information Server 4.0 provides a Browser Capability object that can be used from an ASP to tailor your output to take advantage of specific browser features, such as ActiveX, Java, or Dynamic HTML.

- Less network traffic

    If a component manipulates data that is located on the Internet server or on a server connected to the same LAN, it is likely that you will gain performance by running the component on the server side, instead of transferring large amounts of data across slow links.

- Better performance

    Active Server Pages provide better performance than other server-side technologies, such as CGI. Active Server Pages are multithreaded and run inside the Internet Information Server process. This conserves memory and processor time, particularly when multiple users are accessing a Web page.

- Easier maintainability

    The Active Server Page itself is automatically recompiled by Internet Information Server the first time it is accessed after a change. Like an HTML file, it does not need to be explicitly compiled. This makes modifications to business logic easy.

- Logic cannot be viewed

    The only code the browser knows about is that which is downloaded as HTML. Therefore, viewing the source code through the browser will only display the HTML that is transmitted. Any logic in your scripts or components is private.

Intrinsic Active Server Pages Objects

Active Server Pages have several intrinsic objects. These objects will be overviewed, but not discussed in detail. The intrinsic objects are:

- Request

    The Request object allows you to find out information, such as arguments passed in the URL, information from cookies and forms, and any HTTP headers. You will see how to use the Request object to retrieve URL arguments later in the chapter.

- Response

    The Response object can be used to display text or to open a different URL.

- Server

    The Server object is used to access features of the Internet Information Server. As you will see a little later, the Server object is required to create an instance of a server-side component.

- Application

    This object is used to store information that is common to all users accessing the Web. A common use of the Application object is to lock and unlock resources so that they are not modified at the same time by two different users.

- Session

    The Session object is used to maintain state when moving between Web pages. For example, you may have a series of forms that gather various types of information from the user. This information can be stored in the Session object and retrieved by any of the pages until the session is closed.

Creating an Active Server Page

An Active Server Page is like an HTML document, except that it uses some special tags and is saved with an .asp extension. An Active Server Page should contain a header that looks like this:

```
<%@ LANGUAGE="VBSCRIPT" %>

<HTML>

<HEAD>

<META NAME="GENERATOR" Content="Microsoft Visual InterDev 1.0">

<META HTTP-EQUIV="Content-Type" content="text/html; charset=iso-
    8859-1">

<TITLE>Document Title</TITLE>

</HEAD>

<BODY>

<!-- Insert HTML here -->

</BODY>

</HTML>
```

Notice that the language is noted as VBScript. You could also use JavaScript or any other Active scripting language hosted by Internet Information Server.

Scripting an Active Server Page

ASP Component Access

Active Server Pages (ASP) use *properties* and *methods* to access components. Properties control the state of an object. Methods are *functions* that operate on the object.

The example VBScript procedure uses an object that retrieves the date of the user's last order from a database.

```
<%
Dim OrderDate
Set objOrder = Server.CreateObject("OrderWiz.Retriever")
objOrder.LastName = "Reese"
objOrder.FillLastOrderInfo
OrderDate = objOrder.LastOrderDate
Response.Write = "You placed your last order on " & OrderDate
%>
```

The <% and %> symbols indicate that the script should be run by the server rather than by the client. The Server object is an intrinsic object. Its **CreateObject** method is called to create an instance of the object of class OrderWiz.Retriever. This is an object class that must be registered properly in the registry of the machine running Internet Information Server. Once the instance of the object is created, its **LastName** property is set. Next the script calls the **FillLastOrderInfo** method, which locates the last order made by someone with the last name of Reese. Next the script retrieves the value of the **LastOrderDate** property. The **Write** method of the intrinsic Response object outputs the text as plain HTML.

This script has been simplified for the purposes of this course. In actuality, you would need more information to reliably locate the last order of the person using your Web site.

However, using ActiveX components on the server deserves a littler closer look.

Creating Object Instances

When you're using ActiveX components from an Active Server Page, you need to specifically ask the server to create an instance of the object for you. The Server object has a **CreateObject** method for this purpose. It has the syntax:

```
Set Variable = Server.CreateObject(Libname.Class)
```

The server locates the object's programmatic identifier in the registry and launches the server either in-process (for DLLs) or out-of-process (for EXEs). It is best to use a multithreaded in-process component with Active Server Pages.

Once the instance of the object is created, use the variable containing its reference to access properties and methods.

The first time the server loads the object, it keeps it in memory so that overhead is not incurred every time a user connects to the Web server. While this provides a performance boost, it does mean that the object cannot be replaced unless you specifically unload it. One way to do this is to stop the WWW Publishing Service.

Now let's look at how your Active Server Page can be passed information through its URL.

URL Arguments

It is likely that you may have an Active Server Page that is called via a hyperlink from another Active Server Page or an HTML page. If this is the case, you may want to pass information to the Active Server Page so that it can process the information and return a result to the user. Fortunately, the Active Server Page Request object makes this fairly easy.

An Active Server Page URL can include arguments that are passed as follows:

```
server/directory/file.asp?arg1=value&arg2=value
```

The question mark specifies that an argument list follows. Arguments are separated with the ampersand (&). For example, you may want to pass the item number selected to an inventory ASP. The URL you use for the hyperlink would look something like this:

```
www.mystore.com/inventory/check.asp?Item=820A
```

Inside the Active Server Page, you would use the **QueryString** method of the Request object to retrieve the value of the argument. Your code would look like this:

```
<%Item=Request.QueryString("Item")%>
```

Once you have retrieved the values, you can use the variable just as you would any other.

Virtual Directory Permissions

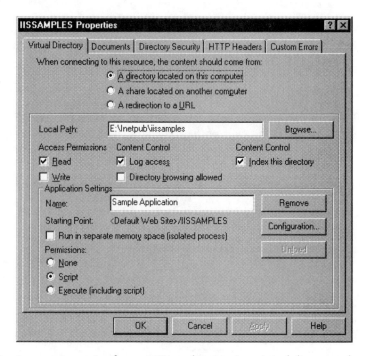

The application starting point for an ASP application is a virtual directory that has been configured as an application. In addition to assigning user- and group-specific NTFS permissions to all directories, files, and component files the ASP will need to access, you also need to assign appropriate Web permissions. To determine the appropriate permissions, think about the types of files that are in the virtual directory.

- Only .asp files

    You can get by with either Read or Script permissions.

- Multiple file types, including .asp files (for example, .htm and .asp files)

    You will need to specify both Read and Script permissions.

- Executables or dynamic link libraries (ActiveX component files)

    You will need to specify both Read and Execute permissions.

DATA ACCESS

Many Web sites are taking advantage of relational databases as a way to provide dynamic information to users. Internet Information Server provides several object models that you can use to interface your Web page with a database. In addition, there are some underlying technologies that provide an interface with the databases. This section will look at the following:

- ODBC
- Internet Data Connector
- ActiveX Data Objects
- Remote Data Services

Let's take a look at each of these.

ODBC

Open Database Connectivity (ODBC) provides an interface that applications can use to talk to various data sources. The ODBC Driver Manager is responsible for finding the appropriate driver to access a database. The examples given in this book reference a SQL data source. However, any source with an ODBC driver could be used, including Oracle, Sybase, or Microsoft Access databases. Let's look at how ODBC datasources can be configured.

ODBC Administrator

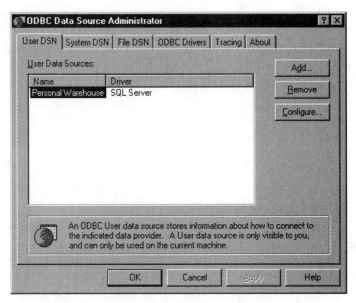

The ODBC Data Source Administrator is launched by double-clicking on the ODBC icon in the Control Panel. It allows you to configure data sources on a per-user or per-system basis. To configure a data source, click on **Add**. You will be prompted to choose the driver for your data source. If you choose the SQL Server driver, the ODBC SQL Server Setup dialog will be displayed.

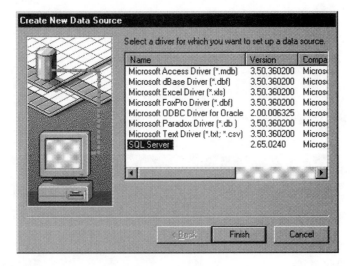

ODBC SQL Server Setup

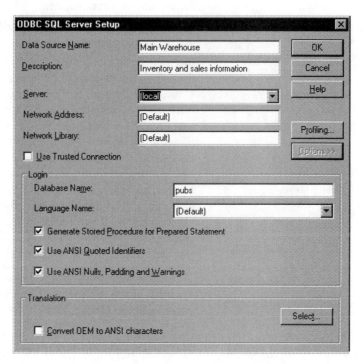

The ODBC SQL Server Setup dialog box allows users to configure a SQL Server data source. The fields should be filled in as follows:

Data Source Name	This is the name by which you will refer to the data source when opening the database.
Description	This is a textual description of the database.
Server	This is the machine name of the server running Microsoft SQL Server. If SQL Server is running on the local machine, specify "local."

Network Address   This is the address of the SQL Server. If you are
                       configuring a Microsoft SQL Server data source, you can
                       usually use the default setting.

Network Library   This is the name of the NetLibrary that the SQL Server
                       driver will use to communicate with the network. If you
                       specify default, it will use the Net-Library that is set up as
                       the default driver in the SQL Server Client Configuration
                       Utility (usually Named Pipes). Using the Named Pipes
                       NetLibrary is sufficient in most cases. Named Pipes runs
                       over TCP/IP, as well as several other protocols and it
                       allows integrated security and trusted connections.
                       However, if your Internet Information Server is on one
                       side of a firewall or proxy server and the SQL Server is on
                       another, you will have to use TCP/IP Sockets as your
                       NetLibrary. The default port for the TCP/IP Sockets
                       library is 1433. If you decide to change it, make sure it is
                       changed consistently on your SQL Server, the firewall,
                       and the Internet Information Server.

Database Name   This is the name of your SQL Server database. This is
                       optional. If it is not specified, you will need to include it
                       in your call to **OpenDatabase**. Otherwise, master will be
                       opened.

Language Name   The language for which SQL Server was configured.

Generate Stored Procedure for Prepared Statement
                       This option specifies that SQL Server should compile a
                       statement when it is prepared and store it as a stored
                       procedure.

Translation   A translator is usually used to translate data between
                       character sets or to provide encryption or decryption.
                       Click on **Select** to choose a translator if applicable.

Convert OEM to ANSI characters
                       Select this option if your client application uses a different
                       code page than that used by the SQL Server that manages
                       the data source.

Data Source Registry Entries

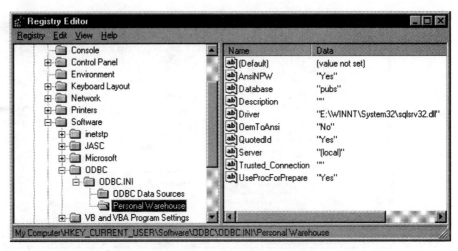

If you configure a user-specific data source, information about it will be stored in the Registry under the HKEY_CURRENT_USER\Software\ODBC\ODBC.INI subkey. Data Source Names are listed under ODBC Data Sources. Each Data Source Name also has its own subkey under which the various attributes needed to connect to the data source are listed. The example above shows the entries created when a data source named Personal Warehouse was created.

If you configure a system-specific data source, information about it will be stored under HKEY_LOCAL_MACHINE\Software\ODBC\ODBC.INI, as shown below:

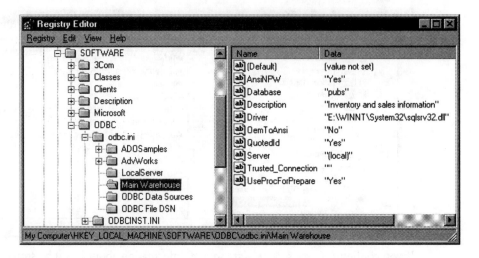

Internet Data Connector

The Internet Data Connector (IDC) is used to retrieve information from a database, format it using a template, and send the resulting HTML to the browser. It requires an ODBC data source name (DSN).

To use the Internet Data Connector, you need to create two files for your query.

IDC file

This file contains the information necessary to query the database. The syntax of the file will look something like this:

```
Datasource: web sql

Username: sa

Template: sample.htx

SQLStatement:

+SELECT au_lname, ytd_sales from pubs.dbo.titleview where
    ytd_sales>5000
```

Notice that the IDC file contains the following four types of information:

- Datasource

  The Datasource is the DSN that has been configured in the ODBC Administrator. Internet Information Server will pass this information to the ODBC Driver Manager. The ODBC Driver Manager will find the DSN in the registry, launch the appropriate driver, and submit the query.

- Username

  This is the name that should be used to log on to the database management system. The username "sa" is the default SQL Administrative name.

- Template

  This is the name of the HTML document that will receive the results of the query.

- SQLStatement

  This is the statement that describes the information that should be returned. This statement is passed on to the database management system, which parses the statement and returns the appropriate results. A detailed discussion of SQL syntax is beyond the scope of this course.

An IDC file is an ASCII file saved with the .idc extension.

Template File

The template file is an HTML document that is saved with the .htx extension. Inside the file, the HTML references the IDC query. The HTML syntax uses special scripting tags <% %>, as well as some keywords to interpret and display the result set. The details of interpreting an IDC result set are beyond the scope of this course.

ADO and OLE DB

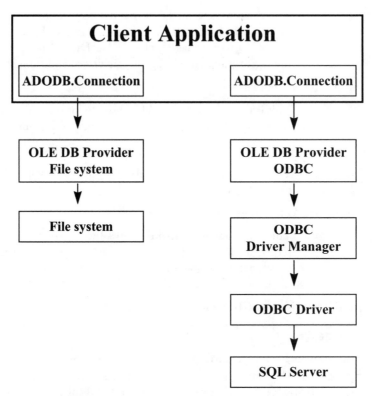

ADO works in conjunction with an OLE DB provider to give a client application access to any type of data, whether it is relational or not. As long as an OLE DB provider exists for a particular data source, ADO can access it. As you can see, this does not mean that ODBC will go away. The ODBC Manager has an OLE DB provider. Its OLE DB provider implements the interfaces that ADO expects an OLE DB provider to implement and passes the request for a connection or query on to the ODBC Manager. From there it works exactly as it always has.

The real difference is that ADO and OLE DB do not require data sources to include an ODBC driver. For non-relational data sources, this greatly reduces the number of layers through which a request must pass.

Currently, the only OLE DB provider available for ADO is the ODBC provider.

ADO Object Model

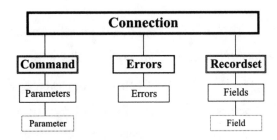

ADO OBJECT MODEL

The ADO object model is composed of ActiveX objects that can be used in any controller, including Internet Information Server, through the use of Active Server Pages. The ADO object model contains seven objects:

Connection	This object is used to create a connection with a Database server.
Command	This object is used to issue queries or execute stored procedures. With non-relational data sources, you may not need to use it.
Recordset	This object stores the result of a query or the data source returned by a provider. This is the object with which you will most frequently interface.
Parameter	The Parameter object provides parameter information and data for the Command object.
Field	A Field object allows access to each data column in the current Recordset record.

Property	The Property object provides information about the characteristics of the Connection, Command, Recordset, and Field objects.
Error	The Error object allows retrieval of provider error information when an error occurs.

The ADO object model also contains four collections:

Fields	A collection of Field objects.
Properties	A collection of Property objects.
Parameters	A collection of Parameter objects.
Errors	A collection of Error objects.

The Connection, Command, and Recordset objects are the central objects in the ADO object model.

Remote Data Service

Internet Information Server 4.0 provides support for Remote Data Service (RDS) 1.5. RDS allows for disconnected result sets on the client. This is useful for situations where the user needs to navigate through and manipulate a set of data. Like ADO, RDS uses OLE DB providers to interface with the data source. This version of RDS also uses the same object model as ADO, making it easy for programmers to adapt server-side code to work with a client-cached result set and vice versa. A detailed discussion of the RDS architecture is beyond the scope of this course.

MICROSOFT TRANSACTION SERVER

One of the challenges of Web solutions is that they often need to be able to support a large number of users simultaneously. This presents a number of challenges for developers. Fortunately, Microsoft recognized the need to provide developers with a simple way to handle some of these issues and developed Microsoft Transaction Server (MTS). This section takes a brief look at Microsoft Transaction server, including:

- What is a Transaction?
- Microsoft Transaction Server Benefits
- Transaction Server Explorer Snap-in

Let's start by looking at the benefits provided by MTS.

What is a Transaction?

You are probably familiar with transactions in the real world. Most classic examples involve money. Consider a credit card transaction. When you make a purchase on your credit card, several things must happen:

- You receive a product or service.
- The credit card company charges your account.
- The credit card company pays the vendor providing the service.

If one of these things fails to happen, the transaction should be *rolled back*. For example, if you ordered a book through the mail and that book never arrived, but the charge appeared on your credit card, you would call the credit card company and ask that the charge be taken off. The credit card company would, in turn, demand that the book publisher either send you the book or refund the payment. One way or another, all aspects of the transaction would either be *committed* or *rolled back*.

The same theory applies to *transactions* that occur on a Web site, particularly if they modify data in a database. Let's look at a quick example.

Suppose you have a retail site. When a customer orders a product, your Web site must receive customer information and order information. Enter the customer information in the Customer table. Verify that the credit card is valid. Verify that the product is in stock. Enter the order information in the Orders table. Send the order to the person who handles shipping. If one of these things fails, the transaction should be rolled back. Prior to MTS, writing the code to handle all of these conditions would have been pretty complex, particularly if there were a lot of user connections involved. Fortunately, MTS can be used to simplify the task.

Microsoft Transaction Server Benefits

In addition to handling transaction commitment and rollback, MTS handles several other issues that arise in a multiple-user environment. These are:

- Thread pooling

    An application with a single thread can only handle a single user. However, writing multithreaded applications is difficult and time-consuming. MTS provides thread management through the use of thread pooling. This simplifies the development process and lets you easily control the number of threads that are running instances of a component.

- Application isolation

    Normally an Active Server Pages application runs in the same process as Internet Information Server. This means that a misbehaving in-process component (DLL) could potentially crash IIS 4.0. To guard against this, MTS allows you to run a Web application inside its own package. If a component in the package misbehaves, only that package will crash. IIS 4.0 will continue to run.

- Integration with Active Server Pages

    It is now easy to build an Active Server Pages application that can take advantage of transactions.

- Integration with Microsoft Message Queue Server (MSMQ)

    The Microsoft Message Queue Server is another server that ships with Windows NT 4.0 Option Pack. This server allows you to queue processes that do not have to occur immediately.

Building transactional Web applications is beyond the scope of this course.

Transaction Server Explorer Snap-in

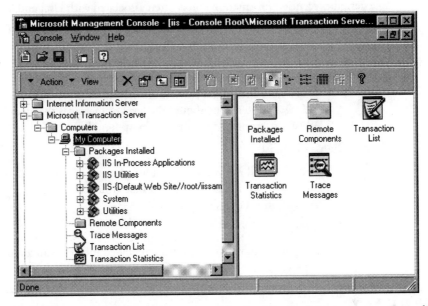

Microsoft Transaction Server can be managed in the Microsoft Management Console by adding the MTS Explorer Snap-in. This snap-in is added by default when Windows NT 4.0 Option Pack is installed.

A Package is the object that contains the components of an application. Each Package contains two folders: one that contains components and the other that contains roles. A role describes security information and is often associated with User and Group accounts. In addition, there are three objects that can be used to view particular types of information about transactions. These are:

- Trace Messages

  This object allows you to view errors, warnings, and informational messages. You can configure the level of messages that are displayed on the Advanced property page of the Computer object.

- Transaction List

  This object allows you to view a list of transactions that are currently running. This is a good place to start troubleshooting if you suspect a transaction is being blocked.

- Transaction Statistics

  This object allows you to retrieve detailed information about a particular transaction.

SUMMARY

During this section, you were introduced to issues you need to think about when deciding how to configure your Internet Information Server to best manage the content it needs to provide. This included:

- HTTP Headers
- Virtual Directories
- Virtual Servers
- Active Server Pages
- ODBC
- Internet Data Connector
- ActiveX Data Objects
- Remote Data Services
- Microsoft Transaction Server

The next chapter will take examine another important server that comes with Windows NT 4.0 Option Pack: Index Server.

POST-TEST QUESTIONS

The answers to these questions are in Appendix A at the end of this manual.

1. Which Microsoft Transaction Server object allows you to view errors that have occurred?

    ....

    ....

2. What do you need to configure in order to use IDC?

    ....

    ....

3. One of the developers has given you an Active Server Pages script to deploy on the Internet. It uses an ActiveX component that is installed in the same directory as the .asp script. What Web permissions should you assign that directory?

    ....

    ....

4. You want to configure separate Web sites for your existing customers and for new customers. However, you only have one IP address available. How can you do this?

    ....

    ....

5. You have configured separate Web sites for your existing and new customers by using host headers. However, when you try to connect to the existing customer site, the site for new customers is displayed. What is the problem?

   ....

   ....

6. You want to run a processor-intensive application when users click on a particular hyperlink. However, when you load test it with only five users, performance for everyone connected to your Web site becomes very sluggish. How can you improve performance for your Web site?

   ....

   ....

7. You run the Web site for a company that provides up-to-the-minute news stories. Recently you have had complaints that some of your stories contain graphic photographs of violent crimes. How can you configure your Web site so that compliant browsers can filter these pages?

   ....

   ....

8. You are running a Web site and you plan to provide content in several different languages. How can you provide error messages in the same language as the Web page being displayed?

   ....

   ....

9. What feature of HTTP 1.1 improves performance by reducing the amount of overhead necessary for establishing connections?

   ....

   ....

CHAPTER 8

Microsoft Index Server 2.0

OBJECTIVES

At the completion of this chapter, you will be able to:

- Describe the features and capabilities of Microsoft Index Server 2.0.

- Identify the search options supported by Index Server 2.0.

- Install and configure Index Server 2.0.

- Identify when Index Server 2.0 will load into memory and run.

- Identify when Index Server 2.0 must be shut down and restarted.

- Restrict the files that are indexed by Index Server 2.0.

- Describe ways in which Index Server 2.0 can be optimized to minimize resource use.

- Determine when re-indexing will occur after file changes.

- Define Index Server 2.0 querying methods.

- Add a new catalog.

- Customize the way Index Server builds an index.

PRE-TEST QUESTIONS

The answers to these questions are in Appendix A at the end of this manual.

1. What Web server feature does Index Server provide?

....

....

2. What is the name of the default catalog?

....

....

3. You have a propriety document format you wish to make available on your Web site. How can you ensure that its contents can be indexed by Index Server?

....

....

4. Can you use Index Server to provide a search if your query form is built by an Active Server Page?

....

....

INTRODUCTION

It doesn't take long for a Web site to grow beyond a few pages. Many companies that establish a presence on the Internet wish to eventually deliver more and more services through public networks. As the number of documents stored on your site grows, it becomes increasingly difficult for users to locate desired content.

Site indexing is an important value-added feature of IIS 4.0. In this section you'll be introduced to the configuration and management of Microsoft Index Server 2.0.

MICROSOFT INDEX SERVER 2.0

Microsoft Index Server 2.0 (MIS 2.0) provides you with the ability to provide indexed searches for information contained on your IIS. Indexing is a valuable feature and proper implementation can produce very professional results. Microsoft Index Server 2.0 is easy to administer and requires relatively low maintenance.

Some features of Microsoft Index Server 2.0 are:

- The ability to index multiple Web Servers, including files on a NetWare server or files in a FAT partition.

....

....

....

....

- Support for full-text and property-value indexing for the following formats:

    Text files (.txt)

    HTML 3.0 and earlier (.htm)

    MS Word 95 and 97 (.doc)

    MS Excel 95 and 97 (.xls)

    MS PowerPoint 95 and 97 (.ppt)

    Binary files (properties only)

Additional file formats can be indexed, provided you install the appropriate content features.

- The ability to support multiple languages by storing index information in Unicode. Supported languages include:

    Dutch

    French

    German

    Italian

    Japanese

    Spanish

    Swedish

    U.K. English

    U.S. English

    Traditional and Simplified Chinese

- Index Server can index your news messages.
- As the site's file structure changes, indexes are automatically updated.
- Index server includes an automatic error detection and recovery system.

System Requirements

Microsoft Index Server 2.0 can be installed on any existing IIS 4.0 Server. The following are suggested memory requirements for Microsoft Index Server 2.0. These requirements are in addition to the those of the Windows NT 4.0 Server operating system and IIS 4.0.

- Fewer than 100,000 Web pages, 32 MB of additional RAM
- 100,000-250,000 Web pages, 64-128 MB of additional RAM
- 250,000-500,000 Web pages, 128-256 MB of additional RAM
- Over 500,000 Web pages, 256 MB or more

Disk space requirements are dependent on the number of files to be indexed. The index *catalog* will be approximately 40% of the total size of the indexed files. Therefore, if you have 1 gigabyte of Web content, you will need about 400 megabytes of disk space to store the catalog.

Performance is based on the number of documents indexed, the size of the *corpus* (a Latin word meaning *body*), search *scope*, processor speed, and other server-related performance issues.

Installing Microsoft Index Server 2.0

The Microsoft Index Server 2.0 is a component of the Windows NT 4.0 Option Pack and is installed by default. It consists of four sub-components:

- Index Server System Files
- Language resources
- Online documentation
- Sample files

NOTE: *Refer to Chapter 4 for more information on IIS 4.0 and Windows NT 4.0 Option Pack installation.*

During the installation process, a *Catalog* directory (catalog.wci) is created below the C:\InetPub directory. The index and property cache files are stored in this directory.

Microsoft Index Server 2.0 is configured and managed with the Microsoft Management Console via the Index Server 2.0 snap-in module.

> *NOTE:* *You may achieve enhanced system performance by installing the Index Server 2.0 component on a different disk drive than the one containing your Web documents.*

Index Server files are copied to the following directories:

\Inetpub\Iissamples\Iissamples	Sample HTML files
\Inetpub\Iisadmin\Iisadmin	Administration files
\Inetpub\Iishelp\Ix	Document Files

Once the Microsoft Index Server 2.0 component is installed, it begins to index all of the files contained in the virtual directories of the Default Web Site.

The Index Server is a Windows NT Service named *Content Index* (cisvc.exe). Launch the Services utility to view information on installed, running, and stopped Services. The Content Index Service runs continuously and automatically updates changes made to your Web site directories and files, even when the WWW Service is not running.

Understanding the Indexing Process

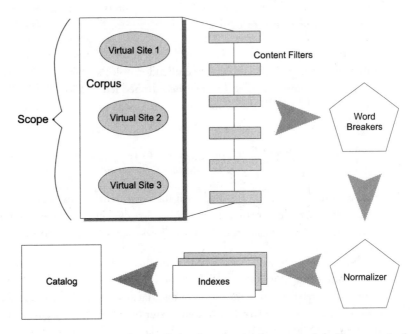

The term *corpus* is used to refer to all the documents that are indexed by a particular catalog. This corpus of documents may be located on the local server or a combination of servers.

A process called CiDaemon is responsible for generating the index. It runs in the background. It creates the index by loading and running the appropriate dynamic link libraries. These DLLs depend on the type of document being indexed, as well as the language in which it was written. Two types of DLLs will be used for each document: Content Filters and Word Breakers.

Content Filters are used to allow the indexing of formatted documents. For example, Microsoft Word uses a different file format than Excel. Microsoft Index Server 2.0 indexes documents based on available Content Filters. It ignores those document formats that it does not recognize.

In addition to text extraction, Content Filters allow Microsoft Index Server 2.0 to recognize language shifts and handle embedded objects. For example, if Microsoft Index Server 2.0 encounters an Excel spreadsheet embedded in a Word document, the server is able to index the text in the Word document as well as text contained in the Excel document.

> *NOTE: Content Filters can be developed by independent software vendors (ISVs) to provide support for additional file formats.*

Once a Content Filter has finished with the document, Index Server uses Word breakers to parse the character stream into individual words. Since different languages separate words differently, language-specific word breakers can be installed.

The Normalizer removes punctuation, capitalization, and words such as *the, of, a, an, and, or,* and other words that have been designated as *noise words*. The pre-identified noise words are stored in a file named noise.dat (for the English language). You can modify the list of noise words or provide your own file. Language-specific noise word files are identified in the Registry under the key: HKEY_LOCAL_MACHINE\SYSTEM\SYSTEM\CurrentControlSet\Control\ContentIndex\Language\<*language*>\NoiseFile.

Once the noise words have been removed, a word list is created in memory. When there are a certain number of word lists in memory, they are merged into a persistent index. The persistent index is stored in the catalog, along with a list of properties.

A *catalog* is associated with a single site. During installation, the Index Server creates a catalog named Web. By default, this catalog is associated with the Default Web Site. you can create multiple catalogs. However, Index Server performs a query on an individual catalog. Therefore, queries cannot be performed across sites.

MICROSOFT INDEX SERVER 2.0 MANAGEMENT

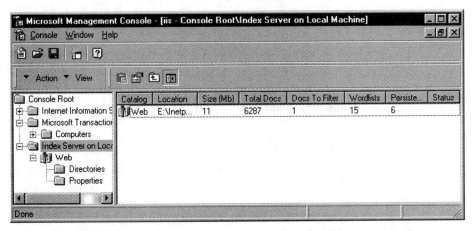

Microsoft Index Server 2.0 Manager is a snap-in to Microsoft Management Console (MMC). The MMC is launched automatically when you start the Index Server Manager. However, you can also add it to any other console, using the procedures described earlier in the course. The following eight parameters are displayed when you select an Index Server:

- Catalog

  The name for the catalogs associated with this Index Server. Separate statistics are maintained for every catalog.

- Location

  The root path for the catalog.

- Size (Mb)

  The amount of space required to hold an index for the cataloged documents.

- Total Docs

    The total number of documents in the catalog directory.

- Docs to Filter

    The number of documents to be filtered.

- Wordlists

    The number of temporary word lists that Index Server has created for the Catalog. When there are 14 to 20 such lists they are merged into a persistent index.

- Persistent Indexes

    The number of permanent indexes for the catalog. Index Server may create additional persistent indexes, which will eventually be merged.

- Status

    The status of the catalog, such as up-to-date or malfunctioning. This parameter is only present when the Index Server is performing an operation on the catalog. If the Status field displays a scan message, you should re-scan the directories in the catalog.

Configuring Global Properties

To view the Properties of your server, right-click on the Index Server folder, then select Properties.

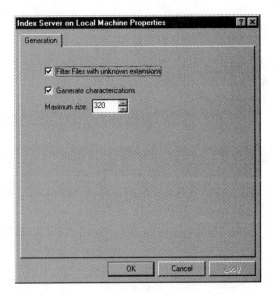

Generation Properties

- Filter Files with unknown extensions

    Enable this option to prevent certain files (.exe, .gif, etc.) that do not contain text from being posted to the results view.

- Generate characterizations

    Enable this option to have the Index Server create a summary for every file in a search result. A summary provides users with an idea of what to expect when they select a particular link. The summary does consume additional CPU cycles and may not produce more usable information than the document title.

- Maximum size

    This option is used to determine the maximum number of characters that are returned in a summary.

NOTE: You make global property changes by configuring the Index Server Properties.

Configuring Catalog Properties

To view the Properties of a catalog, open the Index Server folder, right-click on the Catalog directory and select **Properties**.

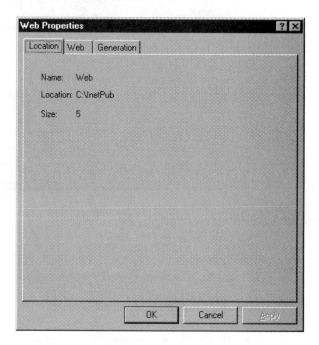

Location Properties

- Name

    The name of the catalog as it appears in the Management **Console**,

- Location

    The physical location for the catalog.

- Size

    The size of the catalog in megabytes.

NOTE: The Property values for a catalog override those of the Index Server.

Web Properties

Click on the **Web** tab to view tracking options.

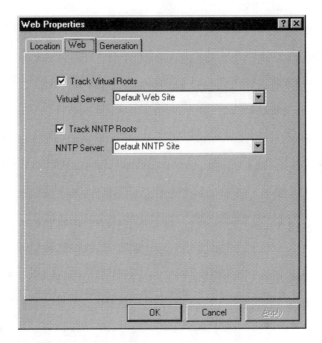

- Track Virtual Roots

  Enable this option to identify the virtual Web server for which the catalog holds information.

- Track NNTP Roots

  Enable this option to index message content from the News server as part of the overall index.

Generation Properties

Click on the **Web** tab to view tracking options.

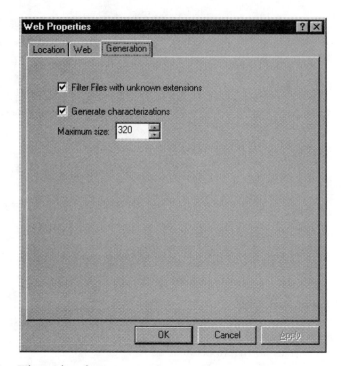

- Filter Files with unknown extensions

    Enable this option to prevent certain files (exe, gif, etc.) that do not contain text from being posted to the results view.

- Generate characterizations

    Enable this option to have the Index Server create a summary for every file in a search result. A summary provides users with an idea of what to expect when they select a particular link. The summary does consume additional CPU cycles and may not produce more usable information than the document title.

- Maximum size

    This option is used to determine the maximum number of characters that are returned in a summary.

NOTE: Characterizations for catalogs can be disabled. This would result in no summaries or abstracts being displayed for files listed on the Results page of a search.

Exercise 8-1:
Creating a New Catalog

In this exercise you use the Index Server Manager to create a new Index Server Catalog. Next, you will stop the Service and re-start it.

1. Launch Windows NT Explorer and browse to the C:\InetPub\wwwroot directory. Select **New/Folder** from the **File** menu and create a folder named Catalog.

2. Click on **Start/Programs/Windows NT 4.0 Option Pack/Microsoft Index Server/Index Server Manager**.

3. Expand the console by clicking the plus symbol (+) next to the Index Server On Local Machine folder.

4. Right-click on the Index Server On Local Machine folder and select **New/Catalog**.

5. Enter New Catalog in the Name field.

6. Click on **Browse** and browse to the C:\InetPub\wwwroot\Catalog folder.

7. Select the Catalog directory and click on **OK**. Click on **OK**.

8. Click on **OK** when prompted with the message: Catalog will remain off line until Index Server is restarted.

9. Select the Index Server in the Scope pane. Click on the **Action** button and select **Stop**.

10. Click on the **Action** button and select **Start**.

Microsoft Index Server 2.0 Performance Issues

Index Server performance issues include:

- Property Cache
- Number of Indexed Directories

Adjusting the Property Cache

For values that are frequently queried you can cache the properties on your server. Adding the tag META="AutoProduct" VALUE="*Product name*" to your HTML document allows you to create queries that will look for items that match a specific name.

Adding and Removing Directories

You should not index your entire server. The Index Server therefore needs to know exactly what directories to incorporate. You can add and remove physical directories from a catalog's scope.

When you create a new content directory that you wish to be indexed, you should add the directory to the Index Server's scope. To do so, right-click on either the Catalog or the Directory folder inside it and run **New/Directory**. Browse to locate the physical directory you wish to index.

To remove a physical directory from the catalog, right-click on the directory and run **Delete**. This does not actually delete the directory from the hard drive. It only prevents the documents inside it from being indexed.

> *NOTE:*   *Indexing and searching in Index Server is based on virtual roots. You exclude Virtual Directories from being indexed through the Internet Service Manager. Select the Home Directory Properties page and clear the check from the **Index this Directory** box.*

Exercise 8-2:
Adding Directories To Catalogs

In this exercise you use the Index Server Manager to add a directory to a catalog.

1. Launch Windows NT Explorer and browse to the root of drive C:. Select **New Folder** from the **File** menu and create a folder named Indexed.

2. Run **Start/Programs/Windows NT 4.0 Option Pack/Microsoft Index Server/ Index Server Manager**.

3. Expand the console by clicking the plus symbol (+) until you see the Directories folder below Web.

4. Double-click on the Directories folder to view the list of indexed directories.

5. Right-click on the Directories folder and select **New/Directory**.

6. Enter C:\Indexed in the Path field, then click on **OK**.

7. Double-click on the Directories folder to verify that the directory has been successfully added.

8. Exit the MMC.

Forcing a Scan

You need to force Index Server to scan directories when you make global changes such as:

*   Adding or removing a filter.
*   Enabling or disabling filtering documents with unknown extensions.
*   Adding a new word breaker.
*   Changing the size of the characterization summary.

Exercise 8-3:
Forcing a Scan

In this exercise you will force an Index Server scan.

1. Run **Start/Programs/Windows NT 4.0 Option Pack/Microsoft Index Server/ Index Server Manager**.

2. Right-click on the Web catalog and run **Properties**.

3. Click on the **Generation** tab.

4. Turn off **Generate characterizations**.

5. Click on **OK**.

6. Expand the console by clicking on the plus symbol (+) until you see the Directories folder below Web.

7. Double-click on the Directories folder to view the list of indexed directories.

8. Right-click on the *systemdrive:*\InetPub\wwwroot directory and select **Rescan**.

9. Click on **Yes**.

10. Exit the MMC.

Forcing a Merge

When server response time slows down for queries, it may be necessary to free resources by combining indexes. Combining smaller indexes into larger ones frees up server memory and disk space.

Exercise 8-4:
Forcing a Merge

In this exercise you will force an Index Server merge.

1. Click on **Start/Programs/Windows NT 4.0 Option Pack/Microsoft Index Server/Index Server Manager**.

2. Expand the console by clicking the plus symbol (+) until you see the Directories folder below Web.

3. Right-click on the Web Catalog and select **Merge**.

5. Click on **Yes**.

6. Exit the MMC.

Microsoft Index Server 2.0 Query Features

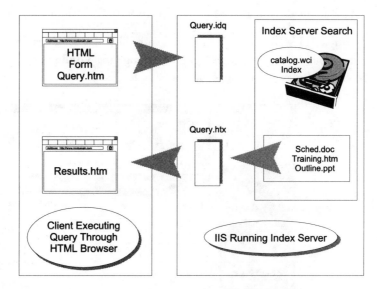

If you have used the Web to search for information, you have probably used a query form. These forms allow users to search your site.

The *Query Scope* defines which documents should be included in the search.

Content query restrictions specify the file properties that should be included in the search. This can include size, modification dates, file names, and authors, among others.

Hit Highlights identifies which parts of each document contain the words defined by the search.

Query Logging can be performed by Internet Information Server, just as any other access logging. Logging will be discussed later in the course.

Query Elements

Let's examine the way that Microsoft Index Server 2.0 handles queries.

A sample HTML query form included with the Index Server can be used to search the indexed files. To view this file, run **Start/Programs/Windows NT 4.0 Option Pack/ Microsoft Index Server/Index Server Sample Query Form**.

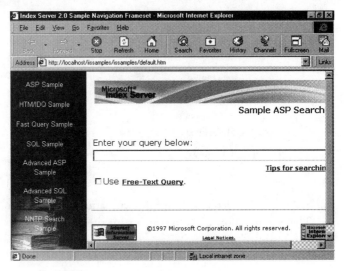

This will launch Internet Explorer and display the query form.

If you receive an error message indicating that the location cannot be found, enter the following in the Address field:

```
C:\InetPub\iissamples\ISSamples\default.htm
```

A Microsoft Index Server 2.0 query is comprised of four components:

- HTML Query form

    Displays a Web page in which the user can enter the query parameters. It will also display the query results.

- Internet Data Query File (IDQ)

    This is the intermediate form that the Index Server will run to search the index for the user's request.

- The HTML Extension File (HTX)

    This is an HTML file containing the result of the search.

- Hit Highlighting information

    This information is contained in a file with the extension .htw. It is combined with the .htx file and formatted appropriately. The resulting HTML is downloaded to the browser.

Query Forms

When using a Web browser, queries are generated by completing the fields in an HTML form. Sample forms are provided with Index Server and can be copied and tailored for your individual needs. Microsoft Index Server 2.0 allows:

- Users to search for words and phrases.

- Users to search by author, subject, file size, and date.

- Users to search with wildcard characters * and ?.

- Users to search by using Boolean operators (AND, OR, NOT).

- Automatic updates when documents are changed.

- User restrictions for document security, ensuring users view only the documents they have permission to view.

Active Server Pages Queries

You can also build query pages with ASP. Use SQL extensions to build the query and ADO to retrieve the data. Then use VBScript or another ActiveX scripting language to format the data. Send the information to the browser using the standard ASP syntax.

Exercise 8-5:
Generating a Query

In this exercise you will use forms to generate a query.

1. Launch NT Explorer and browse to the C:\InetPub\iissamples\ISSamples folder.

2. Press *CONTROL+A* to select all files.

3. Press *CONTROL+C* to copy the selected files.

4. Browse to the C:\AutoParts folder and select **Paste** from the **Edit** menu.

5. Launch Internet Explorer and enter the following address in the **Address** field:

   `http://192.168.211.213/default.htm`

6. Enter the following in the form's Search field and click on **Go**:

   `auto`

7. View the results of the query.

8. Exit Internet Explorer.

Microsoft Index Server 2.0 Security Issues

When the default catalog is created by the Index Server, its Access Control List (ACL) grants access only to Administrators and system services. If you create an additional catalog, make sure to assign the appropriate permissions to guard against unauthorized access.

When filtering documents, Index Server 2.0 also saves the associated Access Control properties created in the NTFS file system. This Access Control information is used by the Index Server to determine if a user is allowed to access a file. If a user has not been granted the necessary permissions to access the file, the file will not appear in the results set.

It is usually a good idea to authenticate users prior to initiating the query. One way to do this is to establish NTFS permissions for the query form (.htm) that initiates the query.

If anonymous logon is allowed, the anonymous user will be used by default as long as all files accessed by the client can be accessed by the anonymous user. Whenever an attempt is made to access a document for which access is denied, an authentication dialog box will be displayed.

SUMMARY

During this chapter you were introduced to Microsoft Index Server 2.0. This included:

- Adding catalogs
- Adding and deleting directories
- Forcing a scan
- Forcing a merge
- Performing a query

In the next chapter, you'll be introduced to two important IIS 4.0 services: SMTP and NNTP.

POST-TEST QUESTIONS

The answers to these questions are in Appendix A at the end of this manual.

1. What is one tool that can be used for administering your Index Server?

   ....

   ....

2. How much RAM does Index Server need if your Web site contains 10,000 documents?

   ....

   ....

3. Which four file types are used to execute an Index Server query from the browser?

    ....

    ....

4. What effect does the number of indexed directories have on server performance?

    ....

    ....

5. Can you use Index Server 2.0 to index News messages?

    ....

    ....

6. You are running Web sites for multiple companies. How can you ensure that each one can provide search capability?

    ....

    ....

7. You have virtual directories on several servers. Can you use Index Server to catalog their contents?

    ....

    ....

8. Your company's name appears in every document. How can you prevent it from being listed in the catalog?

    ....

    ....

CHAPTER 9

SMTP and NNTP

OBJECTIVES

During this chapter, you will be given the information you need to complete the following:

- Identify situations in which using SMTP is an appropriate choice.
- Install and configure SMTP.
- Describe how SMTP handles incoming and outgoing messages.
- Describe the use of domains in SMTP.
- Identify situations in which NNTP is an appropriate choice.
- Install and configure NNTP.
- Configure NNTP to host a newsgroup.

PRE-TEST QUESTIONS

The answers to these questions are in Appendix A at the end of this manual.

1. What allows you to manage SMTP through the Microsoft Management Console?

   ....

   ....

2. Where does SMTP put messages that are addressed to a local domain?

   ....

   ....

3. You are configuring a directory that will be used to host a newsgroup. What file system should you use?

   ....

   ....

4. By default, who can create a newsgroup on an NNTP server?

   ....

   ....

INTRODUCTION

Whether you are implementing a corporate intranet or an Internet presence, it is likely that one of the reasons you are interested in Internet Information Server is to provide better communication with either your customers or your coworkers. So far, the course has focused on how to do this through the WWW service and the FTP service. Now let's look at two more services you can provide with Internet Information Server: messaging and newsgroups.

The chapter begins with a look at Microsoft's implementation of the Simple Mail Transfer Protocol (SMTP). You will see how messages are handled by SMTP and how to configure it to meet your specific needs. Next, the chapter focuses on Network News Transfer Protocol (NNTP). You will learn how to configure the NNTP service so that your Internet Information Server can host a newsgroup.

SMTP OVERVIEW

SMTP is one of the most widely used protocols on the Internet. This section looks at what it does. This includes:

- SMTP Defined
- Sending Messages
- Receiving Messages
- Some Appropriate Uses

Let's start by looking at how SMTP is defined.

SMTP Defined

As its name suggests, Simple Mail Transfer Protocol (SMTP) was designed to handle the transfer of messages from one host to another. One of the most widely used protocols on the Internet, it is described by RFCs 821 and 822. Keep in mind that SMTP is a mail transfer protocol, not a mail system. It does not provide for individual mailboxes for users or other mail features provided by mail systems like Microsoft Exchange. It simply provides a mechanism for transferring messages between hosts, for queuing messages until a message can be forwarded (store and forward), and for notifying the sender when mail cannot be delivered.

Sending Messages

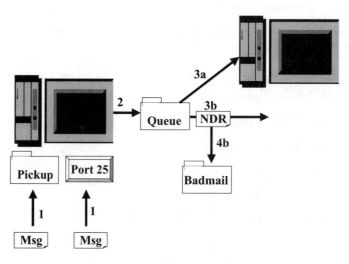

A message can be sent either by saving a text file in the directory named Pickup on the Internet Information Server that is running SMTP or by sending it to the port that has been configured for outgoing mail. By default, this port is Port 25. When the server receives a message, it places it in the Queue folder until it is able to make the necessary connection to deliver it. If it cannot be delivered within the specified amount of time, a non-delivery report (NDR) is sent to the sender. If the NDR cannot be delivered, the message is copied to the Badmail directory.

Receiving Messages

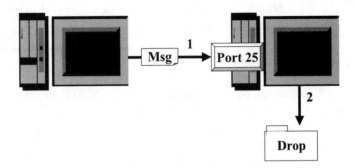

When a message is received in the port designated as the incoming port (port 25 by default), SMTP determines if the final destination of the message is on one of its domains and if it is, deposits that message in the Drop directory. As you can see, this is not a very efficient way to handle mail for a number of recipients. Without a mail system to retrieve those messages and route them to the appropriate users, SMTP is not an appropriate solution for handling incoming mail for multiple users.

Some Appropriate Uses

The SMTP Service is primarily designed for the following purposes:

- To allow users to send a message from your Web site.

   You can configure SMTP and your Web site to allow users to send an e-mail message to the Web administrator. This is appropriate for general-purpose comments or even for technical support questions. Keep in mind that all incoming messages for your domain will be copied to the Drop directory, not to an actual mailbox.

- To allow mail-enabled applications to send outgoing mail.

    Mail-enabled applications can send Internet mail through your SMTP service. The SMTP service can be configured to route the mail to the appropriate domain.

INSTALLING AND CONFIGURING SMTP

This section covers how to install and configure SMTP on your Internet Information Server. The following topics will be covered:

- Installing SMTP
- The SMTP Management Extension
- SMTP Objects
- Site Properties
- SMTP Site Properties
- Operators
- Messages
- Delivery
- Directory Security
- Domain Properties

Let's start by looking at how SMTP is installed.

Installing SMTP

The SMTP service can be installed either during Internet Information Server installation or after. To add it after, insert the Windows NT 4.0 Option Pack CD-ROM and allow it to launch **AutoPlay**. Click on **Install**. Click on **Install Windows NT 4.0 Option Pack**. After Setup loads, click on **Next** then click on **Add/Remove**. Select Internet Information Server. Click on **Show Subcomponents**.

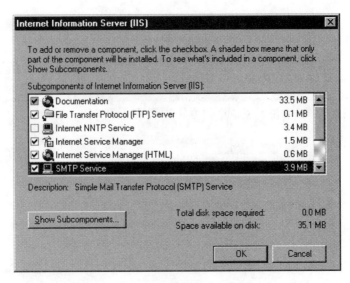

Select SMTP Service and click on **OK**. Click on **Next**.

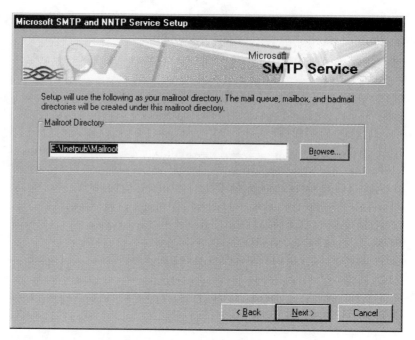

You will be prompted to enter the location where you'd like to install your *mailroot* directory. This is the directory that will contain the Queue, Drop, and Badmail directories. By default, this directory is created at *systemdrive:*\InetPub\Mailroot. It is recommended that you select an NTFS partition for this directory. Click on **Next** to begin reconfiguration and file copy. After the files have been copied, click on **Finish**. Click on **Yes** to restart the computer.

The Microsoft SMTP Service will be started automatically when the computer starts.

The SMTP Management Extension

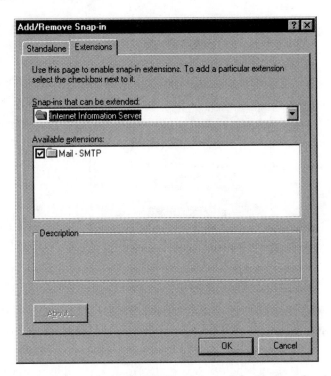

SMTP can be managed through the SMTP Extension of the Internet Service Manager snap-in. This means that like the FTP and WWW services, SMTP can be managed through the Microsoft Management Console.

SMTP Objects

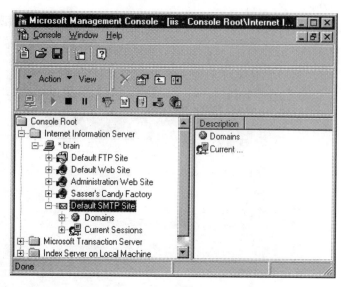

When the SMTP service is installed, three objects are created. These are:

*   Default SMTP Site

    This is the Site object in which you will create domains. The SMTP service can handle only one site. You cannot add additional sites or delete sites.

*   Domains

    This object will contain the local and remote domains you create. By default, a local domain is created with the same name as your machine. This is the default domain for your SMTP site.

*   Current Sessions

    This object will allow you to view information about current SMTP connections.

Site Properties

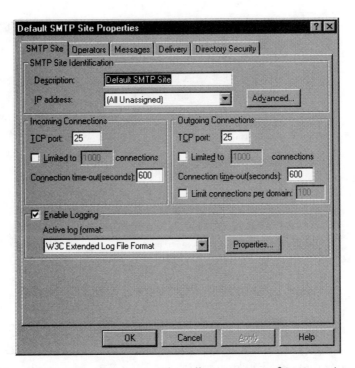

The Site object has five property sheets. They allow you to configure a variety of settings that affect how your SMTP site operates. Some of these are similar to the types of settings you can make to WWW and FTP sites. Some are unique to SMTP sites. Let's look first at the properties you can set on the SMTP Site property page.

SMTP Site Properties

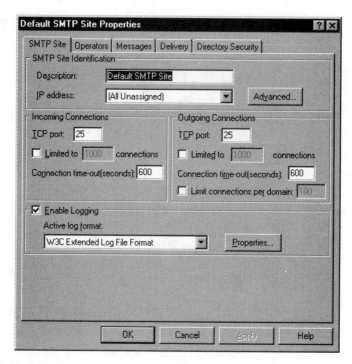

The **SMTP Site** tab allows you to set properties that identify the site and limit the connections. These properties are:

• Description

This is the name of the site. You can keep it at default or change it to something more descriptive.

- IP Address

    This is set to All Unassigned by default. However, you can specify a
    particular IP address if more than one is configured for the computer. As
    with WWW and FTP sites, you can configure multiple identities for this
    site.

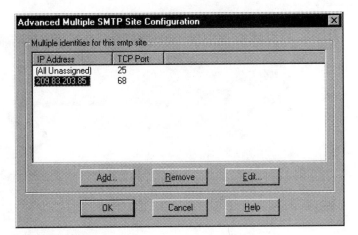

- Incoming Connections

    You can specify the port number, the number of simultaneous connections,
    and the connection timeout value for incoming connections. By default,
    the number of simultaneous connections is limited to 1000 and the timeout
    value is set to 600. The default port number is 25.

- Outgoing Connections

    You can specify the port number, the number of simultaneous connections,
    the number of simultaneous connections per domain, and the connection
    timeout value for incoming connections. By default, the number of
    simultaneous connections is limited to 1000 (100 per domain) and the
    timeout value is set to 600. The default port number is 25. Incoming and
    outgoing connections can use the same port or different ports.

- Enable Logging

    This setting works the same as for the FTP and WWW services. Logging will be discussed later in the course.

Operators

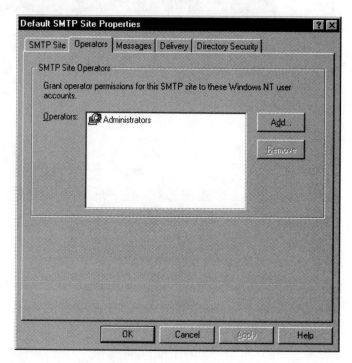

This property page is similar to that for FTP and WWW sites. You can grant specific Windows NT users and groups the ability to perform some administrative activities on the site.

Messages

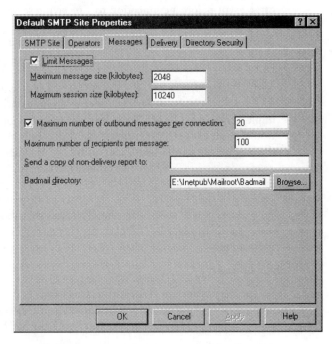

This property page allows you to configure settings related to how messages are handled by the site. Settings include:

- Limit message size

    This value sets the recommended limit for a message. A client can send a message larger than this amount without closing the connection, as long as the maximum session size is not exceeded.

- Limit session size

    This setting is the actual limit for the size of a session. If a client sends a message that is larger than this amount, the connection will be closed.

- Maximum number of outbound messages per connection

  This setting determines the maximum number of outbound messages that can be sent before a connection to a receiving server is closed. By setting this number lower than the usual number of messages transmitted during a connection, you can actually improve performance. This is because multiple connections can be used to deliver messages simultaneously.

- Maximum number of recipients per message

  This is set to 100 by default in order to comply with RFC 821. In some implementations of SMTP, sending a message to more than 100 recipients would result in the 101st recipient (and all others after) being dropped from the list and the sender being sent an NDR. In Microsoft's implementation, a new connection is opened to handle the remaining recipients.

- Send a copy of non-delivery report to

  This allows you to specify an e-mail address that should receive copies of each NDR. It might be useful to provide a mail administrator's e-mail address here.

- Badmail directory

  If a message cannot be delivered to a recipient and its NDR cannot be sent to the sender, the message will be copied to the directory specified here. By default, this is set to *systemdrive:*\InetPub\Mailroot\Badmail.

Delivery Properties

Default SMTP Site Properties   [?][X]

| SMTP Site | Operators | Messages | Delivery | Directory Security |

┌─ Local queue ──────────────────────┐ ┌─ Remote queue ──────────────────────┐
│ Maximum retries: [48]   │ │ Maximum retries: [48]   │
│   │ │   │
│ Retry interval (minutes): [60]   │ │ Retry interval (minutes): [60]   │
└─────────────────────────────────────┘ └─────────────────────────────────────┘

Maximum hop count: [15]

Masquerade domain: [   ]

Fully qualified domain name: [brain   ]

Smart host   [   ]

[ ] Attempt direct delivery before sending to smart host

[ ] Perform reverse DNS lookup on incoming messages

[Outbound Security...]

[OK   ]   [Cancel]   [Apply]   [Help   ]

The settings on the **Delivery** property page can affect how reliable your SMTP service is. They include:

- Maximum retries

  This is the number of times the SMTP service will attempt to send a particular message before issuing an NDR. This is 48 by default. This can be set separately for messages destined for a remote domain than for those destined for a local domain.

- Retry interval

  This is the number of minutes that should elapse between attempts to send a particular domain's messages. It is set to 1 hour by default. When taken together, the maximum retries and the retry interval determine how soon an NDR will be sent if a message is undeliverable. By default, the NDR would not be sent until 2 days after the message had originally been sent.

- Maximum hop count

  This is the number of SMTP servers through which an outgoing message can pass before reaching its destination. If the number is exceeded along the message route, an NDR will be returned.

- Masquerade domain

  This setting replaces the sender's domain with the name specified here. This is useful because it guarantees that replies to the message will come back to the SMTP server. This setting is only used when this SMTP server is the first hop on the message's journey.

- Fully qualified domain name

  This is usually the name set in the Domain field of the TCP/IP property sheet's **DNS** tab. However, you can override that value here. Keep in mind that if you do, you should also change the MX record on the DNS server. Specifying a fully qualified domain name will speed name resolution.

- Smart host

  You can specify that all outgoing mail be sent to a particular host instead of directly to the domain. This allows another computer to take care of choosing the best route for a particular domain. You can use either a host name or an IP address for this value. However, if you use an IP address, enclosing it in square brackets will optimize performance.

- Perform reverse DNS lookup on incoming messages

  This option allows you to ensure that the host name on an incoming message actually matches the IP address from which the message originated. While this can help authenticate the identity of the sender, it can also decrease performance.

- Outbound Security

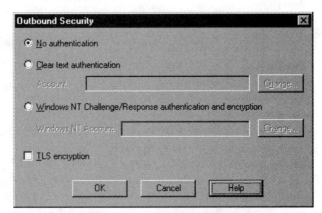

Some servers may require that authentication credentials be passed with the message. If the majority of the domains to which you send messages require a particular type of authentication or encryption, set it here. Otherwise, you will probably want to set these options on a domain-specific basis.

You have already been introduced to Basic Authentication and Windows NT Challenge/Response. TLS encryption is Transport Layer Security encryption. In order to use this type of encryption, you will need to ensure that the recipient server also supports TLS encryption.

Directory Security

This property page allows you to set security restrictions on the messages that are received or relayed by the site.

Anonymous Access and Authentication Control

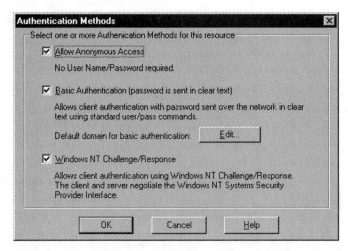

This allows you to determine whether or not to accept incoming messages from the anonymous user account and whether to validate a message originator based on Basic Authentication and/or Windows NT Challenge/Response authentication.

Secure Communications

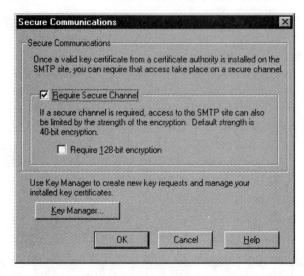

This option allows you to specify that communication can only take place over SSL. Your SMTP site and the remote domain must each have the appropriate keys. If you are in the United States or Canada, you can also specify that you wish to use 128-bit encryption, instead of the 40-bit default.

IP Address and Domain Name Restrictions

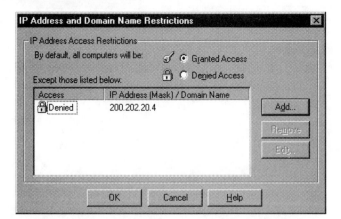

This option can be used to limit or grant access based on IP address, subnet mask, or domain name. As with the WWW and FTP services, restricting or granting access by domain name will diminish performance.

Relay Restrictions

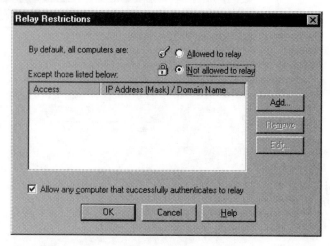

This property page allows you to configure which computers, if any, are allowed to use your SMTP site for message relay. Allowing all computers to relay messages through your site will leave you open to those who wish to distribute Unsolicited Commercial E-mail (UCE). However, you may wish to grant certain computers the ability to use your site for message relay. To do so, specify the IP address for those sites here.

Domains

Local Domains

As previously mentioned, a single local domain is created when you install SMTP. This domain is known as the default domain. The property page for the default domain provides the path to the Drop directory.

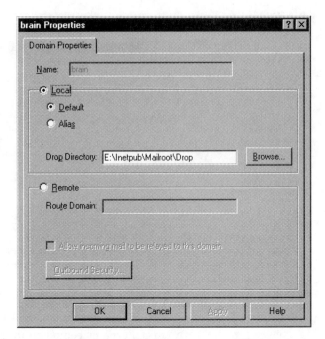

You can create local alias domains as well. These domains provide an alternate name for the default domain. However, mail for all local domains is stored in the Drop directory. If you change an alias domain to the default domain, the current default domain will be changed to an alias domain. You can only have one default domain for any site.

Remote Domains

You can also create remote domains. A remote domain allows you to override certain site settings when a message is delivered to a particular domain. You can:

- Specify a route

  Any route specified here will override the default route. If a smart host is configured for the site, it will be ignored when mail is sent to this domain.

- Allow incoming mail to be relayed to this domain

  This will enable your SMTP site to serve as a relay host for mail destined to this particular domain.

- Configure outbound security

  This button will display a dialog where you can configure specific security settings for mail that is destined for this domain. These settings will override those set for the site.

NETWORK NEWS TRANSFER PROTOCOL

The Network News Transfer Protocol (NNTP) Service allows you to act as a news server by providing newsgroup services to NNTP clients. You can configure custom, secured newsgroups on your IIS 4.0 computer.

This section looks at NTTP installation and configuration. The following topics will be discussed:

- Installing NNTP
- About NNTP
- News Site Properties
- Security Accounts Properties
- NNTP Settings Properties
- Home Directory Properties
- Directory Security
- Groups
- NNTP Expiration Policy

Let's start by looking at how the NNTP Service can be installed.

Installing NNTP

The NNTP Service can be installed either during Internet Information Server installation or after. To add it after, insert the Windows NT 4.0 Option Pack CD-ROM and allow it to launch **AutoPlay**. Click on **Install**. Click on **Install Windows NT 4.0 Option Pack**. After Setup loads, click on **Next** then click on **Add/Remove**. Select Internet Information Server. Click on **Show Subcomponents**.

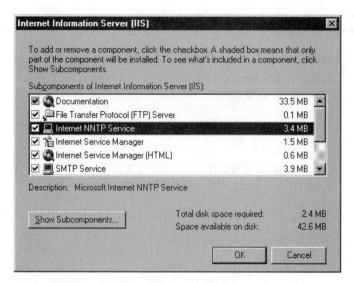

Select the Internet NNTP Service and click on **OK**. Click on **Next**.

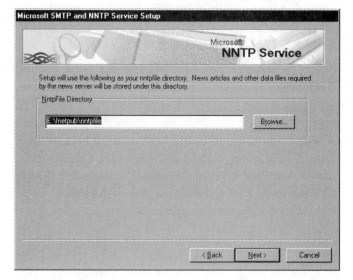

You will be prompted for the directory that should store the news articles. By default, this file is *systemdrive*:\InetPub\nntpfile. It is recommended that you use a directory that is on an NTFS partition. Click on **Next** to begin configuring Internet Information Server and installing the files. After the files have copied, click on **Finish**. You will be prompted to restart your computer. When the computer reboots, the Microsoft NNTP Service will be started automatically.

News Site Properties

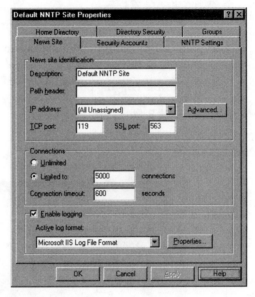

The **News Site** tab allows you to:

- Enter a Description for your site. This is the site name that is displayed by the Microsoft Management Console utility.

- Enter a value for the Path Header option. This is the string that is displayed in the **Path** line in each news posting.

- Enter the server's IP Address. This is the IP address of the NNTP server.

- Configure **Advanced** IP addressing. Select this option to assign multiple IP addresses for this news site

- Select the TCP Port number for the NNTP Service. The default port value is 119.

- Select the SSL Port number for the NNTP Service. The default port value is 563.

- Specify a value for the Connections option. You set a limit on the number of simultaneous NNTP client connections and a time limit on active connections.

- Specify a value for the Connection timeout option. This parameter is used to set time a limit for an inactive news client. The default value is 600 seconds.

- Configure the **Enable Logging** option.

- Configure the Active log format option.

Security Accounts Properties

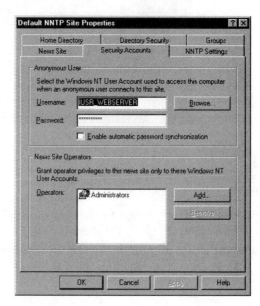

The **Security Accounts** tab allows you to:

- Enable Anonymous User access.

    Use this option to select the account used for anonymous access. The default is IUSR_*Computername*. The permissions granted the account determine which newsgroups are available to anonymous users.

- Assign News Site Operators.

    Use this option to assign one or more operators to the NNTP Service.

NNTP Settings Properties

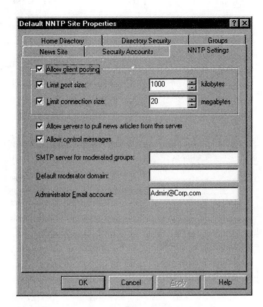

The **NNTP Settings** tab allows you to:

- Enable the **Allow client posting** option.

    Enable this option to allow clients to post articles to the news site.

- Configure the **Limit post size** option.

    This option allows you to define the maximum size of news articles that clients can post to the news site.

- Configure the **Limit connection size** option.

    This option determines the maximum size of all the news articles that a client can post in a single session.

- Enable the **Allow servers to pull news articles from this server** option.

     Enable this option to allow other news servers to pull articles from your new site.

- Enable the **Allow control messages** option.

     A control message is one that adds, or deletes an article or newsgroup. You can prevent control messages from being processed by the site or filter who can issue control messages by granting and restricting access to the control.cancel, control.rmgroup, and control.newgroup newsgroups.

     The directories associated with these control newsgroups are created beneath the nntpfile directory under \root\control. Everyone is granted Full Control permission by default. You can use NTFS permissions to grant or revoke access to individual users and groups. As an alternative, you can select to have these groups moderated.

- Configure the SMTP server for moderated groups option.

     Use this option to specify the SMTP mail server where all postings to moderated groups are forwarded. This must be either a valid computer name registered in DNS with a valid IP or a directory on the local hard drive.

- Configure the Default moderator domain option.

    Use this option to specify the default domain for all moderated postings. Articles posted to a moderated newsgroup that does not have a specified moderator are sent to *news_group_name@default_moderator domain,* where the *news_group_name* is the name of the newsgroup to which the article is sent and the *default_moderator_domain* is the value you specified for this domain.

- Configure the Administrator Email Account option.

    Use this option to specify the e-mail address for the recipient of NDRs for moderated newsgroup articles that cannot be delivered to the designated moderator.

You can also moderate newsgroups from a news client. When configured for moderated articles, the NNTP Service sends articles automatically to a specified SMTP server for delivery to the moderator.

If an article cannot be delivered to the moderator, a non-delivery report (NDR) is returned to the Administrator E-mail account address. For these messages to be processed by SMTP, an account must exist on the SMTP server.

Home Directory Properties

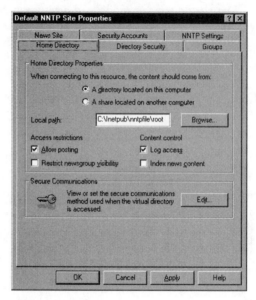

The **Home Directory** tab allows you to:

- Configure the home directory to be **A directory located on this computer** or **A share located on another computer.**

    Remote shares should be entered using a UNC name as shown below:

    \\Servername\sharename

- Configure the Local Path option.

    This is the local directory for the NNTP Service. The default value is C:\Inetpub\nntpfile\root.

- Configure the Network directory option.

    This allows you to specify the network directory where news articles are located. The default value is \\Servername\directory\subdirectory\.

- Enable the **Allow posting** option.

    Enable this option to allow clients to post articles to the home directory.

- Enable the **Log access** option.

    Enable this option to generate a log of news client activity.

- Enable the **Restrict newsgroup visibility** option.

  Enable this option to restrict the viewing of newsgroup lists in this directory to users who have access permission for the newsgroup. (This option adds processing overhead and should not be used for newsgroups that allow anonymous access.)

- Enable the **Index news content** option.

  Enable this option to index newsgroups in this directory with Microsoft Index Server, which allows users to search for specific text.

Secure Communications Settings

This button allows you to configure encryption for outgoing data by requiring the client to use Secure Sockets Layer (SSL) for connections to the NNTP Service. You can:

- Enable the **Require Secure Channel** option.

  This option allows you to ensure that outgoing data is encrypted by requiring the client to use Secure Sockets Layer (SSL) for connections to the NNTP Service.

- Enable the **Require 128-bit Encryption** option.

  This option allows you to limit access to the virtual directory to clients using the 128-bit key strength encryption in SSL. Clients attempting to connect using the 40-bit key strength encryption in SSL are refused. Because of export restrictions, the 128-bit key strength encryption feature is available only in the United States and Canada.

You can create virtual directories to store news articles, which increases the capacity of files that can be stored. Use the Directories option in Internet Service Manager or Internet Service Manager (HTML) to configure virtual directories for specific newsgroups.

The NNTP Service requires approximately 540 bytes per stored article, plus 1 KB for every 128 articles, in addition to the space required for the articles themselves. Select an NNTP home directory location with enough space to accommodate these requirements.

> *NOTE:*   *The home directory must reside on a Microsoft Windows NT Server disk*
> *partition formatted as Windows NT file system (NTFS).*

Directory Security

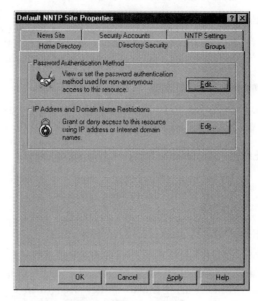

The **Directory Security** tab allows you to:

* Select a Password Authentication Method.

    You can choose one or more authentication methods. Click on **Edit** to view
    the authentication options.

    Enable the **Allow Anonymous** option.

    Enable this option to allow any client access to the contents of this
    directory.

    Enable the **Basic Authentication** option.

    Enable this option to select Basic password authentication. NNTP
    defines an authorization protocol, called AUTHINFO, that is
    based on clear-text passwords. The NNTP Service supports this
    clear-text password authorization protocol as Basic password
    authentication. It also extends the protocol to support delivery of
    confidential data between the NNTP Service and an NNTP client.
    The NNTP Service provides these features as extensions to the
    NNTP AUTHINFO protocol.

Enable the **Windows NT Challenge/Response** option.

Enable this option to select the standard challenge/response security mechanism that is provided with the Microsoft Windows NT Server 4.0 operating system. This security feature makes it possible for businesses to provide secure logon services for their customers. Sites that already use Windows NT Challenge/ Response in an internal system can benefit by using a single, common security mechanism.

Enable the **Enable SSL Client Authentication** option.

By selecting this option you enable secure client authentication using SSL encryption and certificates. This option requires a server certificate from a valid certificate authority (CA).

Enable the **Require SSL Client Authentication** option.

Enable this option to require that clients provide SSL-encrypted user names and passwords.

Enable the **Enable Client Certificate Mappings to Windows NT User Accounts** option.

If the client software has an SSL client certificate installed, the NNTP Service will use the Microsoft Windows NT account that is mapped to that certificate to authenticate users. Choose **Client Mappings** to enter certificates and the Windows NT account names.

- Configure IP Address and Domain Name Restrictions (IP Filtering).

    You have several options for restricting access to newsgroups. Choose **Edit** to view restriction options.

    By default, the news site is accessible from all IP addresses. However, you can grant or deny access to specific IP addresses, while allowing or denying access for a larger group. You can do this by specifying a single IP address, a group of addresses using a subnet mask, or a domain name.

NOTE: Using Windows NT Challenge/Response authentication requires a news client that supports this authentication method. Microsoft Internet Mail and News supports Windows NT Challenge/Response authentication.

Groups

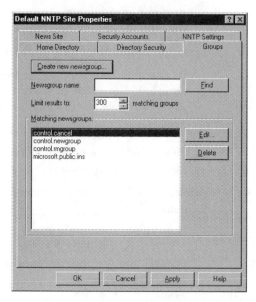

The **Groups** tab allows you to:

- Create newsgroups using the **Create new newsgroup** option.

   Select this option to create a new newsgroup. You can specify whether a newsgroup is to be moderated. When a newsgroup is moderated, articles are sent to the newsgroup moderator for review before they are posted to the newsgroup.

- Use the Newsgroup name option.

   This option allows you to search for a newsgroup by full or partial name.

- Configure the Limit results to option.

   Use this option to limit the number of newsgroups displayed by the **Find** option.

- View the Matching newsgroups list.

   This list displays the newsgroups that were located by the **Find** option.

NNTP Newsgroup Expiration Policy

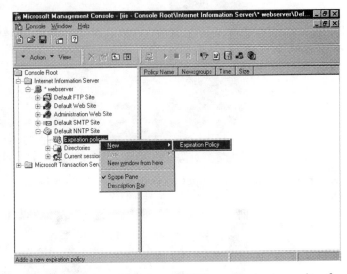

Create NNTP Service Expiration Policies to enforce an expiration policy for any number of newsgroups managed by the NNTP Service. You can define an expiration policy to delete all news articles older than a specified number of days, or to delete the oldest articles when newsgroups reach a specified size, or both.

To create NNTP Expiration Policies, run **Start/Programs/Windows NT 4.0 Option Pack/Microsoft Internet Server/Internet Service Manager** to launch the Internet Service Manager. Open the Internet Information Server folder, then open the webserver computer icon.

Open the Default NNTP Site folder and right-click on **Expiration Policies**. Select **New**, then **Expiration Policy**.

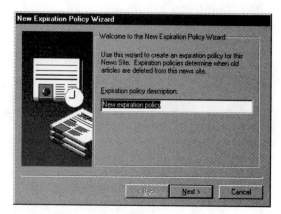

Enter a name for the new expiration policy, then click on **Next**.

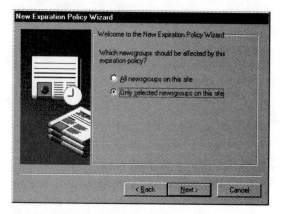

Select the appropriate option to apply the expiration policy to all newsgroups on this NNTP site or to a selected subset of newsgroups.

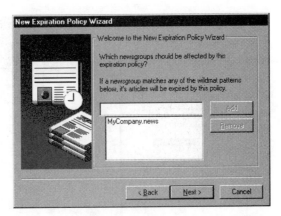

If you selected to apply the expiration policy to a subset of newsgroups, you are prompted to enter the names of the newsgroups to which you wish to apply the policy. Click on **Next** to continue.

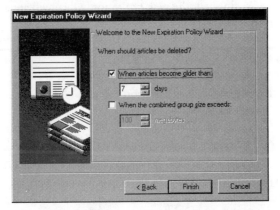

You can enable message expiration by selecting the **When articles become older than** option. This option is enabled by default and the time limit value is set to 7 days. You can also enable a disk space limit on the selected (or all) newsgroups. This option is disabled by default. Click on **Finish**.

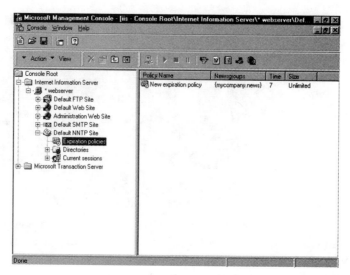

When you are finished, the new expiration policy will appear in the Microsoft Management Console window.

SUMMARY

In this chapter, you learned how you can provide additional features on your Web site. This included:

- Installing SMTP
- Configuring SMTP
- Installing NNTP
- Configuring NNTP
- Adding newsgroups
- Configuring expiration policies

In the next chapter, the focus will turn to day-to-day administrative concerns. You will be shown some options you have when deciding the best way to administer your Internet Information Server.

POST-TEST QUESTIONS

The answers to these questions are in Appendix A at the end of this manual.

1. A user sends a message through your SMTP service. The message cannot be delivered and neither can the NDR. What happens to the message?

    ....

    ....

2. What is the purpose of a remote domain?

    ....

    ....

3. You have created an alias domain named Cust_Srv. You want the mail destined for that domain to be stored in the Cust_Srv directory. How can you configure SMTP to do this?

    ....

    ....

4. What is the disadvantage of enabling DNS Reverse Lookup for your SMTP site?

    ....

    ....

5. What is the purpose of the masquerade domain?

    ....

    ....

6. How can you restrict anonymous users from deleting newsgroups?

    ....

    ....

7. You have created a newsgroup named *President's Update*. How can you cause articles to automatically be deleted after 5 days?

    ....

    ....

8. If a moderator is not defined for a moderated newsgroup, what will happen when an authenticated user posts a message to it?

    ....

    ....

IIS 4.0 Administration Options

OBJECTIVES

At the completion of this chapter, you will be able to:

- Describe the benefits of administering your Web site with a browser.
- List the limits of administration with a browser.
- Administer your Web site with a browser.
- Describe how Windows Scripting Host can be used to automate administrative tasks.
- Write scripts to manage the WWW service.
- Write scripts to manage the FTP service.

PRE-TEST QUESTIONS

The answers to these questions are in Appendix A at the end of this manual.

Q

1. What tool can you use to administer your Index Server across the Internet?

   ....

   ....

2. Which computers are allowed to access the Administrative Web Site by default?

   ....

   ....

3. Which scripting language(s) can you use to administer your FTP site?

   ....

   ....

4. Which executable will run a .vbs file from a command prompt?

   ....

   ....

INTRODUCTION

So far, you have used the Microsoft Management Console to administer your Internet Information Server. However, you have other administrative options available.

The HTML Internet Service Manager (HTML-ISM) program performs the same administrative functions as Internet Service Manager (ISM). You use these HTML files and a Web browser to administer your IIS 4.0 over the Internet. This is one way you can remotely administer your Web server. Both the SMTP and NNTP services have HTML managers, as does the Index Server. The chapter will look at how to use the Internet Service Manager from a browser.

Another important way to automate your Internet Information Server is by writing scripts. The chapter will conclude with a look at how to write and execute administrative scripts. However, keep in mind that a discussion of programming logic and scripting techniques is beyond the scope of this course.

ADMINISTRATION VIA THE INTERNET

The Internet Service Manager includes an HTML-based version that allows you to administer your server over the Internet using your client browser. The following topics will be discussed within this section:

- Internet Service Manager (HTML)
- Remote Site Administration
- Using the HTML ISM Utility

Internet Service Manager (HTML)

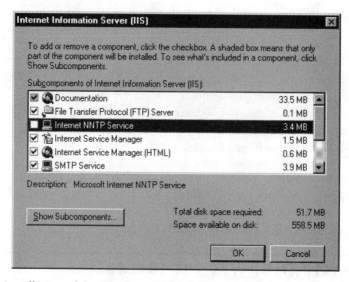

During the installation of the Windows NT 4.0 Option Pack you installed the Internet Service manager (HTML). This option installs the necessary HTML and dynamic link (DLL) files to administer your Web site using a browser.

To launch the HTML version of Internet Service Manager, run **Start/Programs/ Windows NT 4.0 Option Pack/Microsoft Internet Information Server/Internet Service Manager (HTML)**.

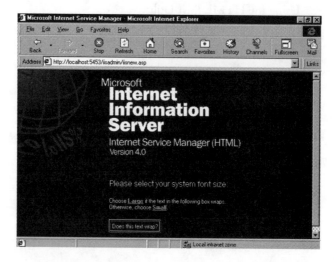

The first time you launch the utility you are prompted to select an appropriate font size to suit your display resolution.

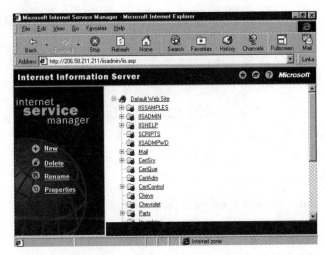

After selecting the font size you are presented with the HTML version of Internet Service Manager.

If you are administering your Web site using any browser except IE, the browser will prompt you for a username and password before the contents of the HTML files in the directory are returned. If you are using IE, it will try to use the current username and password, that is, the username and password used when logging on at the client. If those values aren't valid on the server, you will be prompted for a username and password.

You can also access the HTML version of ISM by launching a browser and entering the following URL:

```
http://computername:<port>/iisadmin/default.htm.
```

The port is the one configured for the Administrative Web Site. This is set to 4867 by default. If you omit the port number from the URL, IIS 4.0 will attempt to identify you as an operator. If you are identified as an operator, you will be able to perform those activities operators are permitted to perform, but will not have all of the permissions of an administrator.

If you have not changed the Directory Security settings on the Administration Web Site and you are running a browser from any computer other than your IIS 4.0, you will receive the following message when attempting to access the Web site:

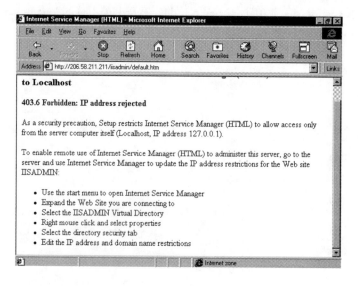

By default, all computers except the localhost (identified by its loopback address 127.0.0.1), are denied access to the administrative site. You must be working at an authorized workstation to use the HTML ISM utility.

Remote Site Administration

To authorize a remote workstation to use the HTML ISM utility, perform the following:

- Launch the Internet Service Manager on your IIS 4.0.
- Locate the Web site you wish to remotely administer.
- Right-click on the Web site and select **Properties**.
- Click on the **Directory Security** tab.
- Click on the **Edit** button for IP Address and Domain Name Restrictions.
- Add the IP address or DNS host name for the remote system you wish to authorize.

Using the HTML ISM Utility

You can perform many site administration tasks using a browser and the HTML ISM utility. From the opening page, you can:

- Create a new directory.
- Delete an existing directory.
- Rename an existing directory.
- View the properties of a Web site.

Creating a Directory

To create a directory, click on the Create link. Enter a name for the directory and click on **OK**.

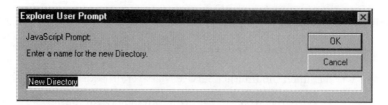

Deleting a Directory

To delete a directory, click on the Delete link. Select the directory to delete, then click on **OK**.

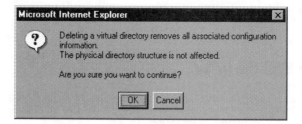

Renaming a Directory

To rename a directory, select the directory to rename and click on the Rename link. Enter the new name for the directory, then click on **OK**.

Viewing and Modifying Site Properties

To view and modify the properties of a Web site, select the site and click on the Properties link.

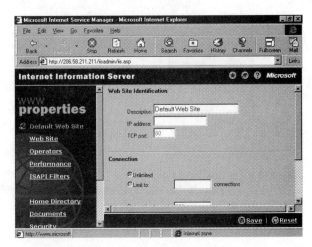

Click on the Operators link to view the Web Site Operators list.

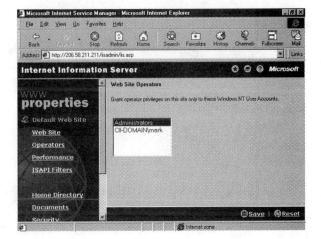

Click on the Performance link to view IIS 4.0 Performance properties.

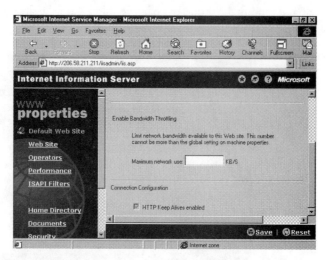

Click on the ISAPI Filters link to view installed ISAPI Filters.

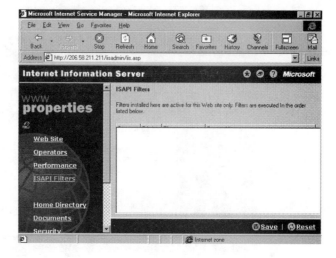

Click on the Home Directory link to manage the site's Directory Properties.

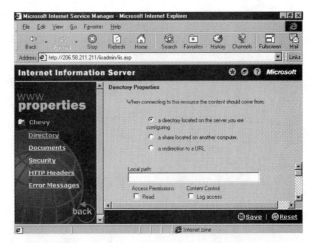

Click on the Documents link to manage the site's Documents properties.

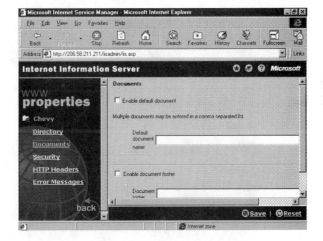

Click on the Security link to manage the site's Security properties.

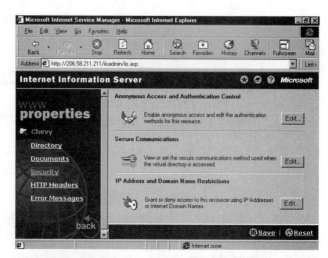

Click on the HTTP Headers link to manage the site's HTTP Headers properties.

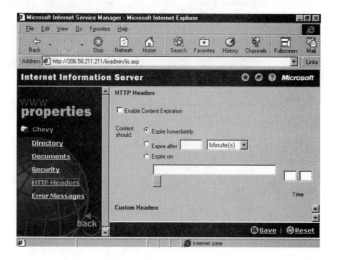

Click on the Error Messages link to view the site's Custom Errors properties.

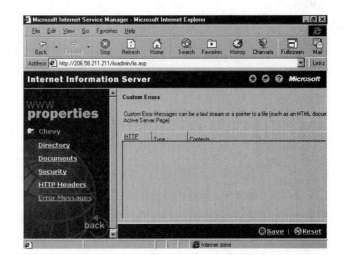

Three important warnings to remember when using the HTML ISM utility:

1. If you are using a non-IE browser, do not turn off Basic Authentication while you are administering IIS 4.0. You will be disconnected and will not be able to log in to remote administration.

2. If you stop the WWW service, you will be disconnected and will not be able to restart it using HTML ISM.

3. If you delete the iisadmin virtual directory on the server you are administering, you will be unable to use HTML-ISM to administer that computer.

Remote management makes it easier to manage multiple servers. Any IIS 4.0 that has HTML ISM installed on it can be managed over the Internet, if you have the proper username and password and the appropriate permissions are configured on the Administrative Web Site.

Exercise 10-1:
Manage Your Web Site with HTML ISM

In this exercise you will use the HTML version of the Internet Service Manager utility to manage your Web site.

1. Click on **Start/Programs/Windows NT 4.0 Option Pack/Microsoft Internet Information Server/Internet Service Manager (HTML)**.

2. Examine the displayed page, then enter the following URL:

   ```
   http://192.168.111.111/iisadmin/default.htm
   ```

3. Is there any difference between launching HTML ISM from the **Start** menu versus accessing the utility by entering a URL in a browser?

4. Enter **Administrator** for the user name and the password you assigned to the Administrator account when you installed the Windows NT 4.0 Server operating system.

5. Click on Default Web Site, then click on the Properties link.

6. Visit each www properties link to determine the administration tasks that can be performed using HTML ISM.

7. If you are in a classroom with other students, repeat this exercise while accessing a different IIS 4.0's IP address.

SCRIPTING

Windows NT 4.0 Option Pack includes the Windows Scripting Host that allows you to execute scripts written in VBScript, JScript, or any other ActiveX scripting language. This section will cover the following topics:

- Scripting Overview
- Windows Scripting Host
- Command Line Scripting Host
- Some Sample Scripts

Let's start with a brief look at the Internet Information Server metabase.

Scripting Overview

Prior to the release of Windows NT 4.0 Option Pack, administrators were limited to writing DOS batch files when they wanted to automate administrative tasks. Part of Microsoft's strategy for future versions of the Windows and Windows NT operating systems is the Zero-Administration Initiative. An important element of this is to provide administrators and developers with powerful scripting abilities and a standard object model they can use to manipulate operating system objects and system services.

You are already somewhat familiar with the ability of Internet Explorer and Internet Information Server to run scripts. This is how they execute VBScript and JScript either on the client or on the server. Windows NT 4.0 Option Pack includes two tools, the Windows Scripting Host and the Command Line Scripting Host, that allow you to run scripts without displaying them in a browser. Let's look at both of these utilities.

Windows Scripting Host

If you select to install the Windows Scripting Host (wscript.exe), it will be installed in the *systemroot*\System32\ directory. It will also be registered as the default application to run when a VBScript (.vbs) or JScript (.js) file is run. You will see a little later how you can change the default scripting host to the Command-Line Scripting Host (cscript.exe).

To run a script that does not require command-line parameters, simply double-click on the icon for the script. If the script requires command-line parameters, you will have to use the **Run** command and type the following:

```
scriptname parameters
```

or

```
wscript scriptname parameters
```

The Windows Scripting Host has several properties you can set to influence how it runs all scripts on the system. To set the Windows Scripting Host's properties, double-click on wscript.exe. The following property page will be displayed:

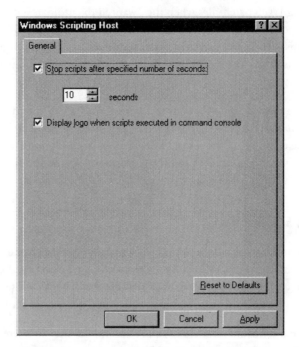

You can set the number of seconds scripts will execute before being terminated, as well as whether or not to display a logo when a script is executed from the command prompt. These properties can also be set on individual scripts by right-clicking on the script and running **Properties**. Click on the **Script** tab. When you close the dialog, a .wsh file with the same name as the script is created. Use this file instead of the .vbs or .js file to run the script using these individualized properties.

Command-Line Scripting Host

The Command-Line Scripting Host can be run from a command prompt. It uses the syntax:

```
CScript scriptname.extension [//option...]  [/arguments...]
```

Each *option* should be preceded by two slashes. Each argument should be preceded by a single slash. The arguments are command-line parameters that are passed to the script. The following options are supported:

//?	Show the options available for the command. Executing CScript with no script name will provide the same result.
//B	Batch Mode: Do not display script errors and user prompts.
//I	Interactive Mode: Display script errors and user prompts.
//H:CScript or **WScript**	Use this option to change the default scripting host to either CScript or WScript.
//S	This option will save the command options used. The next time the current user executes a script, those options will be used by default. This is set on a per-user basis.
//T:*nn*	Timeout: This option sets the maximum number of seconds the script should be allowed to run. This is the same as setting the property for the script.
//logo	Display a banner when the script is executed. This is the option by default.
//nologo	Do not display a banner when the script is executed.

Some Sample Scripts

When the Windows Scripting Host is installed, some sample administrative scripts are installed at *systemroot*\inetsrv\adminsamples. They are not simple scripts for the non-programmer to understand. However, they may prove useful for your day-to-day administrative needs. Information about the arguments they require can be discovered by double-clicking on them.

A detailed discussion of scripting techniques is beyond the scope of this course.

SUMMARY

During this chapter, you were introduced to additional tools to help you administer your Internet Information Server. These included:

- Internet Service Manager (HTML)
- Windows Scripting Host
- Command Line Scripting Host

The next chapter will wrap up the course with a look at tools that will help you optimize performance and provide ongoing maintenance.

POST-TEST QUESTIONS

The answers to these questions are in Appendix A at the end of this manual.

1. What tool is used to remotely administer an IIS 4.0?

   ....

   ....

2. When you are using HTML ISM, under what conditions will your browser not ask you for a username and password?

   ....

   ....

3. What steps must you perform to authorize a remote host to manage your Web server?

   ....

   ....

4. What must you include in the URL to access the Administrative Web Site as an Administrator from a remote computer?

   ....

   ....

5. What service should you not stop while administering an Internet Information Server across the Internet?

   ....

   ....

6. You have written a script to perform routine maintenance on your FTP site every night. You have configured it to run nightly, but on some mornings you find the job only partially complete. What should you check?

   ....

   ....

7. You have several scripts that you configure to run before you leave at night. When you come in the next morning, the second script has hung. You suspect that there is a problem in the script, but you don't have time to troubleshoot it. What can you do to ensure that even if the second script hangs midway through, the third script will be able to execute?

   ....

   ....

CHAPTER 11

Maintenance and Optimization

OBJECTIVES

At the completion of this chapter, you will be able to:

- Describe the purpose and use of a WebMap.

- Use the QuickSearch feature to analyze a Web site.

- Perform IIS 4.0 site analysis using the Site Summary Report.

- Manage and interpret IIS 4.0 log files.

- Describe the purpose of the Usage Analyst Express tool.

- Understand report types and report configurations.

- Analyze IIS 4.0 performance using Performance Monitor.

- Identify counters that reflect WWW, FTP, SMTP, NNTP, and Index Server performance.

- Describe how bandwidth throttling can be used to improve performance.

PRE-TEST QUESTIONS

The answers to these questions are in Appendix A at the end of this manual.

1. What is a WebMap?

   ....

   ....

2. What views are available in the Content Analyzer utility?

   ....

   ....

3. Which files are used by the Usage Import utility?

   ....

   ....

4. Why do ISAPI programs normally provide better performance?

....

....

INTRODUCTION

Once you have set up your Internet Information Server, you have to maintain it. The World Wide Web is dynamic. Content needs to change all the time to keep people coming back. As an administrator, you need to know how those content changes affect your site. For this, you need tools to monitor traffic, Web objects, and performance.

In this chapter you will be introduced to the components and features of Microsoft Site Server Express 2.0. Site Server Express 2.0 allows you to easily view information about the structure of your Web site, content formats, and other pertinent information.

Following that, you'll see how Performance Monitor can provide you with important information about your site's performance. You will also see how you can control the bandwidth used by each site on your server.

MICROSOFT SITE SERVER EXPRESS 2.0

Microsoft Site Server Express 2.0 is included in the Windows NT 4.0 Option Pack. It contains three components that can be used for managing content and site-usage analysis. This section will cover the following topics:

- Installing Microsoft Site Server Express
- Site Server Express Components
- Using the Posting Acceptor

Let's look first at installation.

Installing Microsoft Site Server Express

Microsoft Site Server Express can be installed when you install Internet Information Server or you can add it later. To add it after installation, insert the Windows NT 4.0 Option Pack CD-ROM and let it run **AutoPlay**. Click on **Install**. Click on **Install Windows NT 4.0 Option Pack**. Select to open the file from its current location and click on **OK**. After the Setup program launches, click on **Next**. Click on **Add/Remove**.

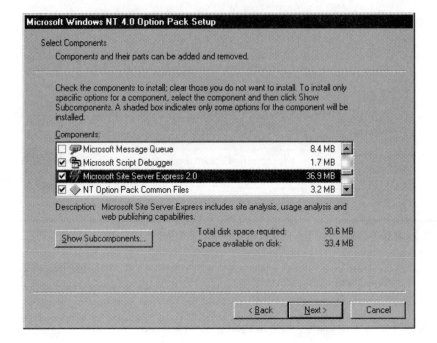

You can select to install all of the components of Microsoft Site Server Express 2.0 or you can view the available subcomponents by clicking on **Show Subcomponents**. The available subcomponents are shown below.

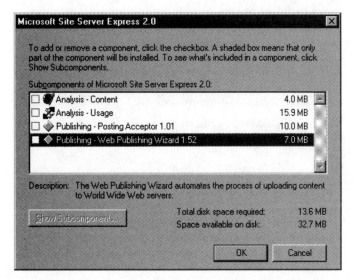

You can select to install the Content Analyzer, the Usage Analyzer, the Posting Acceptor, or the Web Publishing Wizard. The purpose of each of these will be discussed a little later in the chapter. After you have selected the components you wish to install, click on **OK**. Click on **Next**. Your Internet Information Server will be reconfigured and the files will be copied to your disk.

Exercise 11-1

In this exercise, you will install Microsoft Site Server Express from your Windows NT 4.0 Option Pack CD-ROM.

1. Insert the Windows NT 4.0 Option Pack CD-ROM in your CD-ROM drive. Let it run **AutoPlay**.

2. Click on **Install**.

3. Click on **Install Windows NT 4.0 Option Pack**.

4. Select **Open the file from its current location**.

5. Click on **OK**.

6. Click on **Next**.

7. Click on **Add/Remove**.

8. Select Microsoft Site Server Express and click on **OK**.

9. Select **Show Subcomponents**.

10. Select **Analysis - Content** and **Analysis - Usage** and click on **OK**.

11. Click on **Next**.

12. After the files have finished copying, click on **Finish**.

Site Server Express Components

These components are:

*   Content Analyzer

    This component provides a visual representation of a Web site. It can be used to analyze the documents on your Web site to locate broken hypertext links. You can also generate reports in HTML format to view details on Web site content.

*   Usage Import and Report Writer

    Use these components to analyze IIS 4.0 log files.

*   Posting Acceptor 1.01

    This component provides RFC 1867-compliant Web document posting over HTTP.

You can also upgrade to the full version of Microsoft Site Server 3.0 or Microsoft Site Server 3.0 Commerce Edition.

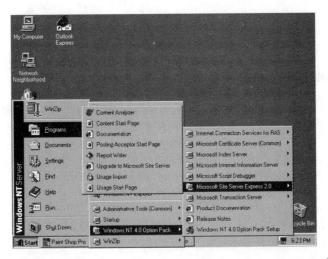

To view the Site Server Express 2.0 components, run **Start/Programs/Windows NT 4.0 Option Pack/Microsoft Site Server Express 2.0.**

Select the **Upgrade to Microsoft Site Server** option to view information on added functionality provided by version 3.0. Your browser will launch and you will be taken to the appropriate location on the Microsoft Web Site.

Using the Posting Acceptor

The Microsoft Posting Acceptor is an add-on tool for IIS 4.0 that allows Web content developers to upload files to your site using HTTP.

IIS 4.0, Microsoft Peer Web Services, and Microsoft Personal Web Server can use the Posting Acceptor to allow the posting of content from a number of sources including:

- Microsoft Web Publishing Wizard/API
- Microsoft Internet Explorer
- Netscape Navigator 2.02 or later

The Posting Acceptor utility can use the Microsoft Content Replication System (CRS) to simultaneously distribute content to multiple servers.

The Content Analyzer

The Content Analyzer can be used to analyze the objects on your Web site or on other Web sites. This section will look at the following topics:

- Running the Content Analyzer
- Using WebMaps
- Tree View WebMap
- Cyberbolic View WebMap
- Using Site Summary Reports
- Site Summary Report Statistics
- Using the Quick Search Feature
- Displaying Pages

Let's start by looking at how to launch the Content Analyzer.

Running the Content Analyzer

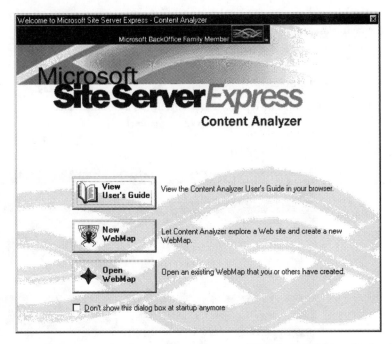

To launch the Content Analyzer, run **Start/Programs/Windows NT 4.0 Option Pack/ Microsoft Site Server Express 2.0/Content Analyzer.**

When you launch the Content Analyzer you are presented with the following options:

- View User's Guide
- New WebMap
- Open WebMap

You can also elect to bypass the opening dialog by selecting the **Don't show this dialog box at startup anymore** option.

Using WebMaps

WebMaps allow you to visualize your Web site's directory structure in two different viewing modes. These are:

- Tree View WebMap
- Cyberbolic View WebMap

To create a new WebMap, launch **Content Analyzer** and select **New** from the **File** menu. You are presented with the option of creating the new WebMap from a URL or from a file.

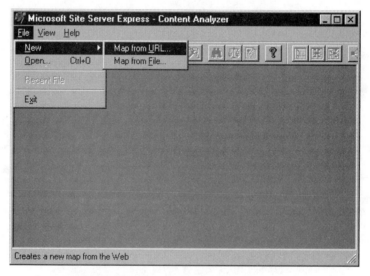

Select the **Map from URL** option.

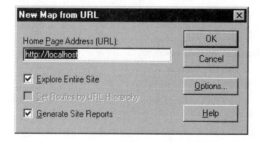

Enter the URL of the site you would like to map. To create a map of the Default Web Site on the local computer, you can use http://localhost for the Home Page Address (URL) value, then click on **OK**. The **Options** button lets you customize several important settings.

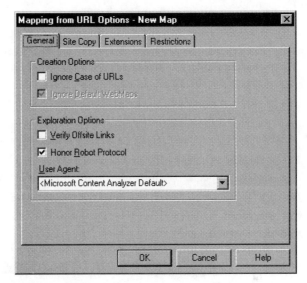

The options you can set include:

- Ignore Case of URLs

    Internet Information Server treats URLs as case-insensitive. This means that the same object might be referred to by uppercase in one document and lowercase in another. If you do not ignore case when creating your WebMap, these will be considered separate objects. If you are creating a WebMap of a UNIX server, you should not ignore case.

- Verify Offsite Links

    It is likely that you provide links to other Web sites. If you select this option, the existence of those objects will be verified. This may be necessary sometimes, but it will increase the amount of time it takes to create the map.

- Honor Robot Protocol

    By default, the Content Analyzer will ignore sites that restrict spiders. To map sites that restrict spiders, turn this option off. Keep in mind, however, that while this might be appropriate when analyzing your own Web site, it is not appropriate when creating a WebMap of a Web site that belongs to some other company.

- User Agent

    This is set to the Microsoft Content Analyzer by default. However, if you provide special handling for certain browsers on your Web site, you will probably want to create a WebMap using various User Agents.

After you have typed the URL of the Web site you would like to analyze, you will be prompted for a destination.

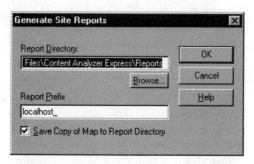

You can view the status of the Content Analyzer as it reads directories and documents.

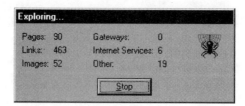

A progress indicator is displayed as the analyzer generates the Site Summary Report.

Internet Explorer launches automatically to display the Site Summary Report.

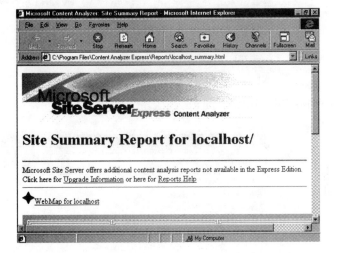

Click on the WebMap for localhost link. This option allows you to save the WebMap to a file.

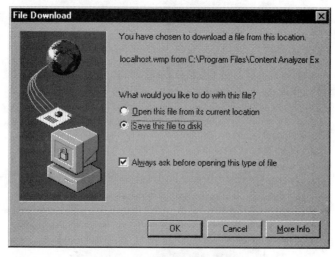

After you have specified a path, click on **Save**.

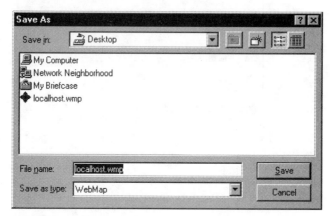

When the WebMap has been saved, click on **OK**.

Scroll down to view the contents of the report. Minimize your browser.

Maximize the Content Analyzer utility.

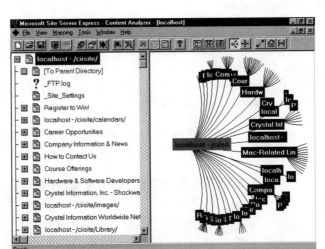

The Tree View WebMap is displayed in the left window pane while the Cyberbolic View WebMap is displayed in the right window pane.

Tree View WebMap

The Tree View WebMap is similar in appearance to the Windows NT Explorer. Icons are assigned to each object. The home page is shown at the top of the window pane. Icons are represented in levels with the home page representing Level 1, similar to a book outline.

Control icons (small gray squares) can contain a plus sign (+), minus sign (-), or question mark (?). By clicking various control icons you can alter the view of the Cyberbolic View WebMap. Click on the plus sign to expand and the minus sign to contract an object. Question marks in control icons indicate that a page has not yet been examined by Content Analyzer.

Cyberbolic View WebMap

The Cyberbolic View WebMap provides a dynamic visualization of a Web site. This view displays relationships between Web objects. By clicking on different control icons you can change the starting point of the Cyberbolic View WebMap. As you click on objects in the Cyberbolic View, the object will move left or right of center. Two toolbar buttons can be used to modify the view's orientation.

You can select the **Display Options** command from the **View** menu to determine which objects to display and other display-related parameters.

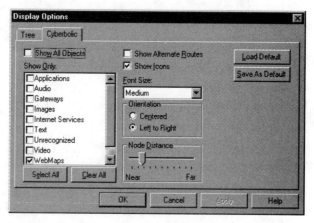

Full-length descriptions are displayed as you move the mouse cursor over an object in the Cyberbolic View.

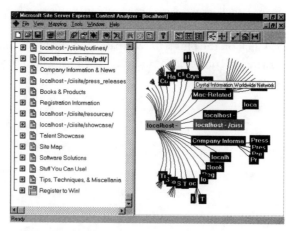

You cannot collapse or expand levels in the Cyberbolic View.

Using Site Summary Reports

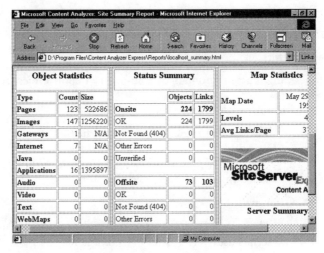

Site Summary Reports are designed to aid your understanding of your Web site's structure and the content types used. Reports include:

- Page, image, and application object counts and sizes.
- The number of objects and links that are broken, missing, or functional.
- Number of levels, starting at the home page.
- Average links per page.

You can generate a Site Summary Report in one of three ways:

- Create a new WebMap and select the **Generate Site Reports** option.
- Click on the **Generate Site Reports** button in the toolbar.
- Select **Generate Site Reports** from the **Tools** menu.

Site Summary Report Statistics

The Site Summary report provides three categories of statistics. These are Object Statistics, Status Summary (Onsite and Offsite), and Map Statistics.

Object Statistics

The following is a description of Site Summary Report Object statistics:

- Pages

    The number pages and their total size

- Images

    The number of images and their total size

- Gateways

    The number of links associated with Common Gateway Interface (CGI) scripts using GET or POST commands

- Internet

    The number of links pointing to Internet services objects

- Java

    The number of links to Java applications and their total size

- Applications

    The number of links to applications and their total size

- Audio

    The number of links to audio objects and their total size

- Video

    The number of links to video objects and their total size

- Text

    The number of links to text objects and their total size

- WebMaps

    The number of links to WebMap objects and their total size

- Other Media

    The number of links to other media objects and their total size

- Totals

    Web site total objects and their total size

Status Summary–Onsite & Offsite

The Status Summary statistics are used to determine the condition of your Web site's links, both Onsite and Offsite. Onsite statistics provide information on local links while Offsite statistics provide information on remote links.

The following is a list of Status Summary Onsite and Offsite statistics:

- OK
- Not found (code 404)
- Other Errors
- Unverified

Map Statistics

Map statistics provide additional information about your Web site including:

- Map Date

    The creation date of the report

- Levels

    The number of Levels of the analyzed site

- Average Links per Page

    The average number of links per page

Using the Quick Search Feature

The Content Analyzer utility includes eight pre-configured Quick Search options to help you detect errors or possible problems on your Web site. To start a Quick Search, select **Quick Search** from the **Tools** menu.

The eight pre-configured Quick Searches are:

- Broken Links

    Locates links whose target is unavailable.

- Home Site Objects

    Displays objects that are in your home page's domain. Determines if damaged objects can be accessed and repaired through the local security structure.

- Images without ALT

    Locates images that do not include the optional ALT text string.

- Load Size Over 32 KB

    Locates resources that are larger than 32 kilobytes in size.

- Non-Home Site Objects

    Displays objects that are not in your home page's domain.

- Not Found Objects (404)

    Locates objects that could not be located when the WebMap was generated.

- Unavailable Objects

    Displays objects that could not be located or were not available when the WebMap was created.

- Unverified Objects

    Displays objects that have not been checked for accessibility.

Displaying Pages

You can load a particular Web page by double-clicking on it in the Cyberbolic View. This is helpful because it allows you to view the page as users will view it. If you click on hyperlinks while in the browser, the current location in the WebMap will also be adjusted.

SITE USAGE REPORTS

Another important feature of Microsoft Web Site Express is the ability to generate reports that show how your site is being used. This section will discuss usage reports. Topics covered will include:

- Generating Log Files
- Log File Management
- Generating a Report From a Log File
- Report Writer
- Detail Reports
- Summary Reports

Let's start with a look at how your site can be configured to generate log files.

Generating Log Files

Site Usage reports are generated by creating and analyzing log files. You must enable logging for your Web site or FTP site in order to generate log files.

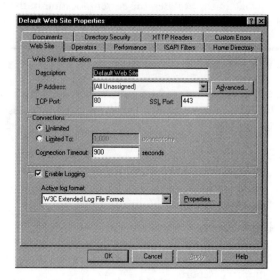

To enable logging, view the Properties of your Web or FTP site. Click on the **Web Site** or **FTP Site** tab and select the **Enable Logging** option. You can select a format for your log file. If you plan to analyze the log file using the Usage Analyzer, you should create the file using W3C Extended Log File Format. The W3C Extended Log File Format is an ASCII file that can be customized to contain various types of information. Selecting ODBC Logging will let you store the logged information in a relational database, but it requires you to create the database and a DSN. Logging to a database will also use more processor time and could impact performance. Choosing NCSA logging creates an ASCII file, but the information is preconfigured and more limited than that provided by the W3C extended format.

Log File Management

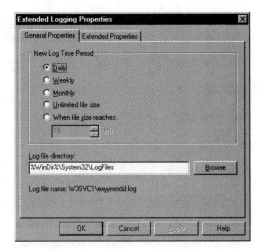

The Extended Logging properties sheet allows you to tailor the tracking and logging of server activity. For most installations the default logging options are acceptable. Log file management is an important component of IIS 4.0 management.

Log files track users who've visited your site, time of visit, documents requested, and downloaded/uploaded files.

The **Extended Properties** page allows you to select from twenty different events that may be logged.

Log File Contents

IIS 4.0 log files are comma-delimited ASCII files that contain hyphens in fields where there is no valid value (empty fields). The order of fields in the file is:

> Client IP Address
>
> Client Username
>
> Date
>
> Time
>
> Service
>
> Computer Name
>
> IP Address of Server
>
> Processing Time
>
> Bytes Received
>
> Bytes Sent

Service Status Code

Windows NT Status Code

Name of Operation

Target of Operation

Because every single Web and FTP access generates a logging entry, log files can grow to be very large. No facility is provided to limit log file size.

Log File Analysis

A tool such as Webtrends (www.webtrends.com) is useful for analyzing log file data.

Exercise 11-2:
Log File Management

In this exercise you will enable weekly logging.

1. Run **Start/Programs/Windows NT 4.0 Option Pack/Microsoft Internet Server/ Internet Service Manager** to launch the Internet Service Manager.

2. Open the Internet Information Server folder, then open the webserver computer icon.

3. Right-click on Default Web Site and select **Properties** or single-click on Default Web Site and click on the **Properties** button on the button bar.

4. Click on the **Web Site** tab.

5. Verify that the **Enable Logging** option is enabled.

6. Click on the **Properties** button next to Active log format. Change the New Log Time Period value from Daily to Weekly.

7. Click on **Apply**, then click on **OK**.

Generating a Report From a Log File

To generate a report from a log file, you need to import the file into the Content Analyzer database. This is done with the Usage Import utility. To launch the Usage Import utility, click on **Start/Programs/Windows NT 4.0 Option Pack/Microsoft Site Server Express 2.0/Usage Import**.

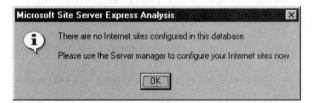

The first time you launch the Usage Import utility you will be informed that no sites have been configured. Click on **OK**.

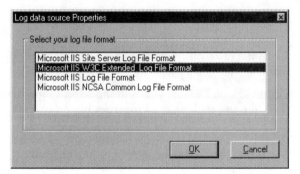

Select the log file format you specified for the Web or FTP site, then click on **OK**.

Enter the name of your DNS domain in the Local domain field, then click on **OK**.

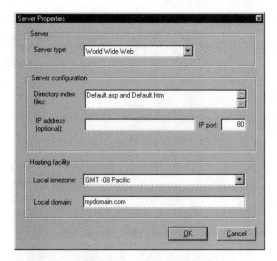

Enter the URL for your home page, such as http://localhost.

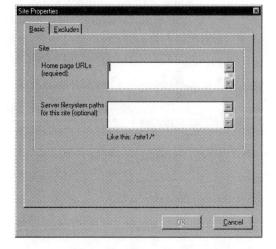

Click on the **Excludes** tab. Select any hosts or image types that you wish to exclude from the report, then click on **OK**.

The Usage Import utility will now finish loading.

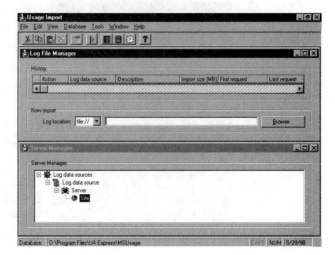

Report Writer

The Report Writer utility is used to analyze and produce reports from your Web or FTP site log files.

To launch the Report Writer utility, click on **Start/Programs/Windows NT 4.0 Option Pack/Microsoft Site Server Express 2.0/Report Writer**.

Click on **OK** to create a report from the Report Writer catalog.

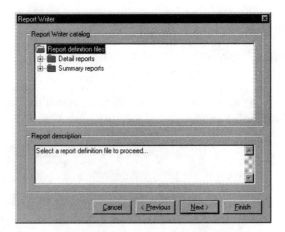

Click on the plus sign (+) next to Detail Reports to expand the list. Scroll down to view the various options.

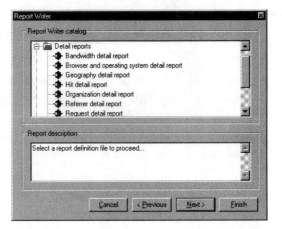

Click on the minus sign (-) next to Detail Reports to contract the list. Click on the plus sign (+) next to Summary Reports to expand the list. Scroll down to view the various options.

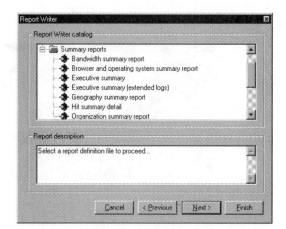

Click on the minus sign (-) next to Detail Reports to contract the list. Re-open the Detail Reports folder and select one of the options, then click on **Next**. We've selected the Browser and operating system detail report.

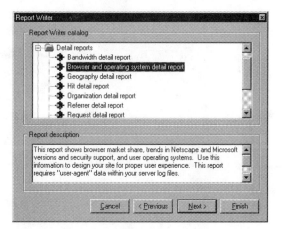

Determine the date scope of the report, then click on **Next**.

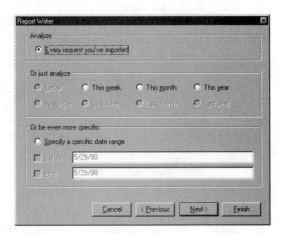

Select any filters you wish to employ to limit the amount of information contained in the report, then click on **Finish**.

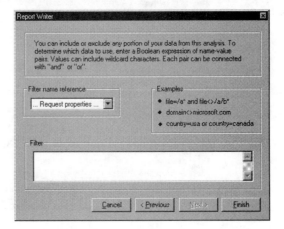

The results of the report are displayed.

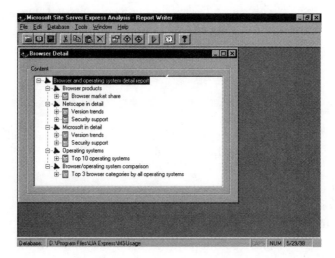

Detail Reports

The Report Writer utility includes nine pre-configured Detail Reports. These are:

- Bandwidth

    This report displays byte transfers in hourly, daily, and weekly increments. You can determine server trends and use the data to create a baseline for your server.

- Browser and Operating System

    This report provides information on client browser market share, versions, security, and local operating system. You can determine the types of browsers and operating systems being used to access your site.

- Geography

    This report displays the cities, states, provinces, and countries of users who have visited your site.

- Hit

    This report displays the number of hits on your server. This report is useful for site expansion and capacity planning.

- Organization

    This report displays the names of the companies of users who have visited your site.

- Referrer

    This report displays the names of sites that have referred users to your site through a hypertext link.

- Request

    This report displays the least/most requested documents on your site.

- User

    This report displays the number of visitors to your site, as well as first-time visitors, users per organization, document requests, and length of stay.

- Visits

    This report displays the requests per visit, average length of stay, pages most likely to be accessed first and last, and visit trends.

Summary Reports

The Report Writer utility includes twelve pre-configured Summary Reports. These are:

- Bandwidth

    This report displays bandwidth used by the site by day of week, hour of day, and work hours vs. non-work hours. This report can be used to determine bandwidth problems, such as abnormal usage or saturation.

- Browser and Operating System

    This report provides information on client browsers and local operating system.

- Executive

    This report provides a summary of Detail Reports information.

- Executive Summary for Extended Logs

    This report provides a summary of extended Log File Detail reports.

- Geography

    This report provides a summary of the Geography Detail report.

- Hit

    This report displays a summary of the Hit Detail report.

- Organization

    This report displays a summary of the Organization Detail report.

- Path

    This report displays the sequence of user page requests over a client session.

- Referrer

    This report displays a summary of the Referrer Detail report.

- Request

    This report displays a summary of the Request Detail report.

- User

    This report displays a summary of the User Detail report.

- Visits

    This report displays a summary of the Visit Detail report.

PERFORMANCE

Another key issue to managing a successful Internet site is making sure that performance does not suffer either because you have insufficient hardware for the amount of traffic you are receiving or because you are running a resource-intensive application on one of your sites. This section will look at the following topics:

- Hardware Performance Issues

- Critical Peripheral Components

- Enhancing IIS 4.0 Performance

- Performance Tuning

Hardware Performance Issues

The Windows NT 4.0 Server operating system requires significant resources to provide satisfactory performance for applications such as the Internet Information Server. You must provide a server hardware platform that is sufficient to service the clients that connect to your Web site.

Specific hardware and software requirements for IIS 4.0 were provided earlier in the course. These should be considered sufficient for lightly accessed servers only. A few important components to consider for high-performance server selection are:

- Server Central Processing Unit (CPU) Type and Speed

    The server CPU type and speed determine the maximum number of instructions per second that the Windows NT Server 4.0 computer can perform. The Windows NT 4.0 Server operating system is available for both Intel and DEC Alpha series CPUs.

    Currently, the highest performance CPU available from Intel is the Pentium II running at 400 MHz. The highest performance Alpha processor available at this time offers a 533-MHz clock speed.

    You should evaluate your overall Web site requirements and select the appropriate processor platform for your needs.

- Server Motherboard Cache RAM

  Cache RAM is high-speed (typically 10 nanoseconds or less), static memory used to buffer data transfers between the server's CPU and main memory. A minimum of 512 KB of cache RAM should be installed. Pentium II-based systems do not use motherboard cache RAM. Instead, Intel has packaged the CPU and cache RAM together in a single package for enhanced performance.

- Server Expansion Bus Type and Speed

  Expansion cards such as network adapters and disk controller boards also play a key role in determining overall system performance. The speed at which data can be transmitted through the server's expansion bus is determined by the bus type, bus width, and bus throughput.

  The most common expansion bus type in use today is the Peripheral Component Interconnect (PCI) bus introduced by Intel. The PCI bus has a maximum data throughput speed of 528 MBps. All Intel Pentium and Pentium II-based motherboards utilize the PCI bus. PCI technology has also been adapted by other manufacturers, including DEC and Apple Computer.

- Server Disk Channel

  The server disk channel is a critical component that has a profound effect on Internet Information Server performance. The primary responsibility of a Web server is to listen for client requests, read documents from a disk storage device, and transmit the document contents to the requesting client through a network interface.

  A slow disk channel will become a significant bottleneck in a Web server. For this reason, you should only install the highest performance disk drives and controllers in your server.

At the low-end of the performance scale are Ultra DMA Integrated Drive Electronics (IDE) and narrow Small Computer Systems Interface (SCSI) disk drives and controllers. Wide, Ultra SCSI drive/controller combinations offer good to moderate performance. You can utilize Redundant Arrays of Inexpensive (or Independent) Devices (RAID) technology for the best possible performance and reliability.

RAID arrays can be configured in several *Levels,* which provide several configuration options. The highest RAID level is Level 5, which offers the highest degree of performance and fault tolerance. Most high-quality disk arrays offer hot-swap capabilities that allow you to replace defective devices without needing to power the system down.

- Server RAM

  A very important factor in maximizing performance is the number of times IIS 4.0 locates the contents of a requested document in server cache memory. The bigger the cache, the better the performance. Adding RAM to your NT server can significantly improve its performance.

Critical Peripheral Components

- Tape Backup System

  A high-performance tape backup system is an absolute requirement for maintaining your Windows NT Server computer. Regular file system backups are an important part of system administration. You should purchase a DAT, DLT, or other high-performance tape backup unit and institute a backup schedule that only performs backups during off-peak hours.

- Uninterruptible Power Supply (UPS)

  All computers running the Windows NT Server 4.0 operating system should be connected to an uninterruptible power supply (UPS). A UPS provides protection against low-voltage conditions (brownouts) and power outages (blackouts). Most units also provide surge suppression to prevent equipment damage due to lightning strikes or other electrical problems.

Enhancing IIS 4.0 Performance

Internet Information Server 4.0 performance is also affected by software parameters that can be adjusted to accommodate various application requirements. To optimize the performance of your Web server, perform the following tasks.

- Use the Performance Tuning option to balance Windows NT Server memory requirements.

- Use the Bandwidth Throttling option to limit the total network bandwidth that can be consumed by the Web Service or by particular Web sites.

- Enable the HTTP Keep-Alives option so that client connections to the Web Service can remain open without timing out.

- Use the Windows NT Performance Monitor to determine overall server usage and create a baseline to assist in troubleshooting and future system expansion planning.

The Internet Service Manager utility is used to configure tuning parameters for Web Services.

Performance Tuning

The first step in optimizing your Web server is to verify that you are not under- or over-allocating server memory resources to IIS 4.0. This is controlled by the Performance Tuning option.

To view the current Performance Tuning configuration for your server, run **Start/ Programs/Windows NT 4.0 Option Pack/Microsoft Internet Server/Internet Service Manager.**

Open the Internet Information Server folder, then open the webserver computer icon.

Right-click on Default Web Site and select **Properties**. Click on the **Performance** tab.

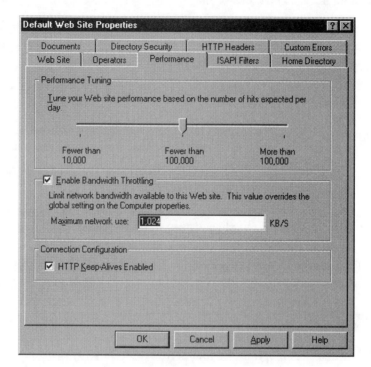

You should adjust the Performance Tuning slider based on the number of anticipated daily Web server document requests (connections). If you set the value slightly higher than the actual number of connections, performance will improve. If you set the value significantly higher than the actual number of connections you will waste server memory and other Services will not achieve peak performance.

Bandwidth Throttling

The allocation and management of network bandwidth is an ongoing issue in the administration of IIS 4.0. World Wide Web, video, audio, and other applications have boomed in popularity, significantly increasing bandwidth requirements on both large and small networks.

The cost of bandwidth varies. Bandwidth on a Local Area Network is relatively inexpensive. The cost of network adapters and hubs that transmit data at 100 Mbps has fallen tremendously. In addition, advanced switching products allow network designers to achieve maximum performance even on busy networks.

On the other hand, the cost of Wide Area Network bandwidth is relatively high and is likely to remain so for some time to come. Internet connectivity options range from 14.4-Kbps dial-up connections through DS-3 (45 Mbps) or faster service.

IIS 4.0 provides the Bandwidth Throttling feature to help you manage network bandwidth. Bandwidth Throttling affects only Web documents containing static information. Active content such as Active Server Pages (ASP), ISAPI Filters, and ISAPI Extensions are not affected.

The Bandwidth Throttling feature offers two forms of bandwidth control:

- Overall Web Site Bandwidth Throttling

    Use this option to reserve a portion of the total bandwidth of your Internet connection for internal network users.

- Individual Site Bandwidth Throttling

    Use this option to limit the maximum bandwidth used by a given Web site.

You must adjust these two options carefully as under- or over-allocating bandwidth to the server or to a particular site could have a negative impact on system performance.

Overall Web Server Bandwidth

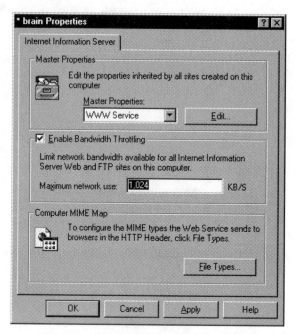

You configure overall Web server bandwidth through the Web Server properties. You enable bandwidth throttling by selecting the **Enable Bandwidth Throttling** option. The default value (when enabled) is 1,024 Kbps. If your Internet connection has enough available bandwidth you may wish to increase this value. If you are using IIS 4.0 to host an Internet Web site, you will probably need to increase this value unless it will have an adverse affect on internal Internet users.

Individual Site Bandwidth Throttling

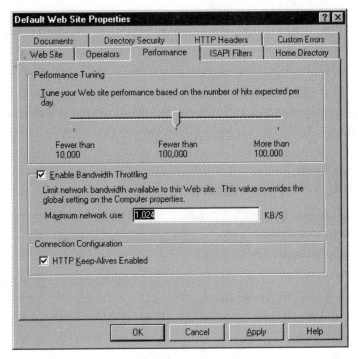

To configure the individual site bandwidth throttling option, right-click on the site's icon and select **Properties**. Click on the **Performance** tab.

You enable bandwidth throttling by selecting the **Enable Bandwidth Throttling** option. The default value (when enabled) is 1,024 Kbps and is likely to be too small for most applications.

HTTP Keep-Alives

When requesting documents from an HTTP server, clients connect to and disconnect from the server many times. This is not necessarily the most efficient method of communicating.

The **HTTP Keep-Alives** option allows client connections to the Web server to remain active rather than establishing a new connection with each additional request. This option is enabled by default and should remain enabled under normal circumstances.

Exercise 11-3:
Configuring Performance Options

In this exercise you will use the Internet Service Manager utility to adjust the Performance Tuning slider. You will then limit bandwidth allocation for your Web server and your overall Web site.

1. Run **Start/Programs/Windows NT 4.0 Option Pack/Microsoft Internet Server/ Internet Service Manager**.

2. Open the Internet Information Server folder, then open the webserver computer icon.

3. Right-click on Default Web Site and select **Properties**. Click on the **Performance** tab.

4. Move the slider to Fewer than 10,000.

5. Select the **Enable Bandwidth Throttling** option. Change the value to 2,048.

6. Verify that the **HTTP Keep-Alives** option is enabled.

7. Click on **Apply**, then click on **OK**.

8. Right-click on webserver and select **Properties**.

9. Select the **Enable Bandwidth Throttling** option. Leave the value set at 1,024.

10. Click on **Apply**, then click on **OK**.

The Effects of CGI and ISAPI on Server Performance

When 100 people access your Web site and request to execute the same ISAPI program, only a single copy of the program is kept in memory. In contrast, when 100 people access your Web site and request to execute the same CGI program, 100 copies of the program may be loaded into memory.

Whenever possible, use ISAPI programs instead of CGI programs.

MONITORING PERFORMANCE

The Performance Monitor utility provides a graphical representation of your system's operating parameters. It is often used to locate and help resolve performance bottlenecks.

Performance Monitor topics to be discussed include:

- Performance Monitor Overview
- Performance Monitor Views
- IIS 4.0-specific Counters
- Suggested Counters
- Performance Report

Careful monitoring is an important part of system optimization. It enables you to locate bottlenecks and to know if your changes have helped to improve performance.

Performance Monitor Overview

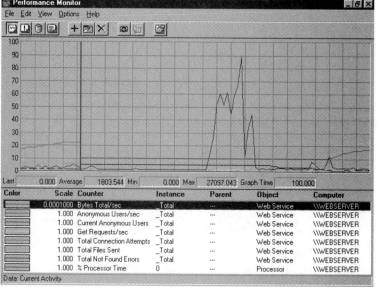

Performance Monitor can be used to:

- Check performance of system objects.

- Compare the performance of different systems.

- Gather data for more detailed analysis.

- Set alerts to occur when selected object parameters hit specified levels.

- Run executable commands or batch files when alerts occur.

- Create report screens displaying exact values in a timely manner.

Windows NT Server includes a standard set of performance counters for objects such as the memory cache, disk usage, processor, processes, and threads. Network counters are installed according to the network software running at the system. Some applications, such as SQL Server for Windows NT or Microsoft Systems Management Server (SMS), also install their own counters.

Performance Monitor Views

The Performance Monitor supports four view options so that you can display information in a format that best suits your needs. The available views are:

- Chart

    In this view, the values of selected counters are displayed as either a line graph or a histogram. The graphical representation makes it easy to monitor available resources or to see performance bottlenecks. This view can become confusing, however, if you try to track too many simultaneous counters.

- Alert

    The Alert view allows you to select counters and instances to be monitored, each with an alert threshold value that you specify. When a counter reaches the threshold, an alert is generated.

- Log

    Creating a log file lets you gather data from selected counters over a period of time and perform offline analysis later. This gives you a way of doing detailed analysis of performance data. Because you can track multiple machines in a single file, you can also perform detailed comparative analysis.

- Report

    The Report view displays the current values for selected counters in a report format. This view allows you to compare exact values, and makes it relatively easy to simultaneously display a larger number of counters and still make sense of them all.

Performance Monitor defaults to the Chart view, displaying data in a line graph format. As you switch between foreground views, those in the background remain active.

Charts

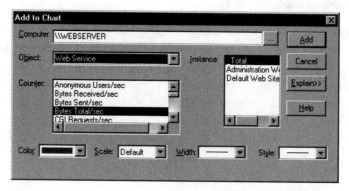

The Add to Chart dialog lets you set the values to be displayed in a chart.

Computer   This is the system from which data is collected.

Object   The object identifies a set of related counters, such as
                  logical disk, physical disk, NetBEUI, and so on.

Counter   This is a list of individual counters available for the
                  selected object.

Instance   If there is more than one instance of an object running,
                  each instance is listed and may be selected separately.

The Color, Scale, Width, and Style selections let you control the appearance of the chart.

Alerts

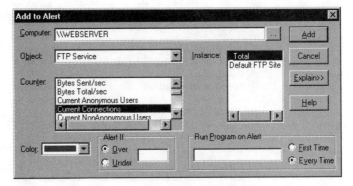

The Alert view lets you monitor system activity and generate an alert when the alert criteria are met or exceeded. Alerts use the same object, counter, and instance selections as charts. You set the value at which an alert is generated. You can also specify a program to run, either an executable or a batch file, when the alert occurs. This can be set to run only on the first occurrence, or on every occurrence of the alert.

Logs

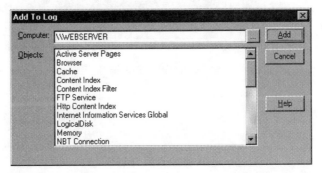

When selecting log contents, you only make object selections. All of the counters for that object are recorded at the interval you set.

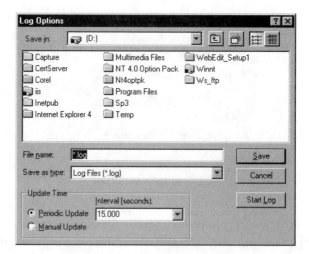

After making your object selections, you must choose **Log** from the **Options** menu, give the log file a name, and click on the **Start Log** button to start recording data.

Report

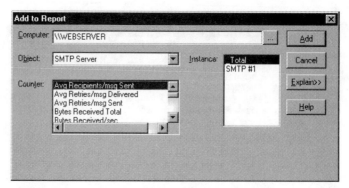

Reports use the same object, counter, and instance selections as charts. The difference is that reports provide you with exact numerical values. You can set the update period, which defaults to updating the report every five seconds.

This is helpful when you need accurate data regarding system activity or want to make exact comparisons between systems.

IIS 4.0 Counters

The following categories contain counters that can be monitored by Performance Monitor:

- Active Server Pages
- Browser
- Cache
- Content Index
- Content Index Filter
- FTP Service
- HTTP Content Index
- Internet Information Services Global
- Logical Disk
- Memory
- NBT Connection
- NNTP Commands
- NNTP Server
- NWLink IPX
- NWLink NetBIOS
- NWLink SPX
- Objects
- Paging File
- Physical Disk
- Process
- Processor

- Redirector

- Server

- Server Work Queues

- SMTP Server

- System

- Telephony

- Thread

- Web Service

Many IIS 4.0-related counters are repeated for the various objects. This is because you will want to track many of the same values for different services.

Using Performance Monitor

To launch the Performance Monitor utility, run **Start/Programs/Administrative Tools (Common)/Performance Monitor**.

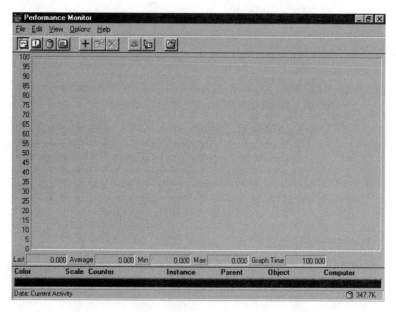

Before any information is displayed, you need to select counters for the parameters you wish to monitor. Click on the **Edit** menu and select **Add to Chart**.

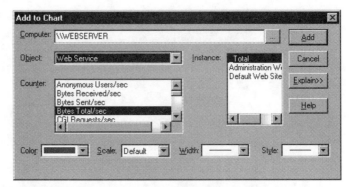

Click on the Object field and select the Web Service object.

If you are not sure what a particular counter is used for, select the counter and click on **Explain** to view a description.

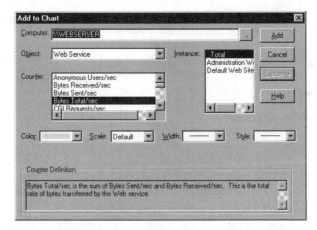

Click on **Add** to add the Bytes Total/sec counter to the chart. Scroll down to select the Current Anonymous Users counter, then click on **Add**. Scroll down to select the Maximum Connections counter, then click on **Add**. Click on **Done** to begin viewing the chart.

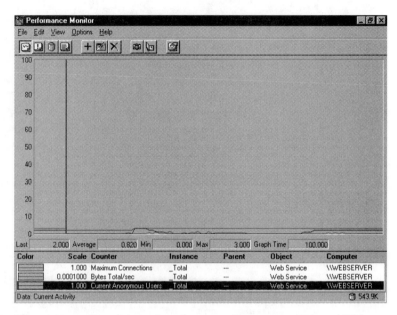

You should not see much activity unless there are clients accessing your Web server.

Exercise 11-4:
Using Performance Monitor

In this exercise you use the Performance Monitor utility to create a chart of counters for your Web and FTP Services.

1. To launch the Performance Monitor utility, run **Start/Programs/Administrative Tools (Common)/Performance Monitor**.

2. Click on the **Edit** menu and select **Add to Chart**.

3. Click on the Object field and select the Web Service object.

4. Click on **Add** to add the Bytes Total/sec counter to the chart.

5. Scroll down to select the Current Anonymous Users counter, then click on **Add**.

6. Scroll down to select the Maximum Connections counter, then click on **Add**.

7. Click on the Object field and select the FTP Service object.

8. Click on **Add** to add the Bytes Total/sec counter to the chart.

9. Scroll down to select the Current Connections counter, then click on **Add**.

10. Scroll down to select the Maximum Connections counter, then click on **Add**.

11. Click on **Done** to begin viewing the chart. View the chart for 10 seconds before continuing.

12. Minimize Performance Monitor and use your browser to access your Web site. Enter http://localhost in the URL field, then press *ENTER*. Click on several hypertext links.

13. Switch back to Performance Monitor to see if the chart shows any activity.

14. Close Performance Monitor.

Performance Report

You can use the Performance Monitor utility to produce a performance report and then export it to a spreadsheet or other application for further analysis. To generate a performance report, select the Report view.

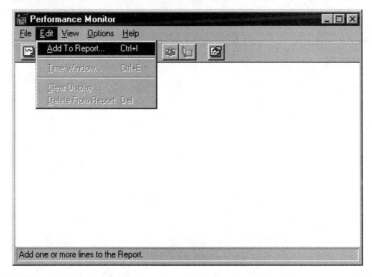

Select **Add to Report** from the **Edit** menu. Add the desired counters, then click on **Done**. To update displayed counters, select **Update Now** from the **Options** menu.

To export report data for use in another application, select **Export Report** from the **File** menu. Reports may be exported in TSV or CSV format.

Exercise 11-5:
Generating a Performance Report

In this exercise you will use the Performance Monitor utility to generate a report and then export the report for use in an analysis application.

1. To launch the Performance Monitor utility, run **Start/Programs/Administrative Tools (Common)/Performance Monitor**.

2. Select **Report** from the **View** menu.

3. Select **Add to Report** from the **Edit** menu.

4. Click on the Object field and select the Web Service object.

5. Click on **Add** to add the Bytes Total/sec counter to the chart.

6. Scroll down to select the Current Anonymous Users counter, then click on **Add**.

7. Scroll down to select the Maximum Connections counter, then click on **Add**.

8. Click on the Object field and select the FTP Service object.

9. Click on **Add** to add the Bytes Total/sec counter to the chart.

10. Scroll down to select the Current Connections counter, then click on **Add**.

11. Scroll down to select the Maximum Connections counter, then click on **Add**.

12. Click on **Done** to begin viewing the report.

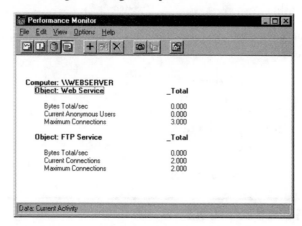

13. Select **Export Report** from the **File** menu. You will be prompted for a filename. Enter the filename:

    c:\perfrep.txt

14. Click on **Save**.

15. Close Performance Monitor.

SUMMARY

During this chapter, you were introduced to several tools and features you can use to monitor, maintain, and optimize your Internet Information Server. These included:

- Content Analyzer
- Usage Analyzer
- Bandwidth Throttling
- HTTP Keep-Alives
- Performance Monitor

POST-TEST QUESTIONS

The answers to these questions are in Appendix A at the end of this manual.

1. What are the four components that comprise Microsoft Site Server Express 2.0?

   ....

   ....

2. Which utility is used to generate the Site Summary report?

   ....

   ....

3. In order to generate Site Usage reports you must first enable _____ .

   ....

   ....

4. What are the categories of reports available in the Report Writer utility?

   ....

   ....

5. Which protocol is used by the Posting Acceptor to upload Web content?

   ....

   ....

6. What is the purpose of the Performance Tuning option?

   ....

   ....

7. What two forms of bandwidth throttling are available in IIS 4.0?

   ....

   ....

8. Which Performance Monitor view provides a realtime display of exact numeric values of selected counters?

   ....

   ....

Appendix A—Answers to Pre-Test and Post-Test Questions

CHAPTER 1

Pre-Test Questions

1. Responds to requests from browsers

2. Netscape Navigator (Communicator) and Microsoft Internet Explorer

3. 4.01

4. Version 4.0 with Service Pack 3 installed (or higher)

Post-Test Questions

1. Windows NT Server 4.0 with Service Pack 3 (or higher)

2. A. False

3. IP address

4. Any browser can use your Web site, provided the Active Server Page running the ActiveX component only outputs standard HTML.

5. The primary advantage of the Java programming language is application portability.

CHAPTER 2

Pre-Test Questions

1. An Internet Service Provider connects you to the Internet.

2. Yes

3. Frame Relay, ISDN, ATM

4. ATM

Post-Test Questions

1. Selecting the wrong ISP can lead to Web server and electronic mail failures, poor performance, and a lack of qualified technical support personnel.

2. Connection type, connection speed, and average usage

3. To change ISPs you must register your new ISP's information with the InterNIC. This is easiest if you have a registered domain name.

4. T-class circuits offer from 1.544 Mbps to 274.176 Mbps of bandwidth.

5. It is important to register your own domain name as it can be very difficult to change ISPs if you use the ISP's domain name for your Web site and e-mail servers.

6. Two 64-Kbps channels are provided with basic ISDN service.

7. An ISP who possesses a T3 connection to the Internet can offer up to 45 Mbps of bandwidth, as opposed to a T1 provider who can only offer 1.544 Mbps of bandwidth.

CHAPTER 3

Pre-Test Questions

1. Transaction logging and file and directory access permissions for Internet access.

2. TCP/IP

3. If you need to be able to boot to DOS to run DOS-based configuration utilities

4. It upgrades Windows NT to the level necessary to install IIS 4.0.

Post-Test Questions

1. The FAT DOS boot partition should be 10 to 20 MB in size if you decide to create one at all.

2. Because some older motherboards cannot perform automatic detection or assign interrupts (IRQs) and I/O addresses to devices, it is sometimes necessary to create a FAT partition that could be used to run MS-DOS configuration and diagnostic utilities.

3. Install NT 4.0, configure TCP/IP, install Service Pack 3 (or a more recent version), install Internet Explorer 4.01, install Windows NT Option Pack

4. IP address, subnet mask, default gateway address, DNS domain name, and DNS server addresses

5. ping.exe, tracert.exe, and ipconfig.exe

CHAPTER 4

Pre-Test Questions

1. 200 MB

2. NTFS

3. Your Web server's default document

Post-Test Questions

1. Pentium 66 MHz

2. 32 MB

3. \InetPub\wwwroot

4. World Wide Web Publishing Service

CHAPTER 5

Pre-Test Questions

1. It provides the user interface shell for management snap-ins, including Internet Service Manager and the Microsoft Transaction Server snap-in.

2. IUSR_*Computername*

3. If Directory Browsing is enabled, a directory listing is displayed. Otherwise, the user receives an error.

4. On the Computer object's property pages

Post-Test Questions

1. The first document in the Documents list that can be located

2. Configure a console with only the Internet Service Manager loaded. Share it in a directory with read-only permissions assigned to the marketing group.

3. Windows NT Challenge/Response

4. Provide the path to the file containing the disclaimer on the Documents property page of the Beta Products Web site.

5. Their e-mail address

6. Display the **FTP Site** property page and click on **Current Sessions**.

7. Change the directory style to UNIX on the Home Directory page of the FTP site.

CHAPTER 6

Pre-Test Questions

1. Full Control for Everyone

2. User Manager for Domains

3. IP Filtering

4. Certificate Server

Post-Test Questions

1. Be synchronized with the password specified in User Manager for Domains

2. It slows performance because a DNS reverse lookup must be performed for each access attempt.

3. She will be denied access.

4. He will be able to view the HTML document in his browser, but he will not be able to upload to the directory.

5. The link is set up to use the "http" protocol instead of the "https" protocol.

6. Install the CA Certificate on their browser.

7. Windows NT Challenge/Response

CHAPTER 7

Pre-Test Questions

1. To host multiple Web sites on a single computer

2. On the same computer as IIS 4.0 or on a different computer on the network

3. Response

4. Remote Data Services

5. Microsoft Transaction Server

Post-Test Questions

1. Trace messages

2. An ODBC data source name (DSN)

3. Read and Execute

4. Use host headers.

5. You need to configure name resolution for the existing customer's site.

6. Create a virtual directory that physically exists on a different computer. Run the application there.

7. Set appropriate content ratings.

8. Provide custom error messages on the appropriate directories.

9. HTTP Keep-Alives

CHAPTER 8

Pre-Test Questions

1. The ability to search a Web site for a document containing certain text

2. Web

3. Provide a content filter DLL

4. Yes

Post-Test Questions

1. Microsoft Management Console

2. 32 MB

3. .htm, .idq, .htx, and .htx

4. It decreases performance as the number gets larger.

5. Yes

6. Create a catalog for each site.

7. Yes

8. Add it to the noise.dat (or other noise word) file.

CHAPTER 9

Pre-Test Questions

1. The SMTP extension to the Internet Service Manager

2. In the Drop directory

3. NTFS

4. Everyone

Post-Test Questions

1. It is copied to the Badmail directory.

2. It allows you to override the SMTP site settings when delivering messages for a particular domain.

3. You can't. All mail for any local domain will be stored in the Drop directory.

4. It will decrease performance because every message received by your server will perform a DNS Reverse Lookup, even if it is just being forwarded.

5. It allows you to guarantee that replies will come to your SMTP server.

6. Set the NTFS permissions on the \nntpfile\root\control\rmgroup folder so that access is denied the IUSR_*Computername* user.

7. Add an expiration policy and associate it with that newsgroup.

8. The message will be sent to the default moderator.

CHAPTER 10

Pre-Test Questions

1. Index Server Manager (HTML)

2. Only the local computer

3. VBScript, JScript, or any other ActiveX scripting language

4. cscript.exe

Post-Test Questions

1. Internet Service Manager (HTML)

2. If you are using Internet Explorer and are already authenticated in as a user with administrative rights.

3. Add the host's IP Address to the list of computers that are granted access to the Administrative Web Site.

4. The Administrative Web Site's Port number

5. WWW Service

6. The timeout value for the Windows Script Host

7. Set a timeout value for the second script and run it using the .wsh file.

CHAPTER 11

Pre-Test Questions

1. A WebMap is a map of the hyperlinks, images, and other content on a Web site.

2. Tree View and Cyberbolic View

3. Log files

4. All instances run in the same process.

Post-Test Questions

1. Content Analyzer, Usage Analyzer, Posting Acceptor, Web Publishing Wizard

2. Usage Analyzer

3. Logging

4. Detail and Summary

5. HTTP

6. It optimizes how Windows NT allocates resources, based on expected traffic.

7. Entire server and per site

8. Chart

SELF STUDY

Glossary

Access Control Entry (ACE)

An access privilege assigned to a user or group. With Windows NT Server, the ACE is stored with the object being protected.

Access Control List (ACL)   Under Windows NT, the Access Control List contains user and group Access Control Entries.

Access Token

A Windows NT object describing a user account and group memberships. The Access Token is used in access validation.

Account SID

A unique value identifying a Windows NT or NT Server user, group account, or object.

Acknowledgment (ACK)

Acknowledgment. A response by the receiver of a communications message indicating the message was received correctly.

ActiveX

ActiveX is an effort by Microsoft to extend the limitations of the web page. It is the name of a technology that consists of Active Controls. ActiveX controls are designed so that they can be written in several different languages.

ActiveX provides interactivity to the page through controls (which are objects) and behavior (controlled by scripts). The ActiveX controls are applications that are downloaded to an Internet browser and then executed. The browser plays host to the file, allowing the availability of editing tools and functions. The behavior of ActiveX controls can be controlled using Visual Basic Script or JavaScript.

ActiveX is a method for creating dynamic Web pages. For example, ActiveX can create controls for animation, audio, and charts with live updating. The controls can be created with existing application development tools like Microsoft Visual Basic and Borland Delphi. Microsoft's Internet Studio also allows for the development of Web pages with ActiveX Controls.

ActiveX is sometimes misunderstood to be Object Linking and Embedding (OLE) under a new name. ActiveX differs from OLE in that the format is not as stringent which allows for smaller files that are suitable for transferring across a distributed network like the Internet.

Active Server Pages

A script that can be compiled and run by Internet Information Server. It is written using an Active scripting language, such as VBScript or JScript. Its output is usually plain HTML that can be displayed by any browser.

Address	A unique designation for the location of data, the identity of an intelligent device, or a logical network address. An address allows each device on a single communications line to respond to its own message.
Address mask	A bit mask used to select bits from an Internet (TCP/IP) address for subnet addressing. The mask is 32 bits long and selects the network portion of the Internet address and two or more bits of the local portion. It is sometimes called subnet mask.
Address resolution	A means for mapping logical addresses to physical addresses.
Address Resolution Protocol (ARP)	
	A protocol used between routers and nodes to determine the MAC or OSI physical layer address when the Network layer (IP) address is known.
Address space	A block of addresses that a process can assign to a particular block of data. The memory allocated from an address space must be backed by physical memory.
Algorithm	The steps that must be performed in order to complete a particular action.
Allocation	Associating a memory address with a block of data and setting aside physical memory to back it.
American National Standards Institute (ANSI)	
	A group of committees formed to establish voluntary commercial and government standards. The committee responsible for computing, data processing, and information technology is ANSI-X3, formerly named USASI (United States of America Standards Institute). ANSI is a member of the International Standards Organization (ISO).
American Standard Code for Information Interchange (ASCII)	
	The American Standard Code for Information Interchange (ASCII) character set is used to translate a byte into a character or number. Devised in 1968, ASCII is used for the purpose of standardizing the transmission of data to achieve hardware and software compatibility.
	ASCII has 128 Characters and uses seven of the eight bits to form these characters. The eighth bit is used for error checking.
	IBM developed the Extended Character Set, which contains 256 characters. In this character set, the eighth bit is used for special symbols, such as bullet points, fractions, and copyright or trademark symbols.
Anonymous FTP	An Internet utility which allows a user to connect to a remote computer as a guest to retrieve documents, files, programs, and other archived data without having a user ID or password on the host system. Users identify themselves as anonymous and skip local security checks.

ANSI character set	The American National Standards Institute 8-bit character set containing 256 characters.

Application Programming Interface (API)

An interface used when proprietary application programs have to talk to communications software or conform to protocols from another vendor's product. API also provides a standardized method of "vertical" communications. Apple Macintosh was the first computer to use the API concept.

Archie	Archie acts as a catalog and index of anonymous FTP sites on the Internet. It was developed by the McGill University School of Computer Science. Archie client sites can be publicly queried and Archie searches Internet FTP sites by program or document name (names appearing on FTP menus). It displays a list of all files containing the search string, as well as the computer address and directories holding the requested information. A user needs to know the exact file name or a substring of it to utilize Archie.
Argument	An argument is a value passed with a procedure containing values needed for procedure execution. The term command option may also be used.

Asymmetric Digital Subscriber Line (ADSL)

ADSL is a technology that increases the amount of data that can be transmitted in a single direction over Plain Old Telephone (POTS) lines. It relies on the fact that multimedia communication involves transmitting a large amount of data in one direction and only small amounts (for control) in the other.

Asynchronous	A form of communication where each transmitted character is preceded by a start bit and followed by a stop bit. This eliminates the need for a particular spacing or timing scheme between characters. Personal computers communicate asynchronously via a serial port.

Asynchronous Transfer Mode (ATM)

ATM is a high-speed (155 - 162 Mbps) communications transport facility capable of carrying voice, data, and video signaling. ATM forms the backbone for broadband ISDN networks.

Backbone	The primary connectivity mechanism of a hierarchical distributed system. All systems which have connectivity to an intermediate system on the backbone are assured connectivity to each other. This does not prevent systems from setting up private arrangements with each other to bypass the backbone for reasons of cost, performance, or security.
Background application	An application that is running but does not have focus and cannot receive user input.

Backup	1. Pertaining to a system, device, file, or facility that can be used to recover data in the event of a malfunction or loss of data.
	2. To copy information, usually onto diskette or tape, for safekeeping.
Bandwidth	The range of frequencies that can be transmitted through a particular circuit.
Baseband	Characteristic of any network technology that uses a single carrier frequency and requires all stations attached to the network to participate in every transmission.
Basic Input/Output System (BIOS)	Software or firmware embedded in chips on the circuit board which determines compatibility. Examples of these are IBM, Compaq, AMI, Award, and Phoenix.
Batch	A method of computer job processing where input is collected and run through the processing programs all at once and outputs produced in the form of files and reports. Batch is the opposite of interactive job processing, in which an operator at a terminal interacts with the processing program directly during data entry. Most personal computers employ interactive processing. Mainframes use batch processing.
Batch program	A text file that contains operating system commands. When you run a batch program, the operating system carries out the commands in the file as if you had typed them at the command prompt.
Baud	1. Abbreviation for Baudot, which gets its name from J. M. Emile Baudot (1845-1903), who invented the code. The Baudot code is a special set of binary characters using five bits per character to form 32 combinations. The number of combinations was increased to 62 through the use of two special shift characters. The Baudot code was mainly used to handle telex messages by common communications carriers such as Western Union. The main disadvantage of the Baudot code is its lack of an error-checking bit.
	2. Used commonly to refer to transfer rates on dial-up lines.
Baud Rate	The data transmission speed setting of a serial device. Typical rates include 300, 1200, 2400. Higher speeds, 9600, 19200, 38400, and 57600 baud, are achieved through data compression. Sometimes referred to simply as baud.
Bits per second (bps)	Usually the number of bits (binary digits) which can be transmitted or transferred each second.

Broadband	A technique for transmitting analog signals along a medium, such as a radio wave, also called wideband. Broadband signaling works the way radio and television work, by splitting up the available frequencies into different channels. The data is transmitted simultaneously and is represented by changes in amplitude, frequency, or phase of the signal.
	Broadband transmission can be used to transmit different combinations of data, voice, and video information along one physical cable with multiple communication channels of different frequencies. In LAN technology, broadband is a system in which multiple channels access a medium, usually coaxial cable, that has a large bandwidth (50 Mbps is typical) using radio-frequency modems.
Broadcast	1. A transmission of a message intended for general reception rather than for a specific station.
	2. In LAN technology, a transmission method used in bus topology networks that sends all messages to all stations even though the messages are addressed to specific stations.
	BrowserThis client program (software) is used to look at various Internet resources and retrieve information.
Bus	1. A pathway on which data travels. Examples of buses in a typical Macintosh computer include the expansion bus (NuBus or PCI), Apple Desktop Bus (ADB), and SCSI bus.
	2. LAN data pathway based on a single cable terminated at both ends.
Byte	Short for "binary digit eight." A unit of information consisting of usually eight bits. A file's size is measured in bytes or potential storage capacity is measured in bytes, but when dealing with very large numbers, the terms kilobyte, megabyte, or gigabyte are used.
Bytes per second (Bps)	Usually the number of bytes which can be transmitted or transferred each second.
Cache	An area of computer memory set aside for frequently used data to speed operations. Some caches are general purpose, while others are for specific operations. A disk cache is an area of system memory reserved for caching disk reads and writes. A CPU cache is a dedicated, high-speed memory array used to cache pending instructions.
Cache memory	This is a dedicated area of RAM memory used for temporary storage of data. It provides faster access and typically improves overall performance. This is a function of most operating systems and many applications. The specific content of the cache memory is operating system and application specific.

Central Processing Unit (CPU)

A highly complex set of electrical circuits that execute stored program instructions. The CPU consists of the control unit and the arithmetic/logic unit (ALU). In a personal computer, the CPU is typically a single, powerful microprocessor chip. CPUs can be measured by the amount of data they can read from memory in one access, the number of operations per second, the total amount of memory supported, and whether more than one job can be run at one time. Sophisticated computer systems can have more than one CPU operating within the same system.

Certified Information Rate (CIR)

When an ISP gives you a Certified Information Rate, it is a guarantee that your bandwidth will never be below that rate.

Checksum

Used in data communications to monitor the number of bits being transmitted between communications devices by means of a simple mathematical algorithm. The checksum is used to ensure that the full complement of bits is received successfully by the receiving device.

Child process

1. A process that is created by another process.

2. A dependent process; contrast with parent process.

Class

In Visual Basic, the Properties window provides you information about any instance of any object in your application. In this window, one can view the Object name, Detail properties, and the object's Class.

The Class defines an object's characteristics, properties, supported events, and methods.

You can change the properties at design time and, in most cases, at run time. This changes characteristics for that particular instance of the object, but the object still retains its class. In other words, it stays the same kind of object. The object class cannot be changed. If the object class were changed, it would then be a different type of object.

Client

1. A client is a workstation that requests services of another computer (server).

2. The portion of a client/server application providing the end-user interface (front-end).

Client/server applications

Applications that have been designed to operate in a network environment. They usually consist of a front-end client application and a back-end server application.

Commit

To specify that a transaction should be completed at once.

Common carrier	In the U.S., a private business or corporation that offers general communication services to the public such as telephone, teletype, or intercomputer communications. All common carriers operate under FCC guidelines and all services offered are subject to tariff schedules filed with and approved by the FCC.
Common Gateway Interface (CGI)	The Common Gateway Interface (CGI) is a transport protocol that allows interactivity to take place between a client and a host operating system through the Web by using Hypertext Transfer Protocol (HTTP). CGI is used for developing executable applications that allow the transmission to and from a World Wide Web server.
	These dynamic documents allow the receipt of data such as product registrations, requests for information, or an interface between a Web server and an application such as a database. CGI applications are multi-platform, and can be developed with Perl, C, C++, C Shell, and Korn Shell.
Communications rate	Also called the transfer rate or the transmission rate. The communications rate cannot exceed the maximum rate that both devices can handle.
Component	Hardware or software that is part of a functional unit.
Component Object Model	A binary specification that allows unrelated objects to communicate with each other. Also known as COM, the Component Object Model is the foundation of OLE technology.
Connection-oriented	The model of interconnection in which communication proceeds through three well-defined phases: connection establishment, data transfer, connection release. Examples include X.25, Internet TCP and OSI TP4, ordinary telephone calls.
Connectionless	The model of interconnection in which communication takes place without first establishing a connection. Sometimes called datagram. Examples: LANs, Internet IP and OSI CLNP, UDP, ordinary postcards.
Controller	An application that can be used to build solutions using ActiveX objects. Visual Basic is a controller.
Controller board	A device, also called a host bus adapter (HBA), that allows a computer to communicate with another device, such as a hard disk or tape drive. It manages input/output and regulates the operating of the other device.
Cracker	This refers to an individual who attempts to illegally break into a computer system. It is often confused with hacker, an expert at solving problems with computers.

Daemon program   Slang for a program not used explicitly, but normally loaded when the system is started, and lying dormant in the background awaiting the occurrence of some condition or conditions.

Data   1. In a database, facts about places, individuals, objects, events, concepts and so on.

2. Used to refer to any stored information.

Data Encryption Standard (DES)
This is an algorithm for coding and decoding data to ensure security.

Data integrity   The data quality that exists as long as accidental or malicious destruction, alteration, or loss of data does not occur.

Data modification   Changing data. Under SQL Server, this is through the SQL Statements INSERT, DELETE and UPDATE.

Data retrieval   Finding and displaying data in the database via queries (SELECT statements).

Data Transfer Rate   The data transfer rate determines how fast a drive or other peripheral can transfer data with its controller. The data transfer rate is a key measurement in drive performance.

Database   A collection of interrelated data stored together that is fundamental to a system or enterprise. A data structure for accepting, storing, and providing on-demand data for multiple independent users.

Database Management System (DBMS)
The software that manages the storage and access to the data in the databases.

Datagram   A message transmitted in a network, requiring no response or acknowledgment.

Datatype   1. In SQL Server, identifies the type of data stored in a column and allows for calculating the amount of storage required to hold such a column value.

2. In Visual Basic and other programming languages, defines the type of data that can be stored in a variable.

Debugger   An application that allows a programmer to see the statement that is being executed and the contents of variables or registers to facilitate the location of programming errors.

Default   One of a set of operating conditions that is automatically used when a device such as a printer or computer is turned on or reset. Pertaining to an attribute, value, or option when none is explicitly specified.

Defense Advanced Research Projects Agency (DARPA)
The U.S. government agency that funded the ARPANET.

Defense Communications Agency (DCA)

> The government agency responsible for the Defense Data Network (DDN).

Defense Data Network (DDN)

> This is a collection of networks, including MILNET, portions of the Internet, and classified networks used for military purposes. DDN is managed by the Defense Information Systems Agency (DISA).

Defense Information Systems Agency

> This is the U.S. government agency that manages the DDN portion of the Internet, including the MILNET. Currently, DISA administers the DDN, and supports the users assistance services of the DDN NIC. It was known as the Defense Communications Agency (DCA).

Dependent service   A service that will not run unless a prerequisite service is loaded.

Device   Any computer peripheral or hardware component (such as printer, mouse, monitor, or disk drive) capable of receiving and/or sending data, generally through the use of a device driver.

Device driver   Hardware-specific software that acts as an interface between the operating system and the hardware attached to a computer. Device drivers allow applications to communicate with hardware in a controlled and orderly fashion. A device driver is installed when the system is initialized, either by the operating system or through an installable device driver. Some examples of installable device drivers are mouse, graphical/video monitor, communications port, printer, and network interface card.

Dialup connection   This is a connection between computers which has been established over standard telephone lines.

Digital   Devices that represent data in the form of digits, based on the binary system where the binary digits (bits) are zero or one. Also, pertaining to data that consists of digits.

Digital Envelope   A digital envelope encrypts a packages for transfer across a network or across the Internet. It is encrypted with a public key and decrypted using the corresponding private key. A digital envelop ensures that only the appropriate recipient can decrypt the package.

Digital Signature   A digital signature verifies that the sender of a package is who they claim to be. A digital signature is encrypted with the private key and verified using the corresponding public key.

Directory   Part of a structure for organizing files on a disk. A directory can contain files and subdirectories. The structure of directories and subdirectories on a disk is called a directory tree. The top-level directory in a directory tree is the root directory.

Directory and file permissions

These permissions, assigned to users and groups, set user access level.

Directory path   Information including the server name, volume name, and name of each directory connected to the file system directory you need to access.

Directory permissions   Access permissions assigned to users or groups.

Disk Partitioning   Hard disk initialization takes care of the physical preparation of the hard disk. The logical disk preparation must also be completed. This involves partitioning the hard disk.

When a hard disk is partitioned, logical divisions are created on the hard disk. This makes the disk storage areas available to the system. Multiple partitions may be created on the same hard disk, including partitions for different operating systems. For example, a hard disk may set up as an OS/2 dual boot system with both DOS and OS/2 disk partitions.

Partitioning creates a partition table for each partition. The partition table contains information such as the partition type (operating system), size, and any logical drives configured within the partition.

When the disk is partitioned, the active partition must be identified. This is the partition that is read by the system during system startup. The active partition is also referred to as the boot (bootable) partition.

Disk partitions may be changed at any time, but extreme care must be taken. Creating, deleting, or modifying the size of disk partitions will cause all of the information in the affected partitions to be lost.

Distributed Component Object Model (DCOM)

DCOM is an extension to the Component Object Model that allows components to be run across machines. It is more optimal than its predecessor, Remote Automation, because it only marshals arguments once. DCOM is only available for 32-bit operating systems.

Distributed processing   A technique for implementing a set of information processing functions within multiple physically separate physical devices.

Domain   1. A logical grouping for file servers within a network, managed as an integrated whole.

2. In the Internet, a domain is a part of the naming hierarchy. The domain name is a sequence of names (separated by periods) that identify host sites. For example: galenp@mail.msen.com

Domain Controller   Server within a domain and storage point for domain-wide security information.

Domain name	A unique domain name designates a location on the Internet. Domain Names always have two or more parts separated by periods. The leftmost part is the most specific, and the part on the right is the most general. A given machine may have more than one Domain Name, but a given Domain Name points to only one machine.

Domain Name System (DNS)

The Domain Name System (DNS) is a hierarchical, distributed method of organizing system and network names on the Internet. DNS administratively groups hosts (systems) into a hierarchy of authority that allows addressing and other information to be widely distributed and maintained. A big advantage of DNS is that using it eliminates dependence on a centrally-maintained file that maps host names to addresses.

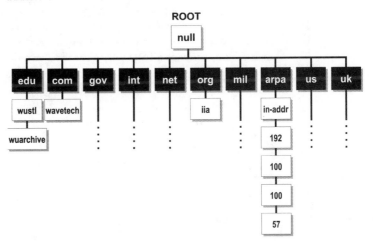

The diagram above shows the hierarchical organization of domain names. The bottom level of the tree structure contains the names of companies or even machines within a company. For example, consider wuarchive.wustl.edu. The bottom of the tree is wuarchive. This is the name of a particular piece of equipment within the wustl domain, which is under the edu domain.

The name of a particular domain is read from the bottom of the tree up to the root. The root is unnamed and is represented with just a period. For example, wavetech.com is a particular domain. If we were to give the fully qualified domain name (FQDN), we would include the unnamed root, so it would be written as "wavetech.com". The final period at the end of the name specifies the root of the tree. The root must always be specified for the host equipment. To make it easy, most software will convert a domain name to an FQDN for the user, by appending any missing domain names all the way to the root.

The top of the tree lists the top-level-domains. These are reserved names. Every domain will have a top-level domain by type or country.

Some of the types are com (commercial), edu (educational), gov (governmental), mil (military), net (network provider), org (non-profit organization), and int (international).

The two-letter country top-level-domains identify the country of a particular Internet site. Most of the countries have formed a similar structure for categorizing site types under the country domains. There is a two-letter country domain for every country. Examples include uk (United Kingdom), za (South Africa), us (United States), de (Germany), fr (France), hk (Hong Kong), jp (Japan), br (Brazil), and mx (Mexico).

When a domain name is registered with the InterNIC, it is added to the tree under a particular top-level-domain. The company registering the name is given control over the sub-domain they've registered. Because control of the sub-domains is given over to the individual registries, they must provide a DNS Server for their own domains. The DNS Server provides the domain name to TCP/IP address resolution. When an Internet user refers to a particular host on the Internet by name, there must be a mapping made between the name entered and the TCP/IP address required for creation of the data packets.

Download

A process where a file is transferred from a host computer to a user's computer. Download is the opposite of upload.

Dynamic link library (DLL)

A module that is linked at load time or run time.

Encryption

Encryption involves encoding a packet's data prior to transmission to ensure data security. The Data Encryption Standard (DES) is an algorithm used for coding and decoding data for security purposes.

Envelope

An envelope is the destination point of an electronic mail message. In other words, the electronic mail message recipient's address.

Event

An action that results in a message being sent or activity in a program. An event can be generated by a user, an application, or the operating system.

Fault tolerance

Operating systems features designed to accommodate failures, therefore improving disk reliability. Related terms are Disk Mirroring, Disk Duplexing, and Disk Striping with Parity.

Fiber Distributed Data Interface (FDDI)

A LAN (Local Area Network) specification from ANSI X3T9.5 committee on computer input/output interface standards. FDDI uses fiber optic cables with token-passing access in a ring topology and transmits at 100 megabits per second across a cable length of up to 62.1 miles with up to 1.24 miles between nodes.

Fiber Optic Cable

Fiber optic networking cable is comprised of light-conducting glass or plastic fibers that are surrounded by a protective cladding and a durable outer sheath.

Fiber Optic Cable

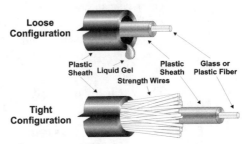

Fiber Optic Cable Connector

The bulk of the expense that characterizes fiber optic cabling systems can be attributed to the interface devices that convert computer signals to and from light pulses. The light pulses are generated by light emitting diodes (LEDs) or injection laser diodes (ILDs). Photo diodes reconvert the light pulses to electrical signals.

Data transfer rates from 100 Mbps to over 2 Gbps are supported at distances from 2 to 25 Km.

Because it doesn't carry electric signals, fiber-optic cabling is ideal for use in hazardous, high-voltage, or secure environments.

Common fiber optic cables are classified based on the diameter of the light-conducting core. Thicker cores allow the signal to reflect from side-to-side and are thus referred to as multi-mode, while narrow core fiber cable is referred to as single-mode.

Most LAN fiber networks use 62.5-micron fiber cable.

There are advantages to using fiber optic cables. It supports extremely high bandwidth, is immune to Electro-Magnetic Interference (EMI), has extremely low attenuation, and is reliable and secure.

There are also disadvantages to this cabling scheme. It is fragile and requires careful handling. Installation is complex, tedious, and expensive. Also, the component parts are relatively expensive.

Fiber optics

Transmission of data in the form of light pulses produced by a laser or light-emitting diode (LED) through glass fiber, plastic, or other electrically non-conductive material. Fiber optics provide high-speed, long-distance transmission at low power.

File Allocation Table (FAT)

> The File Allocation Table (FAT) system is the file system used by DOS machines. Some other operating systems also support the FAT system.
>
> In order to organize your disk, DOS divides it into two parts. The first part is a small system area that DOS uses to keep track of key information about the disk. This system area uses approximately 2% of a floppy diskette, and approximately several tenths of a percent of a hard disk. The second part is the data storage area, which represents the bulk of the disk area.
>
> The system area is divided into three parts called the boot record, FAT, and root directory.

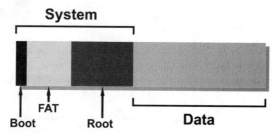

> The boot record holds a very short program that performs the job of beginning the loading of the operating system into the computer's memory.
>
> The next part of the system portion of a disk is called the File Allocation Table (FAT). The operating system divides the disk storage area into logical units called clusters. The FAT contains an entry for each data cluster on the disk. A file's FAT entry points to the first cluster for the file. Each cluster points to the next cluster assigned to the file. The final cluster contains a delimiter of FFF (hex) which signals the end of the file.

File caching

> This improves file access time by using the RAM memory to store recently accessed files.

File compression

> More data can be stored on server hard disks by compressing files that are not being used. NetWare and Windows NT support identifying files and directories to be compressed. With DOS, Windows, and Windows 95, disk partitions are identified for compression.

File Transfer Protocol (FTP)

> The File Transfer Protocol (FTP) is a part of the TCP/IP suite that is used to transfer files between any two computers, provided they support FTP. The two computers do not have to be running the same operating system.

In general, people use FTP to move files from one account or machine to another, or to perform what is called an "anonymous FTP." For example, if storage space on a particular machine is low, the user can free up storage space by using FTP to move the files to a machine with more space. Another reason to move a file to a different account is to print a file to a particular printer. If the file is on a machine that cannot access the desired printer, it must be moved to a machine that does have access.

Whatever the reason for the transfer, FTP requires the user to know the proper login name and the password for both computers to move files between them.

While an anonymous FTP also moves from one computer to another, it has two main differences. An anonymous FTP session usually involves gathering files that a user does not have. Anonymous FTP does not require the user to know a login name and password to access the remote computer.

The Internet has many anonymous FTP sites. Each site consists of an FTP server, a large number of files, and guest login names such as "anonymous" or "FTP." This allows any user to visit these systems and copy files from the FTP site to their personal computer. With the appropriate authority, users can copy files from their system to an anonymous FTP site.

Despite the variety of FTP servers and clients on the Internet and the different operating systems they use, FTP servers and clients generally support the same basic commands. This standard command set allows users to accomplish tasks such as looking at a list of files in the current directory of the remote system, regardless of the operating system in use. Other common commands allow users to change directories, get specific file information, copy files to a local machine, and change parameters.

Graphical web browsers transform the traditional character-based, command-line FTP interface into a point-and-click environment. The only way a user may know that they are in the middle of an FTP session is that the Universal Resources Locator (URL) box in the browser will change from an address that begins with "http://..." to "ftp://...".

Finger

Finger is an Internet software program that retrieves information and allows users to locate a particular user on the local or remote system. It typically shows the full name, last login time, idle time, terminal line, and terminal location (where applicable). In addition, it may display plan and project files defined by the user.

Finger is also sometimes used to give access to non-personal information, but the most common use is to see if a person has an account at a particular Internet site. Many sites do not allow incoming Finger requests.

Fire Wall

A fire wall is a combination of hardware and software that separates a LAN into two or more parts for security purposes. Today, fire walls are commonly used to prevent unauthorized access to a network from the Internet.

Frame relay

Commonly referred to as "bandwidth on demand." Unlike other transmission protocols or processes, frame relay offers users significant benefits over other transmission services, such as T1, by eliminating the processing overhead associated with packets of data moving between packet-forwarding devices.

Gateway

Gateways are the primary linkage between mixed environments such as PC-based LANs and host environments such as SNA.

Gateways generally operate at all seven layers of the OSI Reference Model. They may provide full content conversion between two environments, such as ASCII to EBCDIC, as well as other application and presentation layer conversions.

Gateway Functionality

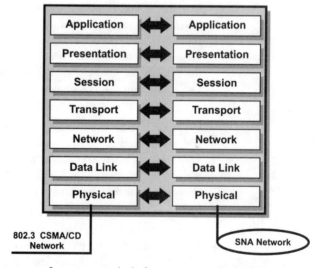

Other types of gateways include fax gateways, which allow users to send and receive faxes from their workstations. These may also be integrated with mail service gateways, which allow communications between users of different mail systems.

Global Group	A group definition allowing permission assignments to local machines or other domains through local group membership of the global group.
Gopher	A hierarchical, menu-based information service developed at the University of Minnesota. It provides access to information collections across the Internet by taking file directories and turning them into easily navigable menus. Gopher also makes file transfer convenient.
	Gopher functions as a client server that connects the user to the menu item(s) selected from the gopher server menu. The user must have a Gopher Client program.
	Although Gopher spread rapidly across the globe in only a couple of years, it is being largely supplanted by Hypertext, also known as WWW (World Wide Web). There are thousands of Gopher Servers on the Internet and they will remain for a while.
Graphics Interchange Format (GIF)	
	Established by Compuserve, GIF is a format for graphics files. In Web documents, IMG links often point to GIF files.
Group	A collection of users. All members get, as implicit rights, any rights assigned to a group.
Hacker	A hacker is a person who is an expert at solving problems with computers. The term is often confused with cracker, which is the name given to a person who illegally attempts to access computer systems or has destructive intentions.
Header	A header contains identifying information.
	Electronic mail message headers contain the message originator's name and address, receiver, subject, date, etc.
	A packet header carries the source and destination addresses along with other information.
Hexadecimal	A base-16 numeric notation system that specifies addresses in computer memory. In hexadecimal notation, the decimal numbers 0 through 15 are represented by the decimal digits 0 through 9 and the characters A through F (A=decimal 10, B=decimal 11, and so on).
Hit count	The number of objects found in the site database that match the query criteria.
Home page	A document coded in HTML (Hypertext Markup Language) that acts as a top level document for an Internet site or a topic. A home page contains hypertext links to related documents.
Hop	Describes routing through a network. A hop is a data packet moving through routers from the point of origination to the destination.

Hop count	The number of cable segments a message packet passes through between its source and network or internetwork destination. The destination can be no more than 16 hops from the source.
Host	A computer that is remotely accessible and provides information or services for users on a network. It is quite common to have one host machine provide several services, such as WWW and USENET. A host computer on the Internet can be accessed by using an application program such as electronic mail, telnet, or FTP. A host computer may also be a bulletin board.
Hostname	The name given to a computer that identifies it as an Internet or other site.
Href	In a link tag, href denotes the address of the target of the link.
HTML Editor	An HTML editor is a tool that automates and simplifies HTML document preparation.
Hyperlink	Words, phrases, images, or characters highlighted in bold indicate connections in a given document to information within another document. The user also has the option to underline these hyperlinks.
Hypermedia	Hypermedia is the name for richly formatted documents containing a variety of information types such as textual, image, movie, and audio. These information types are easily found through hyperlinks.
Hypertext	Hypertext allows users to move from one site or place in a document to another. Hypertext links in World Wide Web documents link the user from terms in one document to the site referenced in the original document.

HyperText Markup Language (HTML)

Standard Generalized Markup Language (SGML) is a worldwide method of representing document formatting. It is also a broad language that is used to define particular markup languages for particular purposes.

The language that the Web uses is a specific application of SGML called HyperText Markup Language (HTML). As HTML has evolved, it has moved away from the SGML conventions. With newer versions of HTML, there has been some effort to rebuild the relationship between the two languages. Because of the worldwide investment in SGML, future versions of HTML will most likely comply with SGML even more closely.

HyperText Markup Language (HTML) is the standard language that the Web uses for creating and recognizing hypermedia documents. Web documents are most often written in HTML and normally have an .html or .htm extension.

Languages such as HTML follow the SGML format and allow document creators to separate document content from document presentation. As a markup language, HTML is more concerned with the structure of a document than with the appearance.

HTML documents are standard 7-bit ASCII files with formatting codes that contain information about layout (document titles, paragraphs, breaks, lists) and hyperlinks. Although most browsers will display any document that is written in plain text, by creating documents using HTML, writers can include links to other files, graphics, and various types of media.

HTML specifies a document's logical organization. While a formatting language, such as Rich Text Format (RTF), indicates typeface, font size, and style of the text in a document, HTML uses tags to mark the headings, normal paragraphs, and lists (and whether or not they are numbered).

While the HTML standard supports simple hypermedia document creation and layout, it is not capable of supporting some of the complex layout techniques found in traditional document publishing. As the Web and HTML gain additional momentum and are used by more people for more purposes, it will most likely gain some of the functionality used in desktop publishing.

HTML has been added to most major Internet browsers. Examples include Netscape Navigator and Microsoft Internet Explorer.

HTML is an evolving language. Different web browsers recognize slightly different HTML tags. Some Web document creators attempt to get around formatting limitations in HTML by using graphics and browser-specific HTML tags. The creators do this in an attempt to make their documents look a certain way in a particular browser. Though approximately 80% of all users view web documents with Netscape or Microsoft browsers, browser-specific documents look bad or can be inaccessible with the other browser.

Even with comprehensive capabilities, HTML is still an easy-to-use language, and is simple enough to type directly into a word processing application without the use of an HTML editor.

Hypertext Transfer Protocol (HTTP)

HTTP is a set of directions for Web servers that tells them how to respond to various events initiated by users. HTTP is the most important protocol used in the World Wide Web (WWW).

The simplest example is clicking on a link to another part of the same file. The server receives the information that the link has been activated, and sends back the designated part of the file for display.

An HTTP client program is required on one end, and an HTTP server program on the other.

Index	A database object that provides efficient access to rows in a table, based on key values.
Inheritance	The means by which a child object can get information from its parent.

Institute of Electrical and Electronics Engineers (IEEE)

A professional ANSI-accredited body of scientists and engineers based in the U.S. IEEE promotes standardization, and consults to the American National Standards Institute on matters relating to electrical and electronic development. The IEEE 802 Standards Committee is the leading official standard organization for LAN (Local Area Networks).

Integrated Services Digital Network (ISDN)

A special kind of telecommunications network designed to handle more than just data. Using existing telephone lines and computer networks, integrated networks can handle video, text, voice, data, facsimile images, graphics, etc.

Integrity	Data consistency and accuracy.
Interface	1. A shared boundary between two functional units, defined by functional characteristics, signal characteristics, and other characteristics, as appropriate. Also, any of the electrical and logical devices that permit computers and peripherals to be interconnected.
	2. A contract between an object and its users.

International Standards Organization (ISO)

Founded in 1946, the ISO promotes the development of international standards for the computer, communications, and other fields. ISO members are the standards organizations of 89 countries. The United States representative is the American National Standards Institute (ANSI).

Internet

An international computer network of networks that connect government, academic and business institutions. Networks on the Internet include MILNET, NSFnet, and other backbone networks, as well as mid-level networks and stub (local) networks.

Internet networks communicate using TCP/IP (Transmission Control Protocol/Internet Protocol). The Internet connects colleges, universities, military organizations and contractors, corporations, government research laboratories, and individuals.

Although parts of the Internet operate under single administrative domains, the Internet as a whole reaches around the globe, connects computers from personal computers to supercomputers, and is not administered by any single authority. The Internet in July of 1995 roughly connected 60,000 independent networks into a vast global Internet.

Used as a descriptive term, an Internet is a collection of interconnected packet-switching networks. Any time you connect two or more networks together, you have an Internet—as in inter-national or inter-state.

Internet Activities Board (IAB)

The IAB is the technical body that oversees the development of the Internet suite of protocols commonly referred to as "TCP/IP." It has two task forces, the IRTF and the IETF, each charged with investigating a particular area.

Internet Address   A 32-bit value written or displayed in numbers that specify a particular network and node on that network.

Internet Control Message Protocol (ICMP)

ICMP is used for error reporting and recovery, and is a required component of any IP implementation.

Internet Engineering Steering Group (IESG)

The IESG is the executive committee of the Internet Engineering Task Force (IETF).

Internet Engineering Task Force (IETF)

One of the task forces of the IAB, the IETF is responsible for solving short-term engineering needs of the Internet. It has over 40 Working Groups.

Internet Gateway Routing Protocol (IGRP)

The Internet Gateway Routing Protocol is a proprietary IGP used by Cisco System's routers.

Internet Information Server (IIS)

Microsoft Internet Information Server is a network file and application server that transmits information in Hypertext Markup Language.

Internet Protocol (IP)   IP is the OSI layer 3 routed protocol used to transmit packetized information on a TCP/IP network.

Internet Relay Chat (IRC) IRC is an Internet protocol that supports real-time conversations between Internet users worldwide.

Internet Research Task Force (IRTF)

> The Internet Research Task Force is one of the task forces of the Internet Activities Board (IAB) that is responsible for research and development of the Internet protocol suite.

Internet Server Application Programming Interface (ISAPI)

> An API that is used to build server-side filters and extensions. When IIS starts up, it loads each ISAPI component into memory. This is the copy of the component that IIS will use each time a user causes the component to run. This is more optimal than CGI applications, which load a new copy every time they are used.

Internet Service Provider (ISP)

> Internet Service Providers are companies that provide an Internet connection for educational institutions, individuals, companies, and organizations.

Internetwork

> Two or more networks connected by a router.

InterNIC

> The Internet Network Information Center (InterNIC) was developed in 1993 by General Atomics, AT&T, and NSI to provide information services to Internet users. It offers a reference desk that provides networking information, referrals to other resources, and associate users with their local NICs. It also provides coordination to share information and activities with U.S. and international organizations; and education services to train midlevel and campus NICs, and to end users to promote Internet use.

Interoperability

> The ability to use products from different vendors in the same system. Communication protocols, such as IP or AFP, can be used in ODI to process information from the network. The user does not have to know each protocol's required method of packet transmission. Interoperability also means an application can share files, even when running on different platforms, such as Macintosh or UNIX.

Interprocess communication

> The exchange of information between processes by means of messages.

Interrupt Request Lines (IRQ)Interrupt Request Lines are normally referred to as IRQ lines, and each line requires a separate IRQ number. Many PC add-in boards and devices require a unique dedicated IRQ line. Some IRQs are assigned to system devices.

> The original IBM PC was an 8-bit system with eight available IRQ lines numbered 0 through 7. These lines support the system timer, keyboard, COM and LPT ports, and the floppy disk controller.

With the 16-bit IBM AT came eight additional IRQ lines which "cascade" through IRQ2. These IRQ lines support the Real Time Clock, hard disk controller, math coprocessor, and other devices. Examples of devices that use these IRQ lines are VGA and network adapters, CD-ROM drives, and SCSI controllers.

Some COM ports share IRQ lines. All odd-numbered COM ports (COM1, COM3, etc.) share IRQ 4, while all even numbered COM ports share IRQ 3.

Intranet

An Intranet is a private Internet, usually within a company, for facilitating information sharing. It looks and acts just like the public Internet.

IP Address

Each host in the network is assigned a unique IP address for each network connection (installed network adapter). The IP address is used to identify packet source and destination hosts.

An IP address is a 32-bit address, written as four octets (bytes) separated by periods. For example, 195.143.67.2.

This way of representing an IP address is also known as dotted decimal notation. Each address will also have an associated subnet mask, dividing the address into its network prefix and host suffix. For example, you might have the following defined as a subnet mask: 255.255.255.0. The subnet mask is used to identify the network and host portions of the address.

The network portion identifies where the host is located, and the host portion identifies the device connected to that network.

When dealing with a network the size of the Internet, address assignments must be carefully coordinated. With millions of hosts operating on thousands of networks, the potential for duplicate addresses is significant. The job of coordinating Internet IP addresses is given to the Network Information Center.

An assigned address is only required if your network is connected to the Internet. If connected to the Internet, your network address will be assigned through the Internetwork Network Information Center, or InterNIC.

To get an Internet address, contact the InterNIC at InterNIC Registration Services, c/o Network Solutions, Inc., 505 Huntmar Park Drive, Herndon, Virginia 22070, (800) 444-4345, or at hostmaster@internic.net.

An organization is assigned a network address. The organization can further divide this into its own subnets and assign the host addresses.

Rather than going to the InterNIC, it is more likely that an organization will work through a local provider for address assignment. The organization will then subdivide the address, if necessary, and assign host addresses.

IP datagram

The IP datagram is the fundamental unit of information passed across the Internet. It contains source and destination addresses, along with data and a number of fields which define the length of the datagram, the header checksum, and flags to indicate whether the datagram can be (or has been) fragmented.

Java

Java is a programming language with a colorful history and a meteoric rise. Java was not designed for the Internet or World Wide Web. It was developed by a team at Sun Microsystems which was developing software for consumer electronics.

Existing languages like C and C++ were inadequate for the purposes of the software the team was developing. C and C++ programs need to be compiled for particular computer chips. When a new chip is released, C and C++ programs must be recompiled to run on the new chip. These programs are not flexible enough to be moved to new software libraries.

In the consumer electronics market, pricing of components is crucial and chips are often replaced with newer, more cost-effective chips at a rapid rate. This swapping of chips is not the ideal environment for C and C++ programs.

Backward compatibility is an issue in consumer electronics because it is not uncommon for somebody to have a TV that is five or ten years old. Reliability is another issue because consumer electronics normally have to be replaced if a component goes bad.

Java was originally named Oak by James Gosling, who was the team leader for the original development project. The name was inspired by a large oak tree outside of Gosling's office. It was discovered that there was another programming language called Oak, and a new name had to be coined for the language. The name Java was an inspiration after some of the team members visited a coffee shop near their office.

The Java market is rapidly expanding with many companies licensing Java technology for integration into their products. For browsers, Netscape Communications Corporation added Java support to their Netscape Navigator 2.0 browser giving Netscape Navigator users the opportunity to view Java-enhanced Web pages. Other browser vendors, like Microsoft, are adding Java support in their browsers. Microsoft has also licensed Java for inclusion in future versions of Windows.

Sun Microsystems has started a new business unit called Javasoft, and has announced the release of new Java development tools. Java WorkShop is a set of Java development tools designed to work within a Java-capable browser. With Java WorkShop, developers have the ability to design, test, and deploy Java applications for the Web. Another new product is Internet WorkShop that includes Java WorkShop, Visual WorkShop for C++, and a Network Object Environment (NOE) for development of powerful Web applications.

Joint Photographic Experts Group (JPEG)

JPEG is a format for storing a graphics file in digital format, and is similar to GIF. It is a standard for images on the Web.

The names of jpeg-formatted files often end in ".jpg". The main differences between gif and jpeg are the manner in which data is compressed. Gif uses lossless compression, while jpeg uses lossy compression. The bit depth is 8-bit for gif, and up to 24-bit for jpeg. More information is available in the JPEG FAQs on the Internet.

Jughead

A jughead is a server that maintains a database of menu items at a gopher site. It allows users to search the site.

Jughead is an acronym for Jonzy's Universal Gopher Hierarchy Excavation and Display.

Kilobit (Kb)

In computing, it refers to 1024 bits. (A bit is the basic unit for storing data in primary storage.) Kilobit is used mainly to express the speed of data transmission.

Kilobits per second (Kbps) Thousands of bits per second.

Kilobyte (KB)

In computing, it refers to 1024 bytes. (A byte is a unit of information consisting of 8 bits.) Kilobyte is mainly used to express the capacity of primary storage.

Kilobytes per second (KBps)

Thousands of bytes per second.

Knowbot

A computer program that automates the searching and gathering of data from distributed databases. The general term is sometimes shortened to bot.

Leased-line

A telephone line reserved for the exclusive use of leasing customers, without interexchange switching arrangements. Also called a Private Line.

Legacy

Older, non-plug and play hardware in use.

Link	Any part of a Web page that is connected to something else. Clicking on or selecting a link will make that something else appear. (This is one major difference between virtual reality and real reality.) The first part of the URL named in a link denotes the method or kind of link. The methods include: file (for local files), ftp, gopher, http, mailto, news, and wais (for some kinds of search).
Local Area Network (LAN)	A Local Area Network (LAN) is a group of computers running specialized communications software, and joined through an external data path.
	A LAN will cover a small geographic area, usually no larger than a single building. The computers have a direct high-speed connection between all workstations and servers, and share hardware resources and data files. A LAN has centralized management of resources and network security.
	PC-based networks can trace their heritage back to what are now often referred to as legacy systems. These systems were mainframe and minicomputer hosts accessed through dumb terminals.
	There are a number of similarities between LANs and these legacy systems, such as centralized storage and backup, access security, and central management of resources. There are, however, a number of differences.
	Traditional host systems are characterized by centralized processing, dumb terminals, custom applications, high expansion costs and management overhead. LANs are characterized by distributed processing, intelligent workstations (PCs), and off-the-shelf applications. LANs are modular, inexpensive to expand, and have more moderate management costs.
Local Group	When discussing Windows NT Server Domains, it is a group definition supporting local domain resource management. When discussing Workstations, it is a group definition supporting local management of a Windows NT workstation.
Locks	A mechanism to prevent multiple concurrent user updates from interfering with one another and causing update anomalies.
Lycos	Lycos is a search engine on the Internet located at www.lycos.com.
Lynx	Lynx is a text-based interface to the World Wide Web.
Mail gateway	A machine that connects to two or more electronic mail systems, including those on different networks, and transfers mail messages among them.
Mailbox	An area on a computer used to receive and store electronic mail messages.

Mailto | In a URL, mailto indicates a link that will allow a user to send e-mail to the person whose address follows in the URL.

Management Information Base (MIB)
A collection of objects that can be accessed via a network management protocol.

Megabit (Mb) | 1,048,576 bits.

Megabits per second (Mbps)
Millions of bits per second (bps).

Megabyte (MB) | 1,048,576 bytes.

Megabytes per second (MBps)
Millions of bytes per second (Bps).

Megahertz (MHz) | A million cycles per second. A CPU that operates at 200 Mhz uses a clock oscillator that runs at 200 million cycles per second.

Memory | A hardware component of a computer system that can store information and applications for later retrieval. Types of memory are RAM (Random Access Memory), ROM (Read Only Memory), conventional, expanded, and extended memory.

Message Store | A server component of an electronic mail system. The Postoffice is the message store under Microsoft Mail.

Message Transfer Agent (MTA)
Electronic mail component which transfers messages between message stores. The external program is the MTA for Microsoft Mail.

Method | A defined behavior for a particular interface. An object that owns an interface must implement its methods.

Military Network (MILNET)
Originally part of the ARPANET, MILNET was split off in 1984 to make it possible for military installations to have reliable network service, while ARPANET continued to be used for research.

Million Instructions Per Second (MIPS)
A measure of the speed of execution of a computer's central processsing unit.

Modem | Modem is an abbreviation for modulator/demodulator. A modem is a peripheral device that permits a personal computer, microcomputer, or mainframe to receive and transmit data in digital format across voice-oriented communications links such as telephone lines.

Mosaic | A software program that supports text and GUI (Graphical User Interface) access to the World Wide Web. Mosaic supports hypertext links to graphics and text.

Mosaic was developed at the National Center for Supercomputing Applications at the University of Illinois. It was the first WWW browser that was available for the Macintosh, Windows, and UNIX with a common user interface. Mosaic started the popularity of the Web.

The source code to Mosaic has been licensed by several companies and several other pieces of software are as good or better than Mosaic. The most notable are Netscape and Internet Explorer.

Motherboard	The electronic circuit board containing the primary computer components such as CPU, RAM, ROMs, etc.
Multi-homed host	A computer connected to more than one physical data link. The data links may or may not be attached to the same network.
Multiprocessing	The ability to execute more than one thread simultaneously.

Multipurpose Internet Mail Extensions (MIME)

The standard for attaching non-text files to standard Internet mail messages. Non-text files include graphics, spreadsheets, formatted word-processor documents, sound files, etc. An e-mail program is said to be "MIME Compliant" if it can both send and receive files using the MIME standard. When non-text files are sent using the MIME standard they are converted (encoded) into text, although the resulting text is not really readable. Generally speaking the MIME standard is a way of specifying both the type of file being sent (e.g., a QuicktimeTM video file), and the method that should be used to turn it back into its original form. Besides e-mail software, the MIME standard is also universally used by Web Servers to identify the files they are sending to Web Clients; in this way new file formats can be accommodated simply by updating the Browsers' list of pairs of MIME-Types and appropriate software for handling each type.

Multitasking	A mode of operation that provides for the concurrent performance or interleaved execution of two or more tasks.
Multithreaded application	An executable that activates more than one thread of execution—for example, a thread to handle user input and one to perform background operations.
Name resolution	The process of mapping a node name into the corresponding network address.
Named pipe	An Application Program Interface which allows an unlimited number of sessions on the network. Named pipe is a much higher-level interface than NetBIOS (Network Basic Input/Output System). A single named pipe function is equal to many NetBIOS calls.

National Center for Supercomputing Applications (NCSA)

NCSA is located at the University of Illinois in Urbana-Champaign, Illinois.

National Information Standards Organization

> An organization that develops standards and promotes the voluntary use of technical standards in libraries, publishing, and information services.

National Institute of Standards and Technology (NIST)

> U.S. governmental agency that assists in developing standards. Formerly the National Bureau of Standards.

National Research and Education Network (NREN)

> A U.S. national computer network outlined in the initiative signed into law in December 1991. NREN is to be built on NSFnet, the National Science Foundation Network connecting national and regional networks. NREN will be able to transmit data at more than 40 times the rate of NSFnet.

National Science Foundation (NSF)

> The National Science Foundation is a U.S. government agency that promotes the advancement of science.

> This foundation funded NSFnet, a high-speed network connecting supercomputing and research facilities in the United States. NFSnet also has connections to Canada, Mexico, Europe, and other geographic locations.

> NSFnet is part of the Internet.

National Science Foundation Network (NSFnet)

> NSFnet is an Internet backbone that began as a project with the National Science Foundation in cooperation with corporate partners IBM, MCI, and the Michigan Strategic Fund. It is now owned by America On-line.

> NSFnet was established to enable researchers and scientists working on complex problems to instantaneously access library resources, supercomputer computation, and databases as well as to exchange information with colleagues worldwide.

> NSFnet links regional networks to each other and to the NSF-sponsored supercomputer networks. These other networks include BARRNET (Stanford University), NCAR/USAN (National Center for Atmospheric Research), NorthWestNet (University of Washington), SDSCNET (San Diego Supercomputer Center), Sesquinet (Rice University), Westnet (Colorado State University), MIDnet (University of Nebraska-Lincoln), NDSA/UIUC (University of Illinois, CNSF (Cornell Theory Center), JvNC (John von Neumann Supercomputer Center), NYSERNet (Syracuse, New York), PSCnet (Pittsburgh Supercomputing Center), and SURAnet (University of Maryland). These networks are based on TCP/IP and are part of the Internet.

Netiquette	Netiquette describes the code of conduct or etiquette governing personal behavior on the Internet. For example, it is considered poor netiquette to use all upper-case letters for casual conversations or messages. Upper case normally conveys the meaning that the originator is shouting angrily.
Netscape Communications Corporation	
	Netscape Communications is the company that produces Netscape Navigator and Netscape Server products.
Network	A group of computers and other devices connected together so they can communicate with each other.
Network adapter	The card that allows a computer to interface with the network. Also known as a Network Interface Card (NIC).
Network address	A network address can also be the network portion of an IP address. For a Class A network, the network address is the first byte of the IP address. For a Class B network, the network address is the first two bytes of the IP address. For a Class C network, the network address is the first three bytes of the IP address. In each case, the remainder is the host address.
Network drive	The common name for a logical drive.
Network Information Center (NIC)	
	A resource providing network administrative support as well as information services and support to users. The most famous of these on the Internet is the InterNIC, which is where new domain names are registered.
Network Interface Card (NIC)	
	Workstations communicate with each other and the network server via this circuit board which is installed in each computer. It can also be referred to as an NIC, LAN card, or network card.
Network News	Network news (also called newsgroups) is a misleading name for this popular function of the Internet. Network news has no relation to the world or local news reports. Although it includes news coverage, a newsgroup's function is far broader than simply reporting events.
	Network news is made up of discussion groups, or forums, where Internet users can browse a multitude of articles (postings) that cover a variety of topics. USENET is a term often used in conjunction with Network News. Network News grew out of USENET, which is a UNIX function that services discussion groups. The two terms are generally used interchangeably.

Users can choose articles on a variety of subjects. In 1995, over 7,000 topics were covered by newsgroups, and new groups are constantly being creating. The group "new.announce.newuser" lists new newsgroup additions. Though the address is similar to the domain name system, it has no relation to domain names. This format is just a convention for identifying newsgroups.

Because there are so many topics, some Internet providers will not download all the possible newsgroups. For example, many providers prohibit any newsgroup with a name that includes the words "sex" or "alt" (which stands for alternative). System administrators also decide how long to maintain postings on network servers. A day's worth of postings may require 50 megabytes or more of disk space. It is unusual for administrators to keep articles that are older than one or two weeks.

The major newsgroup divisions are biz (business and commerce), comp (computers, computer science, and software), sci (scientific subjects, such as astronomy and biology), soc (socializing and social issues), talk (debate on various topics), news (general news and topical subjects), rec (arts, hobbies, and recreational activities), alt (extremely varied subjects), and misc (topics that don't fall under the other categories). These abbreviations are the first part of a newsgroup's name, and provide a very general idea of the newsgroup's subject matter.

The second part of a newsgroup's name identifies the major subject area or topic. For example, one of the "misc" subcategories is "misc.jobs." More additions to the name increase the newsgroup's focus. For example, the following subcategories of "misc.jobs" offer very specific discussion groups, such as "misc.jobs.contract," "misc.jobs.resume," "misc.jobs.offered," "misc.jobs.offered.entry," and "misc.jobs.misc."

If a user is interested in a particular discussion group, he or she can subscribe to that newsgroup and read or post articles as desired. While no one limits the number of newsgroups in which a user can participate, the amount of time required to read and respond to the thousands of daily postings can become prohibitive.

Network news is a separate application from electronic mail. Although e-mail might seem like a convenient way to read newsgroup postings, users would find their mailboxes flooded with thousands of postings daily. The storage space needed to maintain these postings would be enormous. Network news gives users the ability to view unread postings at their leisure and keeps e-mail inboxes free of clutter.

Anyone on the Internet can post an article to a news group, as can people from other sources. When someone posts an article to a newsgroup, the local system sends the article to the central server for that newsgroup. The central server distributes the article to the other network news servers throughout the Internet.

Some discussion groups are moderated. In moderated news groups, someone reviews each article before it is sent to the other servers. The reviewer for a newsgroup does not censor articles, but ensures that articles posted are relevant to that group. Although this method slows down the posting process, the postings on moderated discussion groups stay focused on the issue.

Unmoderated newsgroups have no screening process. Discussions can and do follow a variety of tangents. Junk-mail postings are prevalent. However, unmoderated newsgroups are somewhat policed by the subscribers to that group. For example, if someone were to advertise a car for sale in the middle of a newsgroup on popular music, the poster of the advertisement would be flooded with angry e-mails from subscribers. This can be frustrating for the offender, as he or she will need to delete hundreds of messages a day. It can also be devastating if the offender uses a provider that charges a fee for each item of e-mail received.

Network news
: An electronic news service divided into newsgroups relating to a variety of topics. Users of network news can post messages to an electronic forum and read messages posted by others.

Network News Transfer Protocol (NNTP)
: NNTP is a protocol that defines the distribution, inquiry, and retrieval of news articles on the Internet from TCP/IP sites.

New Technology File System (NTFS)
: This is the native file system for Windows NT. NewsgroupsNewsgroups are message centers devoted to a particular topic, such as history or science. They resemble mailing lists except that no one need subscribe to them. Anyone with access to a computer that receives Usenet news may both read and contribute to every newsgroup to which they have access. In URLs, newsgroups are denoted by the prefix "news".

Node
: A device at a physical location that performs a control function and influences the flow of data in a network. Node can also refer to the points of connection in the links of a network. Any single computer connected to a network.

Non-trusted Connection
: SQL Server connection by an IPC method other than named pipes, such as IPX/SPX or TCP/IP sockets.

Object
: An object can be any program, file, or utility that can be accessed by the user.

Object variable
: A variable used to store a reference to an instance of a class in memory.

Packet Internet groper (Ping)
: A program used to test reachability of destinations by sending them an ICMP echo request and waiting for a reply. The term is used as a verb: "Ping host X to see if it is operational!"

Page	A Web "page" isn't literally a page, but an entire document, however long. A home page (often called "home.html" or "index.html") is the first page called up when you enter a Web site or when the URL doesn't give a filename.
Parameter	A variable that is given a constant value for a specified application and that may denote the application; or a variable that is given a constant value for a specific document processing program instruction.
Parent object	Container objects which hold other objects.
Partition	1. An area of storage on a fixed disk that contains a particular operating system or a logical drive where data and programs can be stored.
Plug and Play	The specification for a hardware and software architecture that allows automatic device identification and configuration.
Plug-In	A software utility that conforms to a specific application's add-on software architecture. For example, Adobe Photoshop can be extended through the use of third-party Plug-Ins such as Kai's Power Tools from MetaCreations, Inc.
Point of Presence (POP)	The Point of Presence is the access point to a public data network (PDN). It is a location where a network can be connected to the PDN, often with dialup phone lines.
	If an Internet company says they will soon have a POP in Belgrade, it means that they will soon have a local phone number in Belgrade and/or a place where leased lines can connect to their network.
Port	On the Internet, "port" often refers to a number that is part of a URL, appearing after a colon (:), immediately after the domain name. Every service on an Internet server "listens" on a particular port number on that server. Most services have standard port numbers. Web servers normally listen on port 80. Services can also listen on non-standard ports, in which case the port number must be specified in a URL when accessing the server. You might see a URL of the form: gopher:// peg.cwis.uci.edu:7000/ which shows a gopher server running on a non-standard port (the standard gopher port is 70).
Post	To send a message to a network newsgroup or electronic bulletin board.
Post Office Protocol (POP)	
	Post Office Protocol refers to the way e-mail software, such as Eudora, gets mail from a mail server. When you obtain a SLIP, PPP, or shell account, you normally get a POP account. You set your e-mail software to use this account for receiving mail.

Power On Self Test (POST)

When you first start a PC, it will go through a Power On Self Test (POST). The various parts of the computer are checked in a particular order. If errors are detected, they are reported to the user.

The first part tested is the basic system. This includes the microprocessor, bus, and system memory. The extended system is checked next (the system timer, and, if installed, the ROM BASIC interpreter).

The third group tested is related to the video display. The video signals and display-adapter memory are tested. If there is more than one display adapter installed, only the primary adapter is tested.

The memory is tested next. All addressable memory (conventional and extended) is tested through a write/read test.

The keyboard interface is tested, and the keyboard checked for malfunctioning (stuck) keys.

Finally, the system will then determine if any disk drives (floppy and/or hard disks) are installed. If so, they are then tested.

POST errors are reported as audio beeps and numeric error codes. While many manufacturer's codes are similar, you will want to refer to documentation for your particular system to identify any error messages.

Primary Domain Controller

Windows NT Server which stores the master copy of domain security information. It is the controlling system for the domain.

Priority class

A priority setting for an entire process.

Priority level

A priority setting for a thread within a process.

Procedure

1. A block of program code with or without formal parameters (the execution of which is invoked by means of a procedure call).

2. A set of executable Visual Basic program steps.

Processor

In a computer the processor, or Central Processing Unit (CPU), this is a functional unit that interprets and executes instructions. A processor contains at least an instruction control unit and an arithmetic and logic unit.

Properties

Values related to an object.

Property

A variable containing information about a particular object. Properties can be exposed or private.

Property sheet

A grouping of an object's properties that can be viewed or changed.

Protocol	A set of strict rules (usually developed by a standards committee) that govern the exchange of information between computer devices. Also, a set of semantic and syntactic rules that determine the behavior of hardware and software in achieving communication.
Proxy	Proxy is the mechanism whereby one system "fronts for" another system in responding to protocol requests. Proxy systems are used in network management to avoid implementing full protocol stacks in simple devices, such as modems.

Random Access Memory (RAM)

RAM is the computer's storage area to write, store, and retrieve information and program instructions so they can be used by the central processing unit. The contents of RAM are not permanent.

Real-time	A mode of interaction between the user and a distant facility in which the response to the user's inquiry or comment is apparently immediate.
Record	A set of related fields that describes a specific entity. Also called a "tuple" or "row."

Redundant Array of Independent Disks (RAID)

A Redundant Array of Independent Disks is usually referred to as a RAID system. The "I" originally stood for Inexpensive, but was changed to Independent because RAID systems are typically expensive.

A RAID system is composed of multiple hard disks that can either act independently or emulate one large disk. A RAID disk system allows increased capacity, speed, and reliability.

RAID was defined in nine levels by the RAID Advisory Board. Each level provides a different amount of reliability and fault tolerance. The level numbers do not indicate that one level is superior to another.

For an online RAID Guide, see www.invincible.com/rguide.htm.

Registry	Windows NT and Windows 95 configuration database.
Remote Management	Use of a remote console by a network supervisor or by a remote console operator to perform file server tasks.
Reply	An electronic mail program feature that enables a message receiver to automatically respond to a received message without manually addressing the message.

Request For Comments (RFC)

RFC is the name of the result and process for creating a standard on the Internet. New standards are proposed and published on line, as a Request For Comments.

The Internet Engineering Task Force is a consensus-building body that facilitates discussion and new standards. When a new standard is established, the reference number/name for the standard retains the acronym "RFC." For example, the official standard for e-mail is RFC 822.

Rollback

Cancel a SQL transaction and return the result set to the state it was in prior to the beginning of the transaction.

sa

Sa is the logon name for the SQL Server system administrator account.

Script

A file that contains a sequence of system commands used to automate common tasks.

Search engine

A search engine is a computer or group of computers that provide search capabilities for resources on the Internet.

Secure Sockets Layer (SSL)

Secure Sockets Layer is a transmission scheme proposed by Netscape Communications Corporation. It is a low-level encryption scheme used to encrypt transactions in higher-level protocols such as HTTP and FTP.

Security descriptor

A structure that contains information about which users can access an object and for what purpose. Only objects created under Windows NT can have security descriptors.

Security Identifier (SID)

Unique identifier value used in Windows NT Workstation and NT Server security management.

Share name

The name give to a shared resource. The universal naming convention references machine name and share name.

Simple Gateway Management Protocol (SGMP)

SGMP is the predecessor to SNMP.

Simple Mail Transfer Protocol (SMTP)

The Internet standard protocol for transferring electronic mail messages between computers.

Simple Network Management Protocol (SNMP)

The Simple Network Management Protocol (SNMP) is one of the most comprehensive tools available for TCP/IP network management. It operates through conversations between SNMP agents and management systems. Through these conversations, the SNMP management systems can collect statistics from and modify configuration parameters on agents.

The agents are any component running the SNMP agent service and are capable of being managed remotely. Agents can include mini-computers, mainframes, workstations, servers, bridges, routers, gateways, terminal servers, and wiring hubs.

Management stations are typically more powerful workstations. Common implementations are Windows NT or UNIX stations running a product such as HP OpenView, IBM Systemview/6000, or Cabletron Spectrum. The software provides a graphic representation of the network, allowing you to move through network hierarchy to the individual device level.

There are three basic commands used in SNMP conversations: GET, SET, and TRAP.

The GET command is used by the management station to retrieve a specific parameter value from an SNMP agent. If a combination of parameters is grouped together on an agent, GET-NEXT retrieves the next item in a group. For example, a management system's graphic representation of a hub includes the state of all status lights. This information is gathered through GET and GET-NEXT.

The management system uses SET to change a selected parameter on an SNMP agent. For example, SET would be used by the management system to disable a failing port on a hub.

SNMP agents send TRAP packets to the management system in response to extraordinary events, such as a line failure on a hub. When the hub status light goes red on the management systems representation, it is in response to a TRAP.

An SNMP management station generates GET and SET commands. Agents are able to respond to SET and GET and to generate TRAP commands.

Site   Any location of Internet files and services.

Small Computer Systems Interface (SCSI)

A high-speed interface bus used for disk drives, scanners, printers, CD-ROM drives, digital cameras, and other devices. Available in several versions including SCSI-I, SCSI-II (Fast SCSI), Wide (16-bit data path) or UltraWide.

Standard Generalized Markup Language (SGML)

SGML is an international standard. It is an encoding scheme for creating textual information. HTML is a subset of SGML.

Stored Procedures   Custom SQL Server procedures that have been compiled, an execution plan created, and the procedure stored in the current database.

Structured Query Language (SQL)

An ISO data-definition and data-manipulation language for relational databases. Variations of SQL are offered by most major vendors for their relational database products. SQL is consistent with IBM's Systems Application Architecture and has been standardized by the American National Standards Institute (ANSI).

Subnet	The primary reason to divide a network into subnets is network performance and available bandwidth. Without separate networks, each transmission would be broadcast across the entire internetwork, waiting for the destination system to respond. As the network grows, this causes increases in traffic until it exceeds the available bandwidth.

Subnets

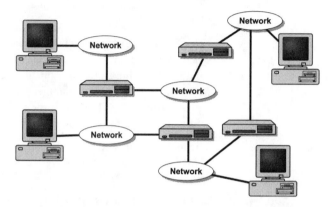

Routers divide, as well as provide communications between the networks. Packets bound for a destination within the local network are kept local. Only packets bound for other networks are broadcast across the network, moving from router to router. Overall traffic levels are reduced.

Subnet Mask	A filter which separates subnetted addresses into network and local entities. Local systems have subnet masks so they can restrict the broadcast to be received on the local network only.
Subnetting	When a complex network is recognized as a single address from outside of the network.
Switched line	A communications link for which the physical path may vary with each usage, such as the public telephone network.
Symmetric Multiprocessing (SMP)	
	In an SMP operating system such as Windows NT, the operating system can run on any processor, or share tasks between several processors. User and applications threads can also be shared between processors, making best use of processor time and reducing bottlenecks.
T1	A leased-line connection capable of carrying data at 1,544,000 bits per second. At maximum theoretical capacity, a T1 line could move a megabyte in less than 10 seconds. That is still not fast enough for full-screen, full-motion video, for which you need at least 10,000,000 bits-per-second. T1 is the fastest speed commonly used to connect networks to the Internet.

T2	A leased-line connection capable of carrying data at 6,312,000 bits per second.
T3	A leased-line connection capable of carrying data at 45,000,000 bits per second. This is more than enough to do full-screen, full-motion video.
T4	An AT&T term for a digital circuit capable of supporting transmissions at a rate of up to 274.176 megabits per second.
Tag	A tag is a string of characters of the form <...> or </...> (the latter is for closing tags only). Tags tell a Web browser how to format text or various bits of texts. For example, the pair of tags <B>... </B> tells the browser to put the text between the two tags in boldface. The single tag <HR> tells the browser to insert a horizontal line. The tag pair <TABLE>... </TABLE> tells the browser to format the material between as a table.

Tagged Image File Format (TIFF)
A file format used to store bitmapped graphics.

Tape backup device	This internal or external tape drive backs up data from hard disks.
Thread	The object of a process that is responsible for executing a block of code. A process can have one or multiple threads.
Time to Live (TTL)	The amount of time between when a packet of data leaves its point of origin and when it reaches its destination. The TTL is encoded in the IP header, and is used as a hop count (to measure the route to the packet's destination).
Traffic	The total information flow in a communications system.
Transaction management	Ensuring that transactions are either completed or canceled so that the database is never left in an inconsistent state.
Transaction Rollback	A process performed during automatic recovery that undoes changes to a database caused by incomplete transactions. This process is performed during automatic recovery, or it can be performed through the ROLLBACK TRAN statement.

Transmission Control Protcol (TCP)
The reliable connection-oriented protocol used by DARPA (Defense Advanced Research Projects Agency) for their internetworking research. TCP uses a three-way handshake with a clock-based sequence number selection to synchronize connecting entities and to minimize the chance of erroneous connections due to delayed messages. TCP is usually used with IP (Internet Protocol), the combination being known as TCP/IP.

Transmission Control Protocol/Internet Protocol (TCP/IP)

Originally designed for WANs (Wide Area Networks), TCP/IP was developed in the 1970's to link the research center of the U.S. Government's Defense Advanced Research Projects Agency. TCP/IP is a protocol that enables communication between the same or different types of computers on a network. TCP/IP can be carried over a wide range of communication channels. The Transmission Control Protocol is connection-oriented and monitors the correct transfer of data between computers. The Internet Protocol is stream-oriented and breaks data into packets.

Transmission rate

The transmission rate is stated in baud or bps. If the connection cannot be made at the selected transmission rate, most modems and communications software will automatically attempt to connect at a slower speed.

Trusted Connection

SQL Server named pipe connection.

Uniform Resource Locator (URL)

A URL is the pathname of a document on the Internet. URLs can be absolute or relative. An absolute URL consists of a prefix denoting a "method" (http for Web sites, gopher for gophers, and so forth). The prefix is followed by a colon and two slashes (://), and an address. The address consists of a domain name followed by a slash and a pathname (or 'username@domain name' for mailto). The last part is an optional anchor which is preceded by a #. The # symbol points to a place within the web page.

Uninterruptible Power Supply (UPS)

If power loss, surges or drops (brownouts) are a significant concern, an Uninterruptible Power Supply (UPS) may be your best option. With a UPS, line voltage is fed into a battery keeping it constantly charged. The computer is, in turn, powered from the battery. Because the computer is already running from the battery, there is no switching time if power is lost. UPS systems supply protection against power events more effectively than most other devices. Uninterruptible Power Supplies are considered essential for network servers. If normal power is lost or interrupted, the UPS allows time to safely shut down the file server. Many UPSs can alert network users to warn when the system is going down.

When selecting a UPS, examine the software and hardware available for the UPS. Options and features vary greatly.

Universal Naming Convention (UNC)

A file-naming convention that uses the *//machine_name/share_name* format.

UNIX	UNIX is a computer operating system originally developed at AT&T's Bell Research Laboratories and later at the University of California Berkeley. It is implemented in a growing number of minicomputer and microcomputer systems.
	UNIX is "multi-user" because it is designed to be used by many people at the same time and has TCP/IP built into the operating system. It is the most common operating system for servers on the Internet.
Upload	A process where a user copies a file "up" to a host computer. Opposite of download.
User Manager	A Windows NT user and group administration utility.
User Manager for Domains	
	User Manager for Domains is a utility installed on all NT Server systems. On additional servers it is operationally identical to the Windows NT Workstation version of the utility, User Manager. The utility is also installed as part of the NT Server remote management tools.
	When User Manager for Domains is started, the current domain users and groups are displayed. Domain Administrators and Account Operators can view and modify users and groups by selecting the appropriate account and running "Properties" from the "User" menu, or by double-clicking on the account. Administrators can manage any account.
	Additional menu selections let you create and manage accounts, select the sort order for account names, manage domain policies, and establish trust relationships.
W3 Consortium	W3C works with the global community to produce specifications and reference software. W3C is funded by industrial members, but its products are freely available to all.
Web browser	A Web browser is a client program that serves as the interface between the user and the resources of the World Wide Web.
WebCrawler	A WebCrawler is a search engine on the Internet, and is located at www.webcrawler.com.
WHOIS	WHOIS is an Internet software program that enables users to register their names and electronic mail addresses, and to query a database of people, domains, networks, and hosts. The database is maintained at the Defense Data Network Network Information Center (DDN NIC) and can be reached through telnet at nic.ddn.mil.

Wide Area Networks (WANs)

Wide Area Networks (WANs) expand the basic LAN model by linking Local Area Networks (LANs), and allowing them to communicate with each other. By traditional definition, a LAN becomes a WAN when it crosses a public right-of-way, requiring a public carrier for data transmission. More current usage of the term usually includes any situation where a network expands beyond one location/building. A WAN is characterized by low- to high-speed communication links, and usually covers a wide geographic area. The remote links may be operational LANs or only groups of workstations. With the exception of a WAN's wider area of operation, the benefits and features of LANs and WANs are the same.

World Wide Web (WWW)

The World Wide Web (WWW) is a recent and fast-growing addition to the Internet.

In 1991, Tim Berners-Lee developed the World Wide Web for the European Council for Nuclear Research (CERN). It was designed as a means of communicating research and ideas between members of the high-energy physics community.

Browsers are the client tools that allow users to view the contents of the Web. The Web at that time had no easily accessible viewing capabilities. The browsers were text-only, line-mode tools that offered no graphical capabilities and few navigation links.

Early in 1993, a team at the National Center for Supercomputing Applications (NCSA) at the University of Illinois at Champaign-Urbana developed an Internet browsing program called Mosaic. The NCSA had no way to disseminate or market the program.

Later that year, a former NCSA graduate student (Tim Krauskopf) offered the University of Illinois a business plan and was given the rights to license Mosaic. The company is called Spyglass. Another company, with the help of former NCSA programmers, created its own Internet browser company and wanted to call it Mosaic Communications, but the NCSA would not allow this. The company was renamed Netscape, and their graphical Web browser, was named Netscape Navigator. Netscape markets their browsers and servers directly to consumers, while Spyglass markets Mosaic to component suppliers such as AT&T, IBM, and Microsoft.

Because the Mosaic project initiated the graphical browser implementation, the term Mosaic is sometimes still used to describe any graphical Web browser.

The Web unifies many of the existing network tools with hypertext (also called hyperlinks). Hypertext gives users the ability to explore paths of information in non-linear ways. Instead of reading through files in a pre-planned sequential arrangement, users can move from item to item in any order they choose.

Some hyperlinks lead to ftp sites, newsgroups, gopher sites, and other Web sites which house additional graphical Web documents. To navigate these Web sites and find links, search engines are available. While current engines can only identify sites that meet the user's criteria, second generation search engines will use artificial intelligence to report to users on information that exactly meets their needs.

The graphical interfaces make the Internet much more appealing, powerful, and simple. Besides being more intuitive than text-based tools, graphical browsers offer full hypermedia support. As recently as 1994, few trade journals mentioned the Web.

Today, Web addresses (URLs) are included in television, radio, magazine, and movie advertisements, and on billboards. By 1995, Web traffic was doubling every four months, and was growing more than twice as fast as general Internet traffic. Entire businesses now reside on the Web and millions of people use it as a communications and educational resources.

Yahoo

Yahoo is a search engine on the Internet, and can be found at www.yahoo.com.

ACRONYMS

-A-

AAL	ATM Adaptation Layer
Abend	Abnormal end
ABR	Automatic Baud Rate Detection
ACDI	Asynchronous Communications Device Interface
ACE	Access Control Entry
ACF/VTAM	Advanced Communications Function/Virtual Telecommunications Access Method
ACK	Acknowledgment
ACL	Access Control List
ACSE	Association Control Service Element
AD	Administrative Domain
ADB	Apple Desktop Bus
ADMD	Administration Management Domain
ADSP	AppleTalk Data Stream Protocol
AEP	AppleTalk Echo Protocol
AFP	AppleTalk Filing Protocol
AIFF	Audio Interchange File Format
ANI	Automatic Number Identification
ANSI	American National Standards Institute
AOW	Asia and Oceania Workshop
APA	All Points Addressable
API	Application Program Interface
APPC	Advanced Program-to-Program Communications
ARA	AppleTalk Remote Access
ARP	Address Resolution Protocol
ARPA	Advanced Research Project Agency
ARPANET	Advanced Research Projects Agency Network
ARQ	Automatic Request for Retransmission
ASCII	American Standard Code for Information Interchange

ASMP	Asymmetric Multiprocessing
ASN.1	Abstract Syntax Notation One
ASP	AppleTalk Session Protocol
ATM	Asynchronous Transfer Mode
ATP	AppleTalk Transaction Protocol
AUI	Attachment Unit Interface
AUP	Acceptable Use Policy
AWG	American Wire Gauge
-B-	
BBS	Bulletin Board System
bcp	Bulk Copy Program
BDC	Backup Domain Controller
BER	Basic Encoding Rules
BIOS	Basic Input/Output System
BISDN	Broadband ISDN
bit	Binary Digit
BITNET	Because It's Time Network
BNC	British Naval Connector
BOC	Bell Operating Company
Bps	Bytes per second
bps	Bits per second
BRI	Basic Rate Interface
BSC	Binary Synchronous Communications
BSD	Berkeley Software Distribution
BTAM	Basic Telecommunications Access Method
-C-	
CAP	Competitive Access Provider
CATV	Community Antenna Television
CBR	Constant Bit Rate
CBT	Computer-Based Training
CCITT	International Consultative Committee for Telegraphy and Telephony
CCL	Common Command Language

CCR	Commitment, Concurrency, and Recovery
CCTV	Closed-Circuit Television
CD-ROM	Compact Disc Read-only Memory
CERN	European Laboratory for Particle Physics
CERT	Computer Emergency Response Team
CGA	Color Graphics Adapter
CGI	Common Gateway Interface
CICS	Customer Information Control System
CIR	Commited Information Rate
CISC	Complex Instruction Set Computer
CIX	Commercial Internet Exchange
CLNP	ConnectionLess Network Protocol
CLTP	ConnectionLess Transport Protocol
CMIP	Common Management Information Protocol
CMOS	Complementary Metal Oxide Semiconductor
CMOT	CMIP Over TCP
CN	Common Name
CO	Central Office
Codec	Coder-decoder
CONP	Connection Oriented Network Protocol
COS	Corporation for Open Systems
COSINE	Cooperation for Open Systems Interconnection Networking in Europe
CPE	Customer Premise Equipment
CPI	Common Programming Interface
cps	Characters per second
CPU	Central Processing Unit
CRC	Cyclic Redundancy Check
CREN	Corporation for Research and Educational Networking
CRT	Cathode Ray Tube
CSMA	Carrier Sense Multiple Access
CSMA/CA	Carrier Sense Multiple Access with Collision Avoidance
CSMA/CD	Carrier Sense Multiple Access with Collision Detection

CSNET	Computer Science Network
CSU	Customer Service Unit
CU	Control Unit
-D-	
DAC	Digital to Analog Converter
DACS	Digital Access Cross Connects
DARPA	Defense Advanced Research Projects Agency
DAV	Digital Audio Video
DB2	IBM Data Base 2
DBCS	Double Byte Character String
DBMS	Database Management System
DBO	Database Owner
DBOO	Database Object Owner
DCA	Defense Communications Agency
DCE	Distributed Computing Environment
DCE	Data Communications Equipment
DD	Double Density
DDE	Dynamic Data Exchange
DDL	Data Definition Language
DDM	Distributed Data Management Architecture
DDN	Defense Data Network
DDP	Datagram Delivery Protocol
DES	Data Encryption Standard
DET	Directory Entry Table
DFT	Distributed Function Terminals
DID	Direct Inward Dial
DIMM	Dual, In-line Memory Module
DISA	Defense Information Systems Agency
DIX	Digital, Intel, Xerox
DLC	Data Link Control
DLCI	Data Link Connection Identifier
DLL	Dynamic-link library

DMA	Direct Memory Access
DMI	Digital Multiplexed Interface
DML	Data Manipulation Language
DNS	Domain Name System
DOS	Disk Operating System
dpi	Dots per inch
DQDB	Distributed Queue Dual Bus
DRAM	Dynamic Random Access Memory
DS	Data set
DS	Double-Sided
DS1	Digital Signaling Level 1
DS2	Digital Signaling Level 2
DS3	Digital Signaling Level 3
DSA	Directory System Agent
DSDD	Double-Sided, Double-Density
DSE	Data Service Equipment
DSHD	Double-Sided, High-Density
DSP	Digital Signal Processor
DSU	Data Service Unit
DTE	Data Terminal Equipment
DTR	Data Terminal Ready
DUA	Directory User Agent
DXF	Drawing interchange Format
DXI	Data Exchange Interface
-E-	
E-mail	Electronic mail
EARN	European Academic and Research Network
EBCDIC	Extended Binary-Coded Decimal Interchange Code
ECF	Enhanced Connectivity Facilities
EDI	Electronic Data Interchange
EEHLLAPI	Entry Emulator High-Level Language Application Program Interface
EFF	Electronic Frontier Foundation

EGA	Enhanced Graphics Adapter
EGP	Exterior Gateway Protocol
EIDE	Enhanced IDE
EMS	Expanded Memory
EPS or EPSF	Encapsulated PostScript File
ER Model	Entity/Relationship Model
ES-IS	End System-Intermediate System
ESDI	Enhanced Industry Standard Architecture
ESF	Extended Super Frame
EUnet	European UNIX Network
EUUG	European UNIX Users Group
EWOS	European Workshop for Open Systems
-F-	
FAQ	Frequently Asked Questions
FARNET	Federation of American Research NETworks
FAT	File Allocation Table
FCB	File Control Block
FCC	Federal Communications Commission
FCS	Frame Check Sequence
FDDI	Fiber Distributed Data Interface
FEP	Front End Processor
FFAPI	File Format API
FIPS	Federal Information Processing Standard
FM	Frequency Modulation
FNC	Federal Networking Council
FPU	Floating Point Unit
FRICC	Federal Research Internet Coordinating Committee
FT1	Fractional T1
FT3	Fractional T3
FTAM	File Transfer, Access, and Management
FTP	File Transfer Protocol
FYI	For Your Information

-G-

GDI	Graphics Device Interface
GIF	Graphics Interchange Format
GOSIP	Government OSI Profile
GUI	Graphical User Interface

-H-

HAL	Hardware Abstraction Layer
HCSS	High Capacity Storage System
HD	High-Density
HDLC	High-level Data Link Control
HDX	Half-duplex
HFS	Hierarchical File System
HLLAPI	High-Level Language Application Program Interface
HMA	High Memory Area
HPFS	High Performance File System
HTML	Hypertext Markup Language
HTTP	Hypertext Transfer Protocol
Hz	Hertz

-I-

IAB	Internet Activities Board
ICMP	Internet Control Message Protocol
IDE	Integrated Drive Electronics
IEEE	Institute of Electrical and Electronics Engineers
IESG	Internet Engineering Steering Group
IETF	Internet Engineering Task Force
IFS	Installable File System
IGP	Interior Gateway Protocol
IGRP	Internet Gateway Routing Protocol
IIS	Internet Information Server
IMHO	In My Humble Opinion
INTAP	Interoperability Technology Association for Information Processing
IONL	Internal Organization of the Network Layer

IP	Internet Protocol
IPX	Internetwork Packet Exchange
IPXODI	Internetwork Packet Exchange Open Data-Link Interface
IRC	Internet Relay Chat
IRQ	Interrupt Request Lines
IRTF	Internet Research Task Force
IS-IS	Intermediate System-Intermediate System
ISAPI	Microsoft Internet Server Application Programming Interface
ISDN	Integrated Services Digital Network
ISO	International Standards Organization
ISODE	ISO Development Environment
ISP	Internet Service Provider
IXC	Inter-exchange Carrier
-J-	
JANET	Joint Academic Network
JPEG	Joint Photographic Experts Group
JUNET	Japan UNIX Network
-K-	
KB	Kilobyte
Kb	Kilobit
KBps	Kilobytes per second
Kbps	Kilobits per second
-L-	
L2PDU	Layer Two Protocol Data Unit
L3PDU	Layer Three Protocol Data Unit
LAN	Local Area Network
LAPB	Link Access Protocol Balanced
LAPD	Link Access Protocol Device
LAPS	LAN Adapter and Protocol Support
LATA	Local Access and Transport Area
LCD	Liquid Crystal Diode
LDT	Local Descriptor Table

LEC	Local Exchange Carriers
LEN	Low Entry Networking
LLAP	LocalTalk Link Access Protocol
LMI	Local Management Interface
lpi	Lines per inch
LSL	Link Support Layer
LU	Logical Unit
-M-	
MAC	Media Access Control Sublayer
MAN	Metropolitan Area Network
MAP	Manufacturing Automation Protocol
MAPI	Messaging API
MAU	Multi-Station Attachment Unit
MB	Megabyte
Mb	Megabit
MBps	Megabytes per second
Mbps	Megabits per second
MCGA	Multi-Color Gate Array
MDI	Multiple Document Interface
MHS	Message Handling System
MHz	Megahertz
MIB	Management Information Base
MIDI	Musical Instrument Digital Interface
MILNET	Military Network
MIME	Multipurpose Internet Mail Extensions
MIPS	Million Instructions Per Second
MLID	Multiple Link Interface Driver
MOO	Mud, Object Oriented
MPEG	Moving Pictures Experts Group
ms	Milliseconds
MTA	Message Transfer Agent
MTU	Maximum Transmission Unit

MUD	Multi-User Dungeon or Dimension
MVS	Multiple Virtual Storage
MVS-CICS	Multiple Virtual Storage-Customer Information Control System
MVS/TSO	Multiple Virtual Storage/Time-Sharing Option
-N-	
NAK	Negative AcKnowledgment
NBP	Name Binding Protocol
NCC	NetWare Control Center
NCP	NetWare Core Protocol
NCP	Network Control Point
NCSA	National Center for Supercomputing Applications
NDS	NetWare Directory Services
NetBEUI	NetBIOS Extended User Interface
NetWare DA	NetWare Desk Accessory
NFS	Network File System
NIC	Network Information Center
NIC	Network Interface Card
NIST	National Institute of Standards and Technology
NLM	NetWare Loadable Module
NLQ	Near Letter Quality
NLSP	NetWare Link Services Protocol
NMS	Network Management Station
NNS	NetWare Name Service
NNTP	Network News Transfer Protocol
NOC	Network Operations Center
NREN	National Research and Education Network
NSAP	Network Service Access Point
NSEPro	Network Support Encyclopedia Professional Volume
NSEPro	Network Support Encyclopedia Professional Edition
NSF	National Science Foundation
NSFnet	National Science Foundation Network
NT	Windows NT

NT1	Network Termination 1
NT2	Network Termination 2
NTAS	Windows NT Advanced Server
NTFS	New Technology File System
NTP	Network Time Protocol
NWADMIN	Network Administrator

-O-

OBS	Optical Bypass Switch
ODI	Open Datalink Interface
OIW	Workshop for Implementors of OSI
OLE	Object Linking and Embedding
ONC	Open Network Computing
OOP	Object-oriented programming
OPAC	Online Public Access Catalog
OSI	Open Systems Interconnection
OSPF	Open Shortest Path First

-P-

PAD	Packet Assembler/Disassembler
PAP	Printer Access Protocol
PBX	Private Branch Exchange
PCI	Peripheral Component Interconnect
PCI	Protocol Control Information
PCL	Printer Control Language
PCM	Pulse code modulation
PCMCIA	Personal Computer Memory Card International Association
PDC	Primary Domain Controller
PDF	Printer Definition Files
PDN	Packet Data Network
PDS	Processor-Direct Slot
PDU	Protocol Data Unit
PID	Process Identification Number
PIF	Program Information File

Ping	Packet internet groper
PMMU	Paged Memory Management Unit
POP	Point of Presence
POP	Post Office Protocol
POSI	Promoting Conference for OSI
POST	Power On Self Test
POTS	Plain Old Telephone Service
ppm	pages per minute
PPP	Point-to-Point Protocol
PPTP	Point-to-Point Tunneling Protocol
PRAM	Parameter RAM
PRI	Primary Rate Interface
PRMD	Private Management Domain
PROFS	Professional Office System
PSN	Packet Switch Node
PU	Physical Unit
PUC	Public Utility Commission
PVC	Permanent Virtual Circuit
-Q-	
QMF	Query Manager Facility
-R-	
RAID	Redundant Array of Independent Disks
RAM	Random Access Memory
RARE	Reseaux Associes pour la Recherche Europeenne
RARP	Reverse Address Resolution Protocol
RAS	Remote Access Service
RAS	Remote Access Server
RBOC	Regional Bell Operating Company
REM	REMARK
RFC	Request For Comments
RFS	Remote File System
RIP	Raster Image Processor

RIP	Router Information Protocol
RIPE	Reseaux IP Europeenne
RISC	Reduced Instruction Set Computer
ROM	Read-Only Memory
ROSE	Remote Operations Service Element
RPC	Remote Procedure Call
RTF	Rich Text Format
RTMP	Routing Table Maintenance Protocol
RTSE	Reliable Transfer Service Element
-S-	
SAA	Systems Application Architecture
SAP	Service Access Point
SAP	Service Advertising Protocol
SAPI	Service Access Point Identifier
SAPS	Service Access Point Stations
SAR	Segmentation and Reassembly protocol
SCSI	Small Computer Systems Interface
SDH	Synchronous Digital Hierarchy
SDI	Storage Device Interface
SDLC	Synchronous Data Link Control
SDN	Software Defined Network
SDU	SMDS Data Unit
SFT	System Fault Tolerance
SGML	Standard Generalized Markup Language
SGMP	Simple Gateway Management Protocol
SID	Security Identifier
SIMM	Single, In-line Memory Module
SIP	SMDS Interface Protocol
SLIP	Serial Line IP
SMDS	Switched Multimegabit Data Service
SMI	Structure of Management Information
SMP	Symmetric Multiprocessing

SMS	Storage Management Services
SMTP	Simple Mail Transfer Protocol
SNA	System Network Architecture
SNMP	Simple Network Management Protocol
SONET	Synchronous Optical Network
SPAG	Standards Promotion and Application Group
SPE	Synchronous Payload Envelope
SPX	Sequenced Packet Exchange
SQL	Structured Query Language
SRAM	Static RAM
SRPI	Server Requester Programming Interface
SS7	Signaling System 7
SSL	Secure Sockets Layer
STDM	Statistical Time Division Multiplexing
STM	Synchronous Transport Module
STS	Synchronous Transport Signal
SVC	Switched Virtual Circuit
Sysop	Systems Operator
-T-	
TA	Terminal Adapter
TAC	Terminal Access Controller
TCP	Transmission Control Protcol
TCP/IP	Transmission Control Protocol/ Internet Protocol
TDM	Time-Division Multiplexor
TE1	Terminal Equipment Type 1
TE2	Terminal Equipment Type 2
Telex	Teleprinter Exchange
TIFF	Tagged Image File Format
TLI	Transport Layer Interface
TNX	Teletypewriter Exchange Service
TP0	OSI Transport Protocol Class 0
TP4	OSI Transport Protocol Class 4

TSA	Target Server Agent
TSR	Terminate and Stay Resident program
TTF	TrueType fonts
TTL	Time to Live
TTS	Transaction Tracking System
TWX	Teletypewriter Exchange Service
-U-	
UA	User Agent
UDP	User Datagram Protocol
UMA	Upper Memory Area
UMBs	Upper Memory Blocks
UNC	Universal Naming Convention
UPS	Uninterruptible Power Supply
URL	Uniform Resource Locator
UUCP	UNIX-to-UNIX Copy Program
-V-	
VBR	Variable Bit Rate
VCI	Virtual Connection Identifier
VDM	Virtual DOS Machine
Veronica	Very Easy Rodent Oriented Net-wide Index to Computerized Archives
VGA	Video Graphics Array
VLM	Virtual Loadable Module
VLSI	Very Large-Scale Integration
VM/CMS	Virtual Machine/Conversational Monitor System
VMM	Virtual Memory Manager
VNET	Virtual Network
VPI	Virtual Path Identifier
VPN	Virtual Private Network
VRAM	Video RAM
VRC	Vertical Redundancy Check
VRML	Virtual Reality Modeling Language
VSE/CICS	Virtual Storage Extended-Customer Information Control System

VT	Virtual Terminal
-W-	
WAIS	Wide Area Information Servers
WAN	Wide Area Network
WATS	Wide Area Telephone Service
WWW	World Wide Web
WYSIWYG	What You See is What You Get
-X-	
XDR	External Data Representation
XMS	Extended Memory
XNS	Xerox Network System
-Z-	
ZIP	Zone Information Protocol

Index